Attachment-Based Family Therapy for Depressed Adolescents

Attachment-Based Family Therapy for Depressed Adolescents

GUY S. DIAMOND
GARY M. DIAMOND
SUZANNE A. LEVY

AMERICAN PSYCHOLOGICAL ASSOCIATION
WASHINGTON, DC

3rd printing, February 2020

Published by
American Psychological Association
750 First Street, NE
Washington, DC 20002
www.apa.org

To order
APA Order Department
P.O. Box 92984
Washington, DC 20090-2984
Tel: (800) 374-2721; Direct: (202) 336-5510
Fax: (202) 336-5502; TDD/TTY: (202) 336-6123
Online: www.apa.org/pubs/books
E-mail: order@apa.org

In the U.K., Europe, Africa, and the Middle East, copies may be ordered from
American Psychological Association
3 Henrietta Street
Covent Garden, London
WC2E 8LU England

Typeset in Goudy by Circle Graphics, Inc., Columbia, MD

Printer: Maple Press, York, PA
Cover Designer: Berg Design, Albany, NY

Library of Congress Cataloging-in-Publication Data

Diamond, Guy S., author.
Attachment-based family therapy for depressed adolescents / Guy S. Diamond, Gary M. Diamond, and Suzanne A. Levy.
pages cm
Includes bibliographical references and index.
ISBN 978-1-4338-1567-6 — ISBN 1-4338-1567-2 1. Depression in adolescence. 2. Parent and teenager—Psychological aspects. 3. Family psychotherapy. I. Diamond, Gary M., author. II. Levy, Suzanne A., author. III. Title.
RJ506.D4D53 2014
616.89'15600835—dc23

2013020138

British Library Cataloguing-in-Publication Data

A CIP record is available from the British Library.

Printed in the United States of America
First Edition

http://dx.doi.org/10.1037/14296-000

CONTENTS

ACKNOWLEDGMENTS

Jay Haley once wrote that most of his ideas about family therapy emerged while driving to and from work with Sal Minuchin and Bralio Montalavo. What fortune he had to have such great colleagues. We three authors feel the same. For 15 years, we have been working together—treating troubled families in randomized clinical trials. These families taught us much of what we know about how to help them. We have sat behind the one-way mirror together and thought deeply about the micro-movements of family interactions and the decisions therapists make to guide them. Many of these conversations became the basis for process research studies that have further embellished our work. We have also all three been teaching the work at home, nationally, and internationally. These trainings have reinforced our belief in the value of the model and have also helped refine our thinking about how to articulate and teach it. This has been and will be an unbelievable journey, and we are fortunate to be on it together.

We have not been alone on this adventure. Many people have helped along the way. In the formative years, Lynne Siqueland made lasting contributions to this approach. More recently, Roger Kobak and Stephaine Ewing joined our team. Both have helped us integrate the language and concepts of attachment theory more deeply into this work. We look forward to many years of collaboration with them both. We also appreciate the students, postdoctoral fellows, and therapists who have come through our Center for Family Intervention Science over the course of these productive 20 years of treatment research. Both Guy and Gary, who trained and worked at the Philadelphia Child Guidance Clinic, had the pleasure of working with master clinicians and teachers such as Joe Micucci, John Brendler, and Wayne Jones. They have all left a lasting impression on us.

Guy also thanks Guillermo Bernal for first exposing him to outcome research and Paul Crits-Christoph, who mentored him at critical moments in his 20 years in psychiatry at the University of Pennsylvania. Gary also thanks Ruth Camhi and Dana Becker for the skilled training and supervision they provided. Suzanne also thanks Karen Reivich, who taught her to be a better trainer, and Andrea Hussong, whose graduate school mentoring laid the foundation for her work today.

Finally, and most of all, Guy and Gary thank Howard Liddle—supervisor, teacher, mentor, and friend. The hours of sitting behind the one-way mirror and listening to his brilliant analysis of the therapy process shaped our intellects and helped us to become the professionals we are today. His belief and confidence in us nurtured the career goals that have brought us to this moment in our work. His guidance is a testament to the power and importance of mentoring the next generation of psychotherapy researchers.

On a personal note, Guy thanks his parents. His mother's career helped him think big about his own work, and his father's support gave him the confidence to achieve it. Guy also thanks his wife, Karen Reivich, and his four children, Aaron, Jacob, Jonathan, and Shayna. These people have taught him more about attachment and child-centered parenting than any book on his shelf.

Gary also thanks his mother and father, Beverly and Stanley; sister, Jodi; brother-in-law, Lenny; and his best friend and partner, Rivi—all of whom provided him with his own secure base. Finally, he thanks his two wonderful sons, Orian and Yahel. They have taught him what it means and takes to be a good-enough parent.

Suzanne thanks her parents, siblings, nieces, nephews, and friends, without whom none of this would be possible. And a special thanks to Brad, her loving husband, who on many nights and weekends came second to her work but was always understanding and provided unconditional love.

Attachment-Based Family Therapy for Depressed Adolescents

INTRODUCTION: THE CONTEXT OF ADOLESCENT DEPRESSION

Adolescence is a dynamic time in the family life cycle. Adolescents embark on a journey of self-discovery—bursting with newfound physical strength and stature and discovering the power of language, increased independence, strong friendships, first love, sexuality, and pop culture. At the same time, parents enter the middle stage of their life, with a history of successes and failures and a future full of challenges in relation to marriage, work, money, aging parents, and awareness of their own mortality. Middle age and adolescence can coexist peacefully in the family, or they can collide. How this unfolds depends on the strength of the secure base relationships between parents and children. When these relationships are strong, the children are said to have a *secure base* in their parents—that is, a source of love and protection.

A secure base provides the essential context for growth and development throughout childhood. In the early years, the cocoon of love nurtures the important interpersonal skills of life. Children learn to value their own

http://dx.doi.org/10.1037/14296-001
Attachment-Based Family Therapy for Depressed Adolescents, by G. S. Diamond, G. M. Diamond, and S. A. Levy

thoughts and feelings and to trust that others will be supportive and available when needed. In this safe holding environment, children learn to express feelings in words, regulate difficult emotions, tolerate conflict, and negotiate autonomy. In these families, parental love is not contingent on obedience. Love is unconditional. Love is dependable. As children become adolescents, their dependency transforms into a partnership—a give-and-take relationship in which parents and adolescents negotiate goals and compromise to maintain the trust and love they both cherish.

Unfortunately, sometimes a secure base never develops or can be shattered. Some parents struggle with depression, drug use, marital conflict, divorce, lack of social support, or economic hardship; these challenges can compromise parents' ability to be responsive and to provide care and protection. Some parents suffer from their own history of attachment ruptures, experiences that have left them emotionally scarred and unable to consistently provide love and validation or set developmentally appropriate limits and expectations. Wounds from emotional isolation, physical or sexual abuse, and abandonment can cause vulnerabilities that are passed on through generations, like family heirlooms. Sometimes the secure base is threatened by stressors from outside the home. Negative peer relationships or community and interpersonal violence can knock an adolescent off course. These kinds of events can destabilize even the strongest of families. Sometimes the secure base is strained because of challenges the child faces and/or his or her personality. Children with chronic illness, physical disabilities, or extreme temperaments can put tremendous stress on family life. Regardless of the source, when stress or trauma damages the secure base, the sanctuary of the attachment relationship becomes compromised. Safety can no longer be assumed. Parental guidance, patience, and protection diminish or disappear. The adolescent begins to doubt that he or she is loved. The bonds of affection are broken. Security is replaced with insecurity, which interrupts normal development.

For adolescents who become depressed, life is dark and lonely. The world becomes unsafe, and they begin to view themselves as unworthy. To protect themselves, they often retreat from parents, friends, and activities. They can become irritable, erratic, angry, and unpredictable. They are vigilant, always on the lookout for rejection and criticism. Some turn to cutting to distract themselves from their pain, to parasuicide as a cry for help, or even to suicide itself in an effort to escape. Many get lost in a cloud of negativity, sinking deeper and deeper into despair and isolation, unable to find their way out. They have lost their interests, lost their passion for life, lost their inner compass, and lost their voice. They do not know how to ask for help and instead have gone silent.

Lacking the expectation that parents will understand their pain and provide a safe haven, depressed adolescents use emotional overregulation to protect themselves from more hurt. Some are ambivalent about their parents, wanting love but fearing rejection. Consumed with blame, disappointment, and rage, these adolescents often use conflict as a means to achieve pseudointimacy and connection. Other depressed adolescents become indifferent and dismissive, protecting themselves by denying their need for attachment security. Still others become "parentified" and spend more time caring for and protecting their parents than having their own needs met. All these coping strategies make it hard for parents to provide adequate comfort and support. Thus, depression disrupts the normative balance of attachment and autonomy during adolescence. Depression reinforces dependency at a time when autonomy should be emerging. Simultaneously, the depression inhibits the adolescent from using his or her parents as a resource during these troubled times.

BRIEF OVERVIEW OF ATTACHMENT-BASED FAMILY THERAPY

The depressed adolescent's need for both attachment and autonomy represents the unique focus of attachment-based family therapy (ABFT), an empirically supported family psychotherapy designed for treating adolescent depression. ABFT has been tested as a 12- to 16-week intervention but can be used as a longer intervention as well. Studies (G. S. Diamond, Reis, Diamond, Siqueland, & Isaacs, 2002; G. S. Diamond, Siqueland, & Diamond, 2003; G. S. Diamond et al., 2010) have demonstrated that ABFT can reduce adolescent depression more effectively than wait-list control or treatment as usual. Data also suggest that ABFT is effective with the most troubled populations, including adolescents who are severely depressed, have parents who are depressed themselves, or who have a history of sexual abuse (G. S. Diamond, Creed, Gillham, Gallop, Hamilton, 2012; G. S. Diamond et al., 2010). ABFT efficacy with these adolescents is especially noteworthy because these groups have not responded well to cognitive–behavioral treatment and/or medication (Asarnow et al., 2009; Barbe, Bridge, Birmaher, Kolko, & Brent, 2004; Curry et al., 2006). Families with gay, lesbian, or bisexual adolescents have also been treated successfully using ABFT (G. M. Diamond et al., 2012).

The rationale for the ABFT approach rests on decades of research on adolescent development and attachment demonstrating that a secure family base (love and protection) during adolescence improves the welfare and functioning of adolescents and young adults (J. P. Allen & Land, 1999; Kobak & Duemmler, 1994; Steinberg, 1990). ABFT also emerges from interpersonal theories that suggest that adolescent depression can be precipitated, exacerbated, or buffered against by the quality of interpersonal relationships in families (Cicchetti & Toth, 1998; Gotlib & Hammen, 2009; Hammen, 2009;

Joiner & Coyne, 1999). Based on these theories and research, ABFT aims to repair interpersonal ruptures in the adolescent–parent relationship that have damaged the secure base and to rebuild an emotionally protective, parent–child relationship. With the secure base on the mend, treatment then turns to promoting adolescent autonomy and responsibility.

The ABFT model is an emotion-focused, trauma-based, process-oriented, and experiential approach. The model provides structure, goals, and a clear road map for therapy. The model consists of five treatment tasks, with each task requiring a single or multiple therapy sessions to complete. In Task I, the relational reframe task, the therapist meets with the parents and adolescent and shifts the focus of therapy from symptom reduction to relationship development. The task is designed to focus the therapy on identifying and repairing attachment injuries and parental empathic failure rather than on behavioral management. In Task II, the adolescent alliance-building task, the therapist meets with the adolescent alone to explore what has damaged trust between the adolescent and his or her parents. Specific, painful attachment rupture events are explored in depth in an effort to formulate a more coherent narrative of painful memories and to access previously avoided primary adaptive emotions. Validating these attachment injuries helps adolescents feel more entitled to express them more directly. After reactivating the adolescent's longing for attachment, the therapist motivates and prepares the adolescent to discuss the ruptures with his or her parents. In Task III, the parent alliance-building task, the therapist meets with one or both parents alone to explore how current stressors and the parents' own history of attachment ruptures impact their parenting. Parents explore their own unresolved losses just enough to help them remember their own attachment needs as a child. This strategy activates and amplifies natural parental caregiving instincts and, thus, increases parents' empathy for their adolescent's unmet emotional needs. In this state of mind, parents become more open to learning attachment-promoting parenting practices, skills necessary to improve effective, emotion-based communication with the adolescent.

After meeting with the adolescent and parents separately to transform their views of self and other, the ABFT therapist brings the family back together for Task IV, the repairing attachment task. In this task, attachment ruptures are put at the heart of the therapeutic dialogue. Issues of trust, betrayal, commitment, and love become the central themes of the conversation—big themes of family life that organize the day-to-day interactions. Adolescents courageously express unmet attachment needs in an honest and regulated manner, and parents remain supportive and empathically attuned. Adolescents discover their own voice and begin to gain trust in their parents' availability and sensitivity. Simultaneously, parents learn to balance guidance and control with empathy and understanding. Parents learn that problem solving begins with self-reflection and that identifying more vulnerable emotions can lead to more authentic conversations. When relevant, many parents apologize for past and present attachment failures, thus deeply acknowledging the adolescent's previously denied experiences.

These conversations become corrective attachment experiences. Children express hurt and longing, and parents provide comfort and protection. These new, relational, in vivo, in-session experiences can lead to revisions of family members' internal working models of self and other. New, positive relational experiences can replace (or at least compete with) previous negative expectations. When successful, at the conclusion of the attachment task, adolescents are thinking, "Maybe my parents can be there for me." Conversation becomes the new vehicle for attachment. The attachment relationship becomes a place where the adolescent can go for help, for guidance, for protection, for understanding, and for self-reflection. Conversation supports adolescents without constraining them. It engages them while allowing them to differentiate.

Finally, in Task V, the promoting autonomy task, the therapist helps the family practice new interpersonal problem-solving skills that can promote autonomy while maintaining attachment. In this phase, families consolidate skills during the context of solving issues related to cooperation in the home or engagement in activities outside the home. Families also discuss any other issues contributing to the adolescent's depression, such as peer problems, school difficulty, or bullying. Conversations also focus on identity formation by addressing issues of race, gender identity, relationships, or sexual orientation. Whereas Tasks I through III prepare family members to work through attachment ruptures, and Task IV actually works through these ruptures, Task V involves having the family respectfully negotiate solutions to difficult day-to-day challenges in a way that protects the adolescent and supports his or her autonomy development. In many ways, the promoting autonomy task is the culmination of the previous four tasks: the proof in the pudding.

The tasks outlined above offer an ideal performance model for resolving core family relational ruptures and building new, successful family relationships. Although every family has its own history, needs, personalities, and dynamics, these five therapy tasks provide a road map that has specific directions, important points of interest along the way, guidance on when to take detours or get back on the main highway, and the end destination. In this way, the model is both generic and idiosyncratic, and the therapist is both collaborative and directive. Therapists encourage very specific strategies and goals but apply them with sensitivity to the culture of the family.

PURPOSE OF THIS BOOK

This book guides the reader through the process of thinking about and implementing the five treatment tasks. It includes theory, clinical guidelines, and examples. We focus on the basic tenets and processes of the model. In-depth applications to families with particular circumstances (e.g., suicide, sexual abuse, parental psychopathology) will likely appear in future books and workshops (see http://www.ABFTtraining.com and https://www.facebook.com/Attachment.Based.Family.Therapy for more information).

The book is intended for therapists in training and those already with at least a master's level education. Learning this model works best when students have some basic knowledge about, and experience doing, family therapy; this is not a basic introduction to family therapy. The book may also be of interest to administrative and clinical directors looking to incorporate an empirically supported treatment model for adolescents with depression and/or other internalizing disorders (e.g., suicide, anxiety, trauma) into outpatient, inpatient, or community settings. As a principle-based approach, the model can be applied in various delivery contexts.

COMMON QUESTIONS ABOUT ATTACHMENT-BASED FAMILY THERAPY

Therapists learning this model often have several initial concerns. This section includes some of the most common questions and our responses.

Will the Structure of the Attachment-Based Family Therapy Model Constrain My Intuition and Creativity as a Therapist?

No, the ABFT model will not constrain the creative spirit of the therapist or lead the therapist to overfocus on techniques at the expense of the relationship or alliance. ABFT is not a recipe. Although some psychoeducational and cognitive–behavioral therapy approaches are highly scripted, with specific exercises to be used at specific times, ABFT is more principle driven than curriculum driven. In this book, we lay out the general principles and goals of treatment, along with various intervention strategies. The therapist then decides on the timing, pacing, and content of these interventions.

Instead of trying to prescribe what the therapist should do, we aim to increase the therapist's intentionality. This is at both the macrolevel of selecting a general therapeutic strategy or theme and the microlevel of moment-to-moment processes in the session. At the microprocess level, the model helps therapists evaluate the general content, affect, and process in the room.

Having a clear framework and set of goals, the therapist can constantly ask himself or herself, "Is the affect right? Is the content right? Is the process right? Is this conversation facilitating attachment repair or is it the same old destructive conversation the family usually has at home?" (Liddle, 2002). Having a road map, having a plan, and working to facilitate specific treatment processes gives the therapist a foundation on which to make important clinical judgments: "What should I focus on? How long do I focus on this? How do I know when this topic is done, and how should I punctuate this so it supports what I am going to focus on next?" Most therapists no longer have a supervisor to call in from behind the mirror or even to meet with once a week. Having a road map offers some form of self-supervision, some voice inside one's head that can say, "Hmmm, is this helpful right now?"

At the level of clinical strategy, ABFT helps therapists think about what change strategies they are using at any given moment. The ABFT approach is an integrative model that relies on psychoeducation, behavioral management, conflict resolution, cognitive restructuring, emotional processing, intergenerational exploration, and experiential learning. At any given moment, the therapist must be aware of which strategy he or she is using and why: "When am I teaching? When am I solving problems? When am I challenging attributions? When am I promoting emotional expression?" And hardest of all, "When am I enacting in vivo, experiential change?" Many of these strategies occur simultaneously and reinforce the delivery and success of each other. Often a therapist is focused on one change process but may briefly shift to another. For example, when a parent becomes resistant to enacting an interpersonal dialogue with his or her teen, the therapist may return to a teaching moment about adolescent development and the need for parents to be a resource to kids. Once the parent remembers that premise (from Task III), the therapist can return to the experiential enactment (Task IV). The ABFT model offers a framework to help evaluate which strategies are most relevant at a given time in treatment.

One challenge we find with using ABFT, especially when therapists are first learning it, is the tendency to overthink what one is doing. Therapists become preoccupied with doing the model "right" rather than using it as a framework. But we view ABFT like learning jazz. You practice and practice the core rudimentary scales and chord progressions (i.e., the tasks). When you get on stage (i.e., in the therapy room), you have the skills and fundamentals, but you are constantly improvising in response to feedback from the other musicians (i.e., family members). ABFT is a song, written specifically for depressed adolescents. The tasks are the chord progressions, and the emotions and attachment themes are the melodies. The rendition of the song is different each time you play it, but it always has the same basic structure.

In general, then, ABFT should help providers become thinking therapists: therapists who can take stock of the direction, success, and failure of the interventions within and between sessions and use internal (therapist reactions) and external (family responses) feedback to adjust. This ability to adjust becomes an essential skill in facilitating the microprocesses that make up therapy. We also hope that this model will help providers become courageous therapists: therapists who can get to the heart of the matter more quickly and effectively.

Are ABFT Therapists Authoritarian or Authoritative?

Being an intentional, directive therapist can be confused with being authoritarian. There has been much debate in the family systems field about being an authoritarian therapist versus a client-centered therapist (Anderson, 1997; Becker, 2005; White & Epston, 1990). But the field has confused *authoritarian* with *authoritative*. *Authoritarian* means to dominate, force, hold all the power, and make all the decisions. No one thinks that is a good way to do therapy. In contrast, *authoritative* means to be knowledgeable, to provide direction and guidance, while also allowing others to express opinions and to make contributions. ABFT therapists are authoritative. They have a map that guides them toward and through essential processes. Using psychological science, they trust that some things are more important to talk about or accomplish than others.

In this regard, ABFT is not a client-centered therapy but, rather, a client-respectful therapy. We do not let the families determine the direction of therapy, at least not early in treatment. Clients have input; they provide content and constant feedback (positive or negative, verbal or nonverbal) that will shape how the therapist will guide the treatment. However, in ABFT, the family is not wandering around on their own hoping to find solutions. The ABFT therapist is a guide who directs the family's attention to important content, feelings, and processes. There may be detours or side trips, and some destinations may even be missed, but we assume the family has lost its way and is looking for guidance. The therapist serves as a guide and a mentor.

How Many Sessions Does It Take to Complete Each Task?

A task is not equated with a session. *Tasks* are a set of organizing principles, strategies, and outcomes. Sometimes tasks are completed in one session, and other times it takes three. The determining factor is whether the task has been accomplished. Each task has a particular goal and outcome, and the therapist has to assess whether the family has met that goal. If not, maybe it is worked on again, or maybe the outcome is good enough to move to the next task.

Do I Have to Follow the Same Sequence of Tasks in the Same Order With All Families?

Tasks build on each other. What is accomplished in one task sets the foundation for the next task. Thus, we propose an ideal order to be followed when possible. For example, trying to do the attachment task (Task IV) before all family members agree that relationship building is the initial goal of treatment (Task I) or before they have acquired new interpersonal skills (Tasks II and III) increases the likelihood of failure.

However, the model is flexible. Sometimes we see parents alone first instead of the adolescent alone first. For example with one family, we had the parents alone in the first session when we recognized their pressing need to tell a long and humiliating history of the adolescent's problems. With another family, the parents could not come for 2 weeks, so we started with the adolescent. In another family, the daughter had some autonomy-building opportunities that needed immediate attention (e.g., signing up for school), so we addressed a Task V issue early on. With another family, we initially refused to see the family unless the father could attend the first session. We did not want to reinforce the father's exclusion from the overenmeshed mother–daughter relationship. We were convinced that the relational reframe needed to involve all family members. However, when the father still did not come in, despite our best attempts at engagement, we saw the mother and daughter anyway. Getting started was more important than rigidly adhering to our ideal strategy.

We believe in the logical order of the five tasks, but we believe more in the guiding principles and goals inherent in the tasks. Therefore, regardless of the order, the principles of the tasks still organize the treatment. As is evident throughout the book, there are no rules in ABFT; instead, there are principles, goals, and strategies that improve the therapist's ability to organize and facilitate effective therapy.

Are We Taking the Adolescent's Side Against the Parents?

Some therapists worry that in ABFT the therapist sides too much with the adolescent's needs and concerns. This is somewhat accurate, at least initially. One of Howard Liddle's major contributions to family therapy was his understanding that therapists had to engage adolescents in the therapy by making it meaningful to them (Liddle & Diamond, 1991). In fact, one process study using a sample of families receiving multidimensional family therapy found that the alliance with the parent increased retention, while the alliance with the adolescent determined outcome (Shelef, Diamond, Diamond, & Liddle, 2005). Therefore, unlike Minuchin's (e.g., 1974) early work, the initial move of ABFT is not to put parents in charge and have them regain control; rather, it is to create a new context in which adolescents' needs will be understood, considered, and addressed. This may also be the difference between working with adolescents who are depressed versus those with disruptive behaviors (Minuchin, 1974). Youth who are depressed are withdrawn and hopeless. A strong move to help parents manage their behavior will push them deeper into darkness and away from the family. In contrast, we want the adolescent to find a voice and even express assertive anger when called for. Therefore, ABFT therapists attempt to quickly identify the topics that fuel the adolescents' anger, withdrawal, indifference, and despair, and bring those front and center in the therapy.

But this move is more than just about engagement. Once the adolescent feels the therapist is on his or her side, once the adolescent feels there is something in the therapy for him or her (Liddle, 1994), and once his or her issues begin to lead the therapy, the therapist has more leverage to challenge the adolescent. We say to the adolescent directly, "If you want to be taken seriously, you have to be honest, direct, and calm. I will get them to listen, but you have to do your part." So while the adolescent's content takes the lead, the therapist uses her or his alliance with the adolescent to challenge him or her to regulate affect, put emotions into words, and be as honest as possible.

For Whom Is ABFT Not Appropriate?

This treatment is not designed for every adolescent who walks into your office. For most adolescents who are depressed, the approach has great relevance. For some, it may not. The therapist has to make that assessment and determination: Are relational ruptures getting in the way of normative developmental support? Have things happened in the family that have damaged trust? Do parents attempt to help in ways that alienate the teen? Does the adolescent express his or her needs in an immature manner that makes it hard for parents to take him or her seriously? Does the family have difficulty negotiating a healthy balance of attachment and autonomy? If so, ABFT can help this family. We rarely find a family in which the adolescent has developed major depression and some of these negative processes are not at work, even if parents are caring and the adolescent feels close to them. Even when they say they are close, we often find dark corners where problems have been avoided.

But what about other kinds of problems: adolescents who are anxious, oppositional, using illegal substances, acting out sexually, or who have obsessive–compulsive disorder or bipolar disorder? In the early years, family therapy (and all psychotherapies, for that matter) made the mistake of thinking one treatment fits all problems. The assumption was that if one reestablished hierarchy and authority or interrupted the double-bind communication, any problems would resolve. Well, times have changed. The science of psychotherapy has evolved. Empirically supported treatments for specific disorders are emerging. For some disorders, such as anxiety, cognitive–behavioral protocols are particularly helpful. For other disorders, medication may be essential (e.g., bipolar disorder). Increasingly, combination treatments are recommended. We as therapists have to be responsible, well-informed professionals who know the strength and limitations of our trade. ABFT is not a panacea. On the other hand, ABFT identifies some core family processes that may in fact have relevance for families and adolescents struggling with other kinds of problems. As a clinician, the reader has the latitude to apply these principles as they see fit. As scientists, the authors are bound by the data. We cannot advocate this treatment for other problems until empirical evidence indicates it is useful.

OVERVIEW OF THIS BOOK

This book consists of eight chapters. In Chapter 1, we discuss the theoretical and clinical roots of ABFT. We place ABFT in the context of other empirically supported treatments for adolescent depression, other attachment-based psychotherapy models, and the family therapy tradition. Chapter 2 offers a theoretical framework for the model. We review research on attachment between adolescent and parent, adolescent development, emotion regulation, and parenting practices. This is not a comprehensive literature review. Rather, we provide the essential rationale for the proposed mechanisms of the model, which directly informs what therapists do and say in the therapy room.

Chapters 3 through 7 review the structure and procedures of the five treatment tasks, with each chapter covering a different task. The tasks represent essential building blocks of the therapy. Each chapter includes a figure presenting the ideal therapist performance map (i.e., the sequence of the therapists' interventions needed to help the family members traverse through the steps of the task). Each task has an outcome goal. This helps the therapist decide what to focus on and what to avoid during the task and what to aim for by the end of the task. It is not a recipe for the treatment; it is a list of ingredients presented in an ideal order. But do not be fooled: The self of the therapist is critical in the delivery of the model. Therapists need to be emotionally and intellectually present to make the necessary moment-by-moment clinical decisions needed to facilitate the treatment. This approach will resonate well with therapists comfortable with strong emotion, intense interpersonal contact, and trauma-focused therapy. While Chapters 3 through 7 focus on the fine-grained detail of the treatment process, in Chapter 8 we provide a full case study to convey the overall gestalt of the approach.

We believe strongly in the mechanisms of change embedded in each task. We have evidence that many of the mechanisms work, and the overall oucomes are promising. The deeply moving nature of the work also helps us believe in the model. We have seen very difficult families—families that many providers have given up on—work through tremendous pain and resolve deep interpersonal wounds. Perhaps the real lesson in the book is about intentionality. Therapists need a model: a theory of change, a set of intervention skills, and a vision of outcome. These tools create a thinking therapist, one who can be in the here and now of experiential change but can also evaluate—in real time—where they are headed, what is working, and how to change direction if needed. If this book inspires that, then we have accomplished our goal.

1

HISTORICAL ROOTS AND EMPIRICAL SUPPORT FOR ATTACHMENT-BASED FAMILY THERAPY

In this chapter, we describe the historical context and evidence supporting the attachment-based family therapy (ABFT) model. We begin by placing ABFT in the context of several traditions within the field of psychotherapy. Using a historical perspective on family therapy, we describe three waves of development: structural, narrative, and family psychology. Each wave has made important contributions to family therapy but presents some conflicting theories, values, and intervention strategies. Next, we suggest that attachment theory provides a unifying framework that helps resolve some of these differences. In particular, attachment theory offers a transactional model to help explain the mutual influence of internal intrapsychic development and interpersonal experience within family relationships. In Chapter 2, we discuss attachment theory more fully, but here we point out how ABFT and other therapy models use it to guide treatment.

http://dx.doi.org/10.1037/14296-002
Attachment-Based Family Therapy for Depressed Adolescents, by G. S. Diamond, G. M. Diamond, and S. A. Levy

After discussing the theoretical context of ABFT, we next give credit to four clinical models that have shaped our clinical sensibility and intervention strategies: structural family therapy (SFT; Minuchin, 1974; Minuchin & Fishman, 1981), emotion-focused therapy (EFT) for individuals and couples (Greenberg, Auszra, & Herrmann, 2007; Johnson, 2004), contextual family therapy (Böszörményi-Nagy & Spark, 1973), and especially multidimensional family therapy (MDFT; Liddle, 2002). We then describe how task-based psychotherapy research (Rice & Greenberg, 1984) helped us conceptualize the organization and delivery of ABFT. Finally, we provide a brief overview of the empirical support for ABFT and put our model in the context of other empirically supported treatments for depressed youth.

HISTORICAL CONTEXT OF FAMILY THERAPY

Structural Theory

In the 1950s, innovative therapists such as Salvador Minuchin, Jay Haley, Virginia Satir, and others began to question the psychoanalytic tenet that intrapsychic conflict during early childhood (e.g., the oedipal complex) was the root cause of psychopathology later in life. At the same time, these innovators observed that present interactions between family members in the therapy room seemed to cause or reinforce children's existing difficulties. Thus, they began to focus clinically on the current patterns of interaction that maintained the problem. For example, Minuchin (1974) observed that children acted out more when parents disagreed on how to discipline them. Helping parents work better as a team made the acting out child more cooperative. These innovators also found that neutrality- and insight-oriented interventions promoted by psychoanalysis did little to change family interactions. They recognized that therapists needed to be more directive and, at times, challenging to change family functioning.

To help understand these new clinical observations and techniques, family therapists turned away from the popular psychological theories of the day and looked to systems theory as an explanatory model. General systems theory (Bertalanffy, 2003), initially used to understand biological ecosystems, helped theorists and therapists conceptualize how components (family members) within a system (the family) interacted to affect the overall functioning of the system. Dysfunctional organization of the system (e.g., inverted hierarchy, diffuse boundaries, weak leadership) reinforced behavioral and emotional problems in children. Similarly, cybernetics (Bateson, 1972; Wiener, 1973), initially a theory for understanding mechanical systems, helped these early thinkers to understand how feedback loops serve to regulate system parameters. The most famous example was the thermostat: If it gets warm in the house, the air conditioner turns on; if it gets cold, the heater turns on. In this way, homeostasis is maintained. Applied to family functioning, if the parents argued, the child would become sicker, causing parents to stop fighting and cooperate, thereby reducing the threat of separation. In fact, children's symptoms were often viewed as serving a regulatory function for the family. Systems theory provided a major theoretical breakthrough by helping family therapists focus on current family structure, interactions, and communication as a means to change child behavior.

Although systems theory was essential to the birth of family therapy, it had limitations. This theory was essentially an organization model equating family members to cogs in a machine or components in a system. This framework did not explain how human needs such as love, protection, and loyalty motivate interpersonal behavior. Because of this, many early family systems approaches ignored family members' emotional needs that drive interpersonal behavior. Certainly, many family therapists do explore emotions and motives, but systems theory did not provide a conceptual framework for understanding and mobilizing these powerful motivational forces in therapy. In contrast, the ABFT therapist uses and highlights these needs and these feelings as motivators for change (e.g., "You love your child and that is why you are working hard in this therapy") and as content to be to be worked through in the therapy (e.g., "You were never there for me, so I no longer trust you").

Systems theory also promoted an authoritarian therapist style. This may have resulted, in part, from viewing families as an organization or mechanical system that—when dysfunctional—needs a strong leader to change it. Minuchin (1998) proposed that systems theory even had an inherent disdain for families, seeing individuals as victims or prisoners that needed to be liberated from dysfunctional, if not oppressive, family dynamics. In ABFT, we take a strengths-based approach, viewing family relationships as curative. The therapist aims to resuscitate family members' instinctual need to be loved (child) and to protect (parent) and leverages these motives to promote more positive interaction. Therefore, ABFT therapists' stances are authoritative (i.e., the therapists have a plan and a direction), but they facilitate that stance through a more collaborative, conversational approach.

Narrative Theory

In the 1980s, constructivism ushered in what some call second-order family therapy (Berger & Luckmann, 1966; Gergen, 1991). Although most constructivists acknowledge that a "real world" exists outside of human consciousness or language, they are more interested in how people construct their realities. From this perspective, people's view of self and other is determined by their experiences in life, their context, and how they understand those experiences (Maturana & Varela, 1984). This perspective led narrative therapists, such as Anderson (1997) and White and Epston (1990), to focus on how individuals' identities and relationship patterns are reflected in and reinforced by the stories or narratives they tell about themselves and others. Understanding these narratives illuminates people's schemas about themselves and others and how such schemas determine their feelings and behaviors. Therapeutic change occurs by expanding these narratives, uncovering missing details, making richer (or "thicker") stories, thus freeing clients up to view themselves and others differently. In this regard, narrative therapy returned family therapists' attention to the psychological processes within an individual, targeting language as the mechanism of change rather than focusing on families and the interactions between family members. Because knowledge about one's self is relative, constructionism also discouraged the therapist from viewing himself or herself as the expert. Instead, the therapist serves as a conversation manager who facilitates family members' becoming more reflective and curious about themselves (Anderson, 1997).

The narrative revolution has helped family therapy focus on the individual, appreciate the value of self-understanding, and reduce the authoritarian tendencies characteristic of the first-generation family therapists. However, ABFT differs from narrative therapy in several important ways. First, this postmodern theory, particularly the more radical constructionist view, discourages therapists from using psychological science to help guide clinical intervention. If knowledge is subjective, universal truths about human development and interaction do not exist (Dallos, 2006). Therefore, the idea of scientific discovery and the accumulation of knowledge about family interaction is undervalued (Pinsof & Lebow, 2005). In contrast, ABFT assumes that there are general principles about human nature and family life in particular. Applied with sensitivity and while recognizing individual and cultural differences, these principles can assist in assessments and interventions with families.

Second, although it may play out differently in practice (Coulehan, Friedlander, & Heatherington, 1998), on paper narrative therapy primarily focuses on cognitive change processes: telling stories, elaborating and exploring different interpretation, and attributions about experience. As in many cognitive-based psychotherapy models, emotional processing and its relation to cognitive and interpersonal change can be ignored. In contrast, ABFT, like EFT (Greenberg, 2011; Johnson, 2004) views emotional processing as a central mechanism of change. Emotions serve as a gateway to deeper, more profound therapeutic content (e.g., unmet attachment needs) and associated action tendencies, facilitating lasting psychological and interpersonal change. Furthermore, research suggests that arousal of primary adaptive emotions has been linked to positive treatment outcome in experiential EFT (Greenberg, Auszra, & Herrmann, 2007), as well as in behavior therapy (Foa, Hembree, & Rothbaum, 2007).

Third, in narrative therapy, the explorative process seems to mostly occur between the therapist and an individual family member rather than between family members themselves (Minuchin, 1998; Minuchin, Nichols, & Lee, 2007). In this regard, narrative therapy, like cognitive therapy, focuses more on changing how clients think about experiences rather than on changing the current interactions that shape that experience. ABFT, like EFT for couples (Johnson, 2004), also explores parents' and adolescents' internal working models (i.e., narrative or schema) about relationships to prime and prepare them for new relational experiences. Then, however, we facilitate actual in-session family interactions designed to create new and positive relational experiences. These experiential learning experiences are understood to be the primary change mechanism in ABFT. We believe (and continue to test) that these new relational experiences help revise internal working models of self and other.

Finally, because knowledge is viewed as subjective in narrative therapy, therapists resist directing the therapy. Narrative therapists let the client lead the discovery process (i.e., client centered). Although ABFT promotes self-reflection and self-understanding, it is not client centered. Instead, it relies on a foundation of psychological science to help identify the most salient and relevant family processes (e.g., attachment ruptures) and how best to change them (e.g., parent–adolescent dialogue). In this regard, therapists view themselves as experts, professionals well trained in the science of family development and psychotherapy change processes. Being an expert, however, does not mean being authoritarian. The change process requires that therapists collaborate with family members. So therapists set the treatment course and define the treatment focus (repairing relational ruptures) but then help family members understand, express, and discuss their own idiosyncratic schemas and emotions.

Family Psychology

In the last 2 decades, family therapy has entered a third wave of development driven by the emergences of family psychology. Although family psychology refers to a much broader discipline than just therapy, we briefly highlight here some of the values this paradigm brings to family therapy. From an epistemological standpoint, family psychology embraces the scientific method as part of its professional mission (Pinsof & Lebow, 2005). Rather than viewing knowledge as subjective and relativistic, intervention models are subjected to experimentation and evaluation. If therapy works, then how it works can and should be examined. How to empirically test systemic ideas presents unique challenges, but that is the task of family intervention science (Liddle, 1987). If family therapy continues to be ambivalent about science (Liddle, Bray, Levant, & Santisteban, 2002), our profession and practice will increasingly be devalued and marginalized in the current health care environment. Empirically supported treatments increasingly receive the most attention, dissemination, and reimbursement, and family therapy should be a part of this tradition.

Besides testing treatment efficacy, family psychology seeks knowledge about basic psychopathology and development in family life. Research on child and family development, parenting practices, emotional processing, and cognitive schemas, as well as social and cultural forces, can help to identify important risk factors and processes that, if targeted, could increase the potency of family intervention. For example, research on Expressed Emotion (EE; negative and critical views of the child) demonstrates that EE is a risk factor for depression; can be modified by intervention; and if reduced, prevents relapse (Asarnow, Tompson, Hamilton, & Goldstein, 1994; Hooley, Orley, & Teasdale, 1986). This is an example of how family science can inform and enhance family intervention.

Family psychology also provides a scaffold for understanding and tracking the multiple change processes that occur simultaneously in family therapy (Liddle, 2010). At any given moment, family therapists are assessing cognitive, emotional, historical, social, and cultural processes in multiple individuals, as well as the interactions between family members. At any given moment family therapists are providing psychoeducation, challenging attributions, promoting self-reflection, facilitating emotional processes, shaping interactional sequences, monitoring communication style, and/or guiding experiential change. This complexity is inherent to working with a multiperson therapeutic system like a family. Having some understanding of these complex processes helps therapists decide what to focus on, when, and for how long. Focusing on the transactional relationship between intrapsychic and interactional experience, family psychology takes a both/and approach to the systems/individual dilemma. Where systems theory lost sight of the individual, and constructivist therapy lost site of the family, family psychology views both levels, as well as social cultural factors, as important domains for assessment and intervention (Liddle, 1987; Pinsof & Hambright, 2002). Because of its overarching set of principles, we advocate that family psychology should not be limited to or only associated with psychologists. Family psychology is a general scientific and clinical framework that anyone studying or treating families can use. We are trying to understand and improve the psychology of the individuals and their interactions in the context of family life.

ABFT stands firmly in the family psychology tradition. First, ABFT is wedded to the values of empirical science. We use psychological science to inform treatment targets and processes. We are committed to demonstrating treatment efficacy though randomized clinical trials with diverse populations and distinct disorders. We also use the scientific method to study the processes of therapy; the moment-by-moment therapist intervention strategies and client performances that lead to good or bad outcomes. Identifying, testing, and operationalizing effective treatment processes improves our ability to teach therapists how to facilitate them more effectively and more often. ABFT, however, is not an eclectic model. Technical or theoretical eclecticism assumes that therapist have a toolbox of techniques and strategies that are used as needed or, at worse, randomly (e.g., "Maybe today we should do some relaxation techniques"). In contrast, ABFT is truly integrative; our use and implementation of strategies and goals are guided and organized by our overarching theoretical framework: attachment theory.

ATTACHMENT THEORY AS A UNIFYING FRAMEWORK

Attachment theory helps us to understand individual and family development, as well as their interaction. It also helps us conceptualize and guide the therapeutic change processes. Like the early family therapy innovators, John Bowlby, a British psychiatrist and psychoanalyst, believed that psychoanalytic theory focused too much on children's internal fantasy and not enough on what actually transpired between children and parents (Bowlby, 1969, 1988). Bowlby was shunned by his contemporaries for rejecting the core tenets of psychoanalysis, but his ideas found a home in the field of developmental psychology. In collaboration with Mary Ainsworth, the two developed a programmatic research tradition that revealed the importance of children's early attachment as a foundation of healthy development. Although the psychoanalytic community also believed early childhood experience determined psychological development, Bowlby and Ainsworth believed the developmental process was not driven by intrapsychic needs but rather by the influence and impact of real relationships during childhood. Ironically, family therapists also initially rejected Bowlby's ideas. Family therapists believed that current, not early childhood, relational experiences determined behavior.

Attachment theory became more interesting to the psychoanalytic and family systems communities in the 1980s when Mary Main developed the Adult Attachment Interview (Main & Goldwyn, 1998). This assessment tool allowed psychologists to examine adult perceptions of childhood attachment relationships, how these narratives reflected parents' own attachment style or state of mind (e.g., the parents' expectations of relationships as safe or untrustworthy), and how that attachment state of mind impacted current psychiatric distress, marital functioning, and parenting (Hesse, 1999). Suddenly, attachment was no longer understood as simply a childhood phenomenon. Rather, attachment state of mind was related to intrapsychic, interpersonal, and intergenerational processes (e.g., parenting) throughout the life span. With increasing popularity and empirical support, psychodynamic theorists began to use attachment models to explain and facilitate the impact of the therapist–client relationship, how a safe therapeutic relationship could revise internal working models (Fosha, 2000; Holmes, 2001, 2010; Wallin, 2007), and even affect neurological patterns set down by insecure parenting (Fonagy, Gyorgy, Jurist, & Target, 2005; Siegel, 2012). They conceived of the therapeutic process as one of reparenting their clients.

A few family therapists have also turned to attachment theory. Byng-Hall (1995, 1998) understood the importance of the family as a secure base and how therapy could repair it when damaged. He believed that promoting a more coherent understanding of relationships and past attachment ruptures could help resuscitate a more secure attachment state of mind. Dallos (2006) wrote one of the best theoretical integrations of attachment theory, narrative therapy, and systems therapy. He, like us, believes in the process of generating narratives that focus specifically on attachment ruptures. His book, *Attachment Narrative Therapy: Integrating Systemic, Narrative, and Attachment Therapies*, is a must-read for anyone interested in the interface of these three traditions. D. A. Hughes (2007) has also done some important theoretical and clinical modeling of an attachment-focused family intervention. His model shares many of the conceptual goals of ABFT (e.g., creating a more coherent family narrative of trauma). He offers a particular important emphasis on the empathic stance of the therapist to validate clients' avoided or confusing emotionally infused memories. The Circle of Security (Zanetti, Powell, Cooper, & Hoffman, 2011), a parent psychoeducational program, is an early intervention model for parents and young children that teaches parenting skills aimed at promoting secure attachment with young children. Using a group modality, Moretti and Obsuth (2009) also target similar parenting skills, but with parents of adjudicated adolescents. Johnson (2004) has likely done the most to promote attachment concepts as a way of understanding of therapeutic process. Building on the powerful conceptual foundation of EFT (Greenberg, 2002) and its intricately articulated intervention strategies, Johnson has helped highlight the centrality of attachment needs in the context of couples therapy and psychotherapy in general. These psychoanalytic, family therapy, and psychoeducation innovators have inspired the formation of the ideas in ABFT.

ABFT stands within this new tradition of using attachment theory to organize therapeutic conversation and goals. We help adolescents explore and articulate their memories, feelings, and thoughts about their attachment experience. As their awareness and understanding of the experience deepens and becomes more differentiated and coherent, adolescents are better prepared to directly express their unmet attachment needs to their parents. We also explore parents' own history of attachment ruptures, to increase their capacity to reflect on, understand, and empathize with their adolescent's attachment needs, what Fonagy et al. (2005) might call reflective functioning.

We then bring adolescents and parents together to discuss these attachment ruptures that are inhibiting (or undermining) trust and safety in the relationships. As adolescents connect to their feelings and attachment needs associated with past events, and parents listen in a more empathic manner, adolescents' internal working models of their parents are revised. As adolescents speak in a clear, more emotionally regulated manner, parents' working models of their adolescents are revised. These positive, experiential moments of corrective attachment interactions reinforce parents' effective caregiving and adolescents' trust in their parents' availability and sensitivity. With the safe haven on the mend, adolescents will more likely reach out to their parents in times of distress. This provides a secure base to support adolescents' developmentally driven quest for autonomy. Thus, in ABFT, understanding internal working models is in the service of changing interactions. Changing interactions is in the service of revising internal working models.

The attachment-based psychotherapy models share many conceptual and strategic goals (Kobak, Grassetti, Close, & Krauthamer Ewing, 2013). They all appreciate the developmental interaction between internal working models of self and others and the relational experiences between parents and children. In this regard, they discard the empirically false and clinically unhelpful dichotomy between intrapsychic and interpersonal development and functioning. These models also all rest on the assumption that the internal working models are up for revision. In the individual therapies, the therapist provides the corrective attachment experience. In the family-based models, the therapist serves as a transitional object, providing safety, empathy, hope, and guidance to both the adolescent and the parents. With the need and desire for attachment (adolescent) and caregiving (parents) revived, the therapist transitions the responsibility of the reparative process back to the family members.

More rigorous research is required to explore whether these proposed curative mechanisms of attachment-based therapies are in fact active and effective. Or has attachment theory just become a new poetic language to help researchers understand the curative impact of nonspecific therapy factors? Does creating a more coherent attachment narrative improve psychological functioning? Does talking about or exploring attachment narratives between family members improve coherence, and does that lead to a change in adolescents' expectations of their parents (e.g., "they will be there for me" or "they will not be there for me")? Can adolescents work though attachment trauma if the relational environment remains unsafe and unsupportive? How essential is emotional processing to changing internal working models and/or improving family interactions? To what extent do the parents' own attachment styles inhibit them from developing more attachment-promoting parenting skills? What is the relative value of the therapist providing the corrective attachment experience versus the parent providing it? Can parents play a role in repairing their children's attachment state of mind even if their children are now adults? Fortunately, our team is involved in several studies that address these kinds of questions. We hope we can make a contribution to understanding ABFT as well as these other attachment-based interventions.

CLINICAL ROOTS OF ATTACHMENT-BASED FAMILY THERAPY

We must also acknowledge our indebtedness to several clinical traditions. We stand on the shoulders of giants. The four therapy models that have shaped our model are SFT (Minuchin, 1974), EFT (Greenberg, 2002; Johnson, 2004), contextual family therapy (Böszörményi-Nagy & Spark, 1973), and most of all, MDFT (Liddle, 1995).

ABFT grows directly out of SFT. Like SFT, ABFT is built on the belief that effective parenting is essential for healthy child development. Developing his work with young boys who acted out, Minuchin (1974) mainly focused on boundaries and hierarchy. Working with depressed adolescents, we have had to expand our view of effective parenting (see Chapter 3, this volume). The most important contribution of SFT to ABFT, however, is its experiential model of change. Similar to gestalt therapy, Minuchin (1974) encouraged therapists to not just talk about change but to also help families experience new ways of behaving and relating to each other in the therapy session. Minuchin and Fishman (1981) proposed that the "enactment" of new behavior would be a more profound learning experience than just promoting insight or teaching new skills (e.g., psychoeducation). Minuchin, however, tended to focus more on enacting behavioral change episodes (e.g., putting parents in charge, blocking parents intrusiveness). In contrast, ABFT enacts intimate, emotionally laden, genuine moments of conversation about core attachment themes and needs. The experiential learning focuses on affect regulation, direct communication, and building up an expectation of trustworthy interactions between parents and adolescents. Still, SFT remains the cornerstone of our intervention theory and technique.

EFT (Greenberg, 2011) has also greatly influenced ABFT, as it has the field of psychotherapy in general. EFT has helped our profession understand the importance and use of emotions as core psychological and interpersonal processes, and as agents of change in therapy. Informed by contemporary research on emotion, EFT therapists do not think about emotional expression as being cathartic but rather as having a communication function (Greenberg & Safran, 1987). Emotions serve as a doorway to deeper clinical themes and more authentic communication. EFT has been applied to couples therapy (Greenberg & Johnson, 1988; Johnson, 2004), which helped introduce the discussion of emotions in the field of family therapy. The EFT goals of identifying primary adaptive emotions, regulating the expression of emotional needs, and using softer, more vulnerable emotions to facilitate communication has been nothing less than a small revolution in how therapists think about the change process. Johnson (2004) has also made attachment the primary organizing theme of couples therapy, thus helping therapists put the expression and repairing of attachment security at the core of relational intimacy. Repairing this dimension of a relationship resuscitates safety and intimacy and forms the foundation for successful communication and problem solving.

ABFT uses EFT and its techniques but diverges from Johnson's (e.g., 2004) couples work in a profound way. With couples, there is an equal or mutual responsibility between partners to provide love, safety, and protection for one another. In ABFT with adolescents, we aim to rebuild the original parent–child attachment organization. Parents have a natural, inherent, and moral responsibility to meet their child's attachment needs, and not the other way around. Adolescents certainly have to treat their parents with respect, but the natural power differential and inherent responsibility of parents to care for their children must be supported and harnessed. We help parents develop a more authoritative parenting posture that promotes parent–adolescent negotiation of attachment and autonomy.

We also have theoretical lineage to contextual family therapy (Böszörményi-Nagy & Spark, 1973). This underappreciated therapy model views relational justice, fairness, and trust as the fundamental fabric of interpersonal relationships. Rather than being impartial and neutral, the contextual therapist uses multidirected partiality to understand and acknowledge each family member's temperamental, historical, and circumstantial experience to help explain difficulties and motivations that thwart or promote loving parent–child relationships. Contextual family therapy takes into account the mother who had no mother and feels unprepared to parent, the adolescent who cannot forgive his mother for his father's leaving, and the couple who lost their first child and therefore raised their second child with fear and trepidation. Although people have the right to be mad at or distrustful of others, gaining an understanding of the experiences that drive their behavior helps bring perspective and empathy into the complex process of love, respect, and accountability. Forgiveness and exoneration become important topics of conversation when trying to repair attachment ruptures (Böszörményi-Nagy & Spark, 1973; McCullough, Pargament, & Thoresen, 2000). Can family members let go of resentment, indignation, or anger and cease to seek revenge or restitution? In this regard, ABFT can facilitate profound conversations about the existential conditions of family life: Can we go on together? Can we give each other another chance? Is the instinct of attachment and caregiving still alive, even if buried under deep hurt and disappointment? Focusing on these fundamental questions of love, trust, and forgiveness, helps family members enter into profound I–Thou conversations (Buber, 1937), in which blame and defensiveness give way to an appreciation of the tragic circumstances of their family life; a life that should have been filled with love and connection has been dominated by resentment and mistrust. Rather than see each other as enemies, family members see each other as human beings with strengths and weaknesses, good motives and some bad choices. Contextual family therapy helps the ABFT therapist make these existential themes of family life the focus of these reparative conversations.

Finally, we owe our greatest debt to MDFT, developed by Howard Liddle (Liddle, 1999; Liddle et al., 2001). MDFT also emerged from SFT but brought many innovations. First, MDFT was the first family therapy to turn to psychological science to conceptualize its assessment and change processes. Research and theory from child and adolescent development, parenting, cognitions, emotions, social learning, and attachment theory all inform how a therapist thinks about the moment-to-moment decisions of treatment in MDFT.

Second, MDFT helped us incorporate into therapy an appreciation of adolescents' developmental need for autonomy while maintaining attachment. Adolescents are not children to be controlled, but emerging adults that need to have a voice in the treatment. Consequently, therapists actively engage adolescents in the treatment processes as the first agenda of therapy (Liddle, 1995; Liddle & Diamond, 1991). Helping adolescents identify problems that are meaningful to them and helping parents take these concerns seriously are hallmarks of MDFT and fundamental principles in ABFT (G. S. Diamond & Liddle, 1999; Liddle, 1994). ABFT also derives some of its emphasis on emotions from MDFT. MDFT, like EFT (Greenberg, 2011), aims to uncover underlying emotions that drive destructive behavior and helps make them the content and focus of therapy (Liddle, 1994, 2002). Finally, like MDFT, ABFT is a task-based approach. MDFT proposes thinking about four domains of functioning: adolescent's individual functioning, parents' individual functioning, parent–adolescent interaction, and extrafamilial functioning. Work in the individual domains is viewed as preparation for work in the interactional domains, thus laying the foundation for work in the extrafamilial domains. This clinical sensibility directly informs the structure of the ABFT model. MDFT, however, has broad and ambitious conceptual and clinical goals within these domains, whereas ABFT has a more narrow, circumscribed goal: repairing attachment security. We have a strong allegiance to MDFT and are greatly indebted to Dr. Liddle. We hope the reader will hear his voice throughout this book and will be encouraged to read his inspiring writings.

DEVELOPMENT OF THE ATTACHMENT-BASED FAMILY THERAPY MODEL

Possibly the strongest contribution of ABFT is that it offers a model for conceptualizing a profound, interpersonal, trauma-focused, emotionally charged change processes into a fairly well organized set of clinical steps and procedures. To accomplish this, we organize the delivery of ABFT into five treatment tasks: (a) the relational reframe, (b) alliance task with the adolescent, (c) alliance task with the parents, (d) the attachment task, and (e) the promoting-autonomy task. A *treatment task* can be defined as a set of therapist interventions and client processes (or performances) required to accomplish or work through a defined problem state (Rice & Greenberg, 1984). In contrast to specific interventions, tasks provide an overarching structure to guide a progression of distinct, yet interrelated, therapeutic interventions that lead to proximal and distal goals.

The concept of therapeutic tasks evolves from psychotherapy process research developed by Rice and Greenberg (1984). These investigators were interested in studying the most meaningful in-session moments of therapy. They surmised that if these change events could be identified, analyzed, and operationalized, they could be more easily taught and delivered more often and more competently. For example, as a gestalt therapist, Greenberg focused on the empty-chair technique. This technique involves having clients sit in one chair and imagine the person with whom they have a conflict, usually their parent or spouse, in the other, adjacent empty chair. In the empty chair strategy, the client moves back and forth playing both parts. The client then enacts an imaginary conversation with that person about long-standing unresolved issues. Greenberg videotaped these sessions and studied them closely trying to understand what led to successful repair processes, and at times what led to their failure. This included both what the therapist did and how the client performed in successful versus unsuccessful episodes. These videotaped sessions were coded with standardized rating scales to see how objective, observer ratings matched and/or expanded the investigator's clinical impressions. Over time, patterns emerged that reflected the ideal sequence of a successful task. These ideal performance maps could then be shared, taught, and replicated by therapists through training and supervision.

Guy S. Diamond used this change event process methodology for his graduate dissertation under the leadership of Howard Liddle (G. Diamond & Liddle, 1996; G. S. Diamond & Liddle, 1999). In that study, *shift* episodes were identified in therapy: moments when adolescent–parent arguments about behavioral conflicts (e.g., homework, friends, and chores) became so hostile that the therapist stopped trying to solve problems and shifted the conversation to focus on the core relational themes (e.g., abandonment, broken trust) that fueled such conflict. In these shifts, therapists said things like, "Hold on here. . . . Why is there so much hatred expressed over a simple topic as house chores?" And usually turning to the adolescent, "What are you really so angry about? What is underneath this rage?" These shifts were often profound, pivotal moments in the treatment where an adolescent identified core attachment ruptures or experiences of deeply felt relational injustice.

Operationalizing and studying these shift moments helped to focus attention on issues of trust, safety, and relational betrayal. We (the three authors of this volume) then began to apply these strategies with depressed adolescents on the inpatient unit at the Philadelphia Child Guidance Center. We began to ask ourselves how we could make these shift moments happen more quickly and more often. Rather than wait for it to happen by luck, how do we rapidly move from a therapy focused on symptom reduction to a therapy focused on relational issues of love, safety, and trust? We found ourselves increasingly able to organize the therapy around attachment ruptures and repair while becoming more aware of the personal and interpersonal barriers that we needed to overcome to get there. We began to develop intervention techniques to address common and expected challenges. Building on Liddle's (1994) idea of "preparing for enactment," we began to see that rather than a single change event, we were in fact mapping out a series of related change events that systematically built upon each other and ultimately set the foundation for profound life-altering conversations about love, trust, and reconnection (G. S. Diamond & Diamond, 2002).

This process led to the development and operationalization of five specific treatment tasks that serve as the clinical scaffolding for ABFT. These tasks provide an ideal road map to guide the overall direction of the therapy, as well as the within-session processes. The map shows the therapist what to focus on, how to get there, potential barriers and pitfalls, and the desired end point. These tasks give the therapist direction and intentionality within and across sessions and help the therapist to rapidly focus therapy on important, empirically supported, core individual and family processes linked to depression. The clinical chapters that lie ahead (Chapters 3, 4, 5, 6, and 7) represent the "ideal" task performance of the therapist and families as they move through each task. These chapters will not answer every question or map perfectly onto every case. They do, however, provide a set of principles, phases, within-session goals, and end-of-session goals. We use this set of principles as our guide and then modify it on the basis of the idiosyncratic presentation of each family.

DATA SUPPORTING ATTACHMENT-BASED FAMILY THERAPY

Thus far, we have strong data to support the efficacy of ABFT. Several treatment studies have helped validate and refine this approach. An initial open trial of 10 cases demonstrated that ABFT resulted in significant decreases in adolescents' depression and suicidal ideation over 12 weeks (G. S. Diamond, Siqueland, & Diamond, 2003). In a second study, 32 adolescents were randomized to ABFT or a 6-week wait-list control (G. S. Diamond, Reis, Diamond, Siqueland, & Isaacs, 2002). Within the ABFT condition, 81% of adolescents no longer met criteria for major depressive disorder at posttreatment, compared with 47% of the wait-listed cases. In addition, 62% of subjects treated with ABFT met criteria for depression remission, compared with 19% of the control group.

A third study involved randomizing 66 adolescents to 12 weeks of ABFT or to enhanced usual care (EUC; facilitated referral, weekly monitoring) for suicidal ideation and depressive symptoms (G. S. Diamond et al., 2010). Adolescents in ABFT demonstrated significantly greater rates of change on self-reported suicidal ideation at posttreatment, and benefits were maintained at 6 months postbaseline with a strong overall effect size (.97). Treatment effects were similar based on clinicians' ratings. Significantly more adolescents in ABFT displayed clinical improvement on suicide ideation at posttreatment and follow up, with a large effect size (*OR* 4.41). Reduction in depressive symptoms showed a similar pattern. Data also suggest that ABFT is efficacious with the most troubled populations, including adolescents who are severely depressed, have a history of sexual abuse, or have parents who are depressed themselves. The efficacy of ABFT with these adolescents is especially noteworthy because these groups have, historically, not responded well to cognitive–behavioral treatment and/or medication (Asarnow et al., 2009; Barbe, Bridge, Birmaher, Kolko, & Brent, 2004; Curry et al., 2006). Finally, we looked at treatment retention and found that even low-income youth with multiple problems attended, on average, 12 sessions of treatment compared with three sessions of treatment in EUC.

Several small pilot studies have also supported the efficacy of ABFT (these studies will, we hope, lead to larger ones). One study looked at dissemination of ABFT to community providers in a community hospital system in Norway (Israel & Diamond, 2012). We found that we could train these providers and that they produced better outcomes than treatment as usual. Another pilot study demonstrated the feasibility and produced initial data suggesting the efficacy of using ABFT with suicidal gay, lesbian, and bisexual youth (G. M. Diamond et al., 2012). A third study (G. S. Diamond, Levy, & Creed, 2012) used ABFT as an aftercare program for suicidal youth upon discharge from a psychiatric hospital. Compared with treatment as usual, ABFT had fewer adolescents reattempt suicide and/or return to the hospital. Finally, a current study in Israel is comparing ABFT with EFT for adults presenting with unresolved anger toward at least one of their parents. This study is designed to examine the impact of working through unresolved anger through imaginal role play (i.e., chair work) versus attachment-focused enactments with the actual parents.

We also conducted 15 studies looking at a wide range of the proposed mechanisms of change within sessions of ABFT. These process research studies looked within the "black box" of therapy and tried to identify what processes lead to proximal (end-of-session) or distal (end-of-treatment) change. For example, several studies looked at processes within a single task. One study of the reframe task suggested that adolescents generally began therapy with a more interpersonal view of depression than did parents (G. S. Diamond et al., 2003). When therapists successfully elicited the adolescent's more vulnerable emotions associated with the desire to be loved, parents softened and were more likely to embrace a relational goal of therapy. A second study used sequential analytic and bootstrapping techniques to examine the impact of relational reframes on parents' problem constructions, and vice versa, in five sessions focusing on the reframing task. Results showed that relational reframes greatly increased the likelihood that parents would generate interpersonal (rather than intrapersonal) problem constructions and focus on impasses in their relationships with their adolescents (Moran, Diamond, & Diamond, 2005). In a third study using a similar methodology to analyze sessions from 13 different cases of ABFT, findings showed that, in good alliance sessions alone with parents, relational reframes led parents to speak less critically and less dismissively and to take a more understanding, empathic, and affirming posture toward their adolescents (Moran & Diamond, 2008).

In a study of parent–therapist alliance in Task III, we identified a five-stage clinical model of alliance building (Moed, 2002). In the more successful sessions, the clinical pattern progressed through support, empathy, and confrontation, working through and then back to a mix of support and empathy. In a study of successful and unsuccessful attachment tasks (Task IV), G. S. Diamond and Stern (2003) found a nine-stage model of change. This sequence included adolescent disclosure (expression of anger, vulnerable emotions, and problem attributions), parent disclosure (expression of acknowledgment, self-disclosure, and apology), and conversation (exploring adolescents repose, mutual conversation, hopes for the future).

Related to distal changes, one study used observational and self-report measures to examine the correlation between changes in parenting, attachment schema, and adolescent psychological symptoms (Shpigel, Diamond, & Diamond, 2012). Results showed that decreases in maternal psychological control and increases in parental autonomy granting were associated with increased adolescent perception of maternal care. At 3 months, this change in perception was related to reductions of adolescent self-reported attachment-related anxiety and avoidance. Furthermore, reductions in adolescents' perceived maternal control were associated with reductions in adolescent depressive symptoms.

Taken together, these outcome and process studies have earned ABFT a quality of research score of 3.5 for depression and 3.6 for suicide ideation and a 4.0 for readiness for dissemination (based on a scale of 0.0–4.0, with 4.0 being the highest) by the National Registry of Evidence-Based Programs and Practices and recognition by several other review groups (David-Ferdon & Kaslow, 2008; Promising Practices Network, 2011).

PUTTING ATTACHMENT-BASED FAMILY THERAPY IN THE CONTEXT OF OTHER EMPIRICALLY SUPPORTED TREATMENTS FOR DEPRESSED ADOLESCENTS

ABFT should be considered in the context of the many other empirically supported treatment options for adolescent depression. We do not provide a full review here but instead focus on the most salient and robust findings in the field. We encourage ABFT providers to be up-to-date on this clinical information so they are able to accurately explain the benefits and limitations of ABFT to parents and adolescents.

The majority of treatment research and model development for depressed adolescents has focused on psychopharmacology and cognitive–behavioral therapy (CBT). The use of selective serotonin reuptake inhibitors for treating adolescents with depression has generally been positive, especially in combination with psychotherapy. Still, best practice guidelines from the child and adolescent psychiatry and pediatrics associations suggest that, with mild to moderate depression, treatment should begin with supportive therapies; then, if needed, more active psychotherapies (e.g., CBT), and then add medication if progress is not observed within 6 to 8 weeks (Birmaher et al., 2007; C. W. Hughes et al., 2007). For more severe depression, medication can be helpful but may raise the risk of suicide ideation. Therefore, for severely depressed adolescents, the primary recommendation is a combination of psychotherapy and medication. The "Guidelines for Adolescent Depression—Primary Care" (Cheung et al., 2007) and C. W. Hughes et al. (2007) do not recommend medication alone, even though it is likely the most common treatment approach.

We have not conducted clinical trials comparing ABFT with and without medication. In clinical practice, however, we follow best practice guidelines and begin with ABFT. If, however, the depression is particularly severe, we may recommend starting medication immediately to speed the impact of treatment. We explain that the depression is inhibiting the adolescent from engaging in the therapy and rebuilding his or her life. In this way, the medication reinforces the goals of the psychotherapy rather than replace it.

Of the psychotherapies, CBT has received the most scientific attention (David-Ferdon & Kaslow, 2008; Lewinsohn, Clarke, Hops, & Andrews, 1990). The core purported mechanism of CBT is to identify, evaluate, and modify inaccurate or unhelpful thoughts and beliefs to reduce distress and impairment in the adolescent (Beck, 1967). Changes in thinking and beliefs are the proposed mediator of change (Weersing, Rozenman, & González, 2009). Adolescents are coached to problem solve real-world concerns, but these efforts focus on how adolescents might think and act differently in response to these situations, with support from parents when possible (Creed, Reisweber, & Beck, 2011). Traditionally, CBT does not attempt to intervene in the family environment, although in practice many CBT therapists may incorporate family interventions into their work.

CBT has been evaluated for use with child and adolescent depression more than any other psychotherapy. CBT has been shown to be effective for treating mild to moderate depression, as well as for preventing the onset of depression (David-Ferdon & Kaslow, 2008). In the past decade, CBT and pharmacotherapy interventions have been compared and combined in several large adolescent depression studies with severely depressed adolescents (Brent, Emslie, Clarke, Wagner, & Asarnow, 2008; Goodyer et al., 2007; Treatment for Adolescent Depression Study [TADS] Team, 2004). In the most influential of the three studies, TADS (2004), researchers found that the combination of fluoxetine and CBT outperformed each alone in the reduction of adolescent depression. However, although fluoxetine alone did significantly better than the placebo (61% vs. 35%), CBT alone (43%) did not. The low response rate for CBT in this study has generated much controversy and questions about the design of the study and the kind of CBT that was delivered (Hollon, Garber, & Shelton, 2005). Still, the findings were surprising and disappointing for the psychotherapy community.

More specifically, the remission rates (symptom free) in the TADS study at posttreatment were only 37% for the combined treatment, indicating that more than 60% of subjects still had symptoms at the end of treatment. By 9 months, there were no differences between treatment outcomes, suggesting that the type of treatment may affect the rate of response but not its long-term magnitude. It is unfortunate that nearly 50% of subjects who responded to treatment relapsed within a year. These results, and recent findings from a meta-analysis (Weisz, McCarty, & Valeri, 2006), suggest that for depressed adolescents, CBT may not be as potent as researchers had previously hoped. Overall, meta-analytic studies have found that the effect sizes of medication and CBT are more modest than expected or desired (Vitiello, 2009). Effect size for medication was .25 (Bridge et al., 2007) and .34 for CBT (Weisz et al., 2006). Researchers should not be discouraged, but humbled. About one third of depressed adolescents respond to supportive therapy and minimal contact. Another third respond well to active treatment with medication and/or psychotherapy. The other third are treatment resistant and more prone to relapse (Vitiello, 2009). Given this appraisal of the field, many senior investigators have encouraged the exploration of alternative or supplemental treatments that might improve current findings (Brent, 2006; Hollon et al., 2005; Jensen, 2006).

Adding family-targeted treatments to these studies has been one attempt to potentiate CBT interventions. Indeed, some in the research community have integrated a family psychoeducational component into their CBT treatments (Wells & Albano, 2005). Typically, those who have done so educate parents about depression (two sessions) and then teach parenting, communication, and problem-solving skills to the entire family (five sessions). Families do not work through problems in the sessions but are encouraged to use these skills at home. Wells and Albano (2005) reported that most families in TADS presented with severe family conflicts and the family component seemed essential, at least for engagement. However, the family intervention strategies did not potentiate the CBT treatment in TADS, given CBT's poor performance overall (TADS, 2004).

Although family education might be effective for some families, we think an intensive course of ABFT might be a more effective complement or precursor to CBT. On the basis of our clinical experience, we recommend beginning treatment with ABFT to rapidly reduce tension in the family and increase parental support. As the negative family environment diminishes, we find that adolescents become more receptive, psychologically available, and motivated to learn CBT skills. Parents can also then serve as a support system to help reinforce the practice of CBT skills at home.

Interpersonal psychotherapy (IPT; Weissman, Markowitz, & Klerman, 2000) has also yielded some promising results for treating adolescent depression (Mufson, Dorta, Moreau, & Weissman, 2004). Regardless of its etiology, depression affects relationships, and relationships affect mood. Thus, IPT for adolescents aims to improve the interpersonal functioning of the adolescent, with a particular focus on grief, interpersonal disputes, role transition, and interpersonal deficits. Three studies have shown IPT to be better than clinical monitoring or treatment as usual (Mufson, Gallagher, Dorta, & Young, 2004; Mufson, Weissman, Moreau, & Garfinkel, 1999; Rosselló & Bernal, 1999); and in the Rosselló and Bernal (1999) study, IPT demonstrated better recovery rates (82%) than CBT (52%).

Although IPT and ABFT share some common values (viewing depression as an interpersonal problem), the models differ in their intervention techniques and purported change mechanisms. In mostly individual therapy sessions with the adolescent, IPT therapists focus on psychoeducation, emotion regulation training, and interpersonal skill development—some of which are also targets of ABFT. However, in IPT, the main learning occurs between the adolescent and the therapist. The therapist then encourages the adolescent to try these new skills at home or in relationships with peers and significant others. In the adolescent model, there is generally one planned parent session, during which 10 to 15 minutes are spent helping the adolescent talk with the parents about previously identified topics. As becomes clear in the following discussions in this book, the ABFT model turns this process on its head and sees the parent–adolescent conversation as the central change mechanism of the treatment. Still, some of the skills taught in IPT are consistent with the aims of ABFT and could easily be used to supplement individual sessions with the adolescent.

Possibly, one day therapists and researchers will fully understand which treatment, for which clients, and at what time in the course of the illness might produce the best results (Paul, 1967). Some have argued that a family treatment like ABFT might be appropriate only when there is a high level of family conflict. The field knows that family conflict is typically high among families with depressed and suicidal adolescents and is predictive of poor treatment response (Asarnow et al., 2009; Birmaher et al., 2007; Kennard et al., 2006). Whether the deeply meaningful and emotionally charged family context is the most potent and useful environment for working though the challenges of depression, regardless of family conflict, is an empirical question waiting to be explored. One of our goals with this book and our research is to ensure that family-based interventions, such as ABFT, are viewed by the research and clinical community as important and viable alternatives or adjuncts to medication and CBT.

CONCLUSION

We hope that this overview chapter helps put ABFT into the context of other family therapy models and other empirically supported treatments for adolescent depression. As the reader may find, we are not inventors, but innovators. We do not offer radically new ideas or interventions, but rather a next generation of family therapy that is derived from and builds on many old and new traditions: Family Therapy 3.0. We do help put humanistic meaning back into a tradition that has struggled with finding the core motivational processes of family life. Rather than behavioral management or radical constructivism, themes of attachment, love, and trust are the leading edge of this therapy. We also embrace the empirical tradition in a field that has been ambivalent about research (Liddle, Bray, Levant, & Santisteban, 2002) and, in our estimation, has suffered greatly because of it. Family therapy derived great power from its original radical break from tradition. It is unfortunate that it has become somewhat marginalized because it lacks an academic and empirical foundation.

Possibly our greatest contribution is to bring structure to what can often be amorphous. The most common comment we receive at the workshops we give is that we succeed in doing things in 12 to 16 weeks that usually take other therapists 6 months to a year to accomplish. We have identified some of the most potent ingredients in family therapy and packaged them in a way that is easy to learn and deliver in a brief time frame. ABFT helps strengthen therapists' intentionality and provides them a road map to quickly identify and address core, existential, attachment themes that drive intrapersonal and interpersonal behavior. The model also helps therapists stand firm, with courage, in the face of painful attachment-related emotions and deepen those emotions and their expression in a fearless manner. Repairing trust and safety helps parents and adolescents build a new partnership that can help maintain attachment while negotiating autonomy—the central tasks of adolescence. We hope that the chapters ahead give therapists the confidence to accomplish this work. We next provide an in-depth discussion of attachment theory, which guides the focus and decision-making process of ABFT therapists.

2

THEORETICAL FRAMEWORK OF ATTACHMENT-BASED FAMILY THERAPY

A therapist has to have a guiding theory, a theory about etiology and a theory about change. Without a theory, the therapist will not know what to attend to and what to let go, what to promote and what to block. Without a theory, the therapist will not have a clear treatment goal nor will he or she know what it looks like when it has been achieved. Without a theory, the therapist will get lost in the myriad of stories and concerns clients bring to therapy and have no clear path out of this dark forest. Indeed, good therapy involves sorting through the details, finding the core themes, and using these themes to organize the goal and direction of the therapy. This cannot be accomplished without a strong theoretical framework.

Family therapists, especially, need a guiding framework. In the therapy room we have many participants, multiple alliances to manage, conflicting views of the problem, competing treatment goals, and varying levels of motivation and psychological mindedness. Given these multiple forces, family

http://dx.doi.org/10.1037/14296-003
Attachment-Based Family Therapy for Depressed Adolescents, by G. S. Diamond, G. M. Diamond, and S. A. Levy

conversations can become tangential and trivial or quickly escalate into arguments as family members enact in the therapy room the same negative interactions that typically occur at home. Faced with these challenges, therapists working with families need to be directive and goal focused. But therapists cannot be directive without having a theory to guide them. Attachment theory provides the framework for attachment-based family therapy (ABFT).

This chapter provides a theoretical framework to help guide the implementation of the model (Chapters 3–7). We begin by providing a brief introduction to attachment theory for children and adolescents and its contribution to normative adolescent development and emotion regulation. Having a model for normative, secure attachment provides the therapist some generic outcomes or goals for the treatment. We then discuss the parents' contributions to the attachment environment. We review what positive, attachment-promoting parenting might look like and then the risk factors that might undermine that effort. We are not proposing here a comprehensive theory of adolescent depression (Yap, Allen, & Sheeber, 2007); rather, we outline the domains of individual and interactional functioning that serve as the main intervention targets of ABFT. We conclude with a theory of change that builds on these target domains.

INTERNAL WORKING MODELS AND ATTACHMENT SECURITY IN CHILDHOOD

At the heart of attachment theory is the proposition that children have a basic evolutionary instinct to seek out parents for protection and comfort. The young child, scared by something in the playroom, runs back to hold mommy's skirt. If parents attend to the child's needs for comfort and reassurance, the child calms down and returns to play. If this continues over time, the child feels more confident about the parents' availability and thus develops an expectation that parents will positively respond to the child's signals of distress. These children develop a model of their parents as trustworthy, reliable, and available and view themselves as worthy of love and protection. Bowlby (1969) called these *internal working models* of caregivers and self, and more recent scholars have referred to them as *attachment schemas* (Bosmans, Braet, & Van Vlierberghe, 2010; H. S. Waters & Waters, 2006; Young, Klosko, & Weishaar, 2003). These models reflect what people expect or anticipate from relationships, initially from parents, and later in life, from others. If people have been treated well, they expect that to continue. If they have been treated poorly, they expect that to continue. Thus, when parents have been attentive and sensitive, children are more likely to develop a secure attachment style

(Bowlby, 1969; Van IJzendoorn, 1995). Under these conditions, children learn to trust that they can seek out their parents for comfort and support when they face a perceived threat. Confident in their parents' availability and responsiveness, children also more freely recognize their own needs, feel worthy of support, and feel secure enough to explore the world around them (Kobak & Duemmler, 1994). Not surprisingly, attachment security is associated with a variety of adaptive outcomes in children, including higher self-esteem, more positive affect, and better physical health (K. L. Thompson & Gullone, 2008).

Attachment security may contribute to better outcomes in children through promotion of effective emotion regulation strategies (Kobak, Cole, Ferenz-Gillies, Fleming, & Gamble, 1993; Mikulincer & Florian, 2004; S. F. Waters et al., 2010). When children experience fear or worry, the attachment system serves as a behavioral strategy to activate parental caregiving. Emotionally attuned parents can talk about emotions and help their child learn to label her or his emotions, as well as provide validation, support, and comfort to their child. If children feel confident that their parents will listen and understand, they develop greater comfort in expressing emotional needs directly (Garner & Spears, 2000). Over time, these behavioral expressions of emotional needs become verbal expression as children learn to engage in conversation about their thoughts and feelings (Kobak & Duemmler, 1994). Thus, rather than suppress emotions, securely attached children can tolerate negative emotion and express these feelings in words. This not only improves children's ability to use cognitive strategies (e.g., appraisal) to process emotions but also increases their willingness to use the attachment relationship to work through difficult feelings. Thus, many of the interpersonal features of secure attachment promote the normative development of effective emotional regulatory strategies (R. A. Thompson, 2008).

INSECURE ATTACHMENT IN CHILDHOOD

When children do not have sensitive and available attachment figures (e.g., caregivers/parents are neglectful, rejecting, or abusive), they are at increased risk for developing an insecure attachment style. Less confident that parents will respond to their needs, these children are more likely to feel unworthy of being loved and protected. Consequently, they develop attachment strategies that protect them against, or help them cope with, inadequate caregiving (Groh, Roisman, Van IJzendoorn, Bakermans-Kranenburg, & Fearon, 2012; Kobak, Cassidy, Lyons-Ruth, & Ziv, 2006). Three primary insecure attachment styles have been identified. Some children develop an *anxious attachment style*, which arises in response to parents who are intermittently available. This anxious attachment style can be seen as a mechanism aimed at engaging the disengaged parent to maximize opportunities for closeness. Other children develop an *avoidant attachment style*, which arises when parents have been consistently unavailable emotionally. Children with this relational strategy tend to deny attachment needs to avoid further disappointment. Finally, some children develop a *disorganized attachment style*, which arises when parents are not only unavailable or insensitive but have in fact been frightening to children. This is common in children who have experienced maltreatment (abuse, neglect, abandonment). These children have no consistent response strategy and tend to vacillate between trying to engage and withdrawing to protect. In general, attachment styles characterize how children respond under stress in relation to their parent. Insecure attachment styles can also be thought of as defensive strategies, protecting one's self from further relational harm or disappointment (Holmes, 2010).

CULTURE

We must consider culture and ethnicity as part of our understanding of how attachment functions in families. For instance, do the three or four attachment styles show up in other cultures? In cultures where multiple family members help raise the child, does attachment to a parent figure play as important a role? Is a parent's emotional availability as critically important in African American, Asian, or Middle Eastern cultures as it is in White, middle-class American culture?

Fortunately, attachment research has a large body of cross-cultural research to help address these questions. Studies have been done in the United States, multiple African countries, Israel, Japan, and Indonesia (Van IJzendoorn, Bakermans-Kranenburg, & Sagi-Schwartz, 2006).

First, the attachment assessments tools (Strange Situation, Adult Attachment Interview [AAI], self-report) have been effective in identifying attachment styles or states of mind in children and adults in these countries. It is noteworthy that the distribution or percentages of children with specific attachment styles (e.g., secure, anxious, avoidant) are relatively consistent across cultures (Van IJzendoorn & Sagi, 1999). Studies in multiple African countries have found that when a larger community was involved in direct and consistent child care, children displayed attachment behavior to multiple adult figures (proximity seeking in times of distress). However, when the mother was part of this network, she remained the primary attachment figures. When the mother was not available, strong attachment developed with whoever provided the primary parenting environment, be it grandmothers, fathers, or kinsmen.

These studies suggest that children's drive or striving for attachment security is universal. As infants, expression of attachment needs is fairly universal. Babies cry, cling, and reach out when they need comfort. As children get older, however, culture begins to shape this process. For example, in the Gusli tribe in Kenya, older children use a handshake rather than clinging behavior to display attachment needs. In some studies on African American cultures, maternal sensitivity was typically lower than in Caucasian comparisons. Consequently, rates of secure attachment were lower as well. But on deeper analysis, low socioeconomic status accounted for most of the harsher parenting from this community. When poverty was controlled, there were no differences in degrees of sensitive parenting or in rates of secure attachment. Finally, several interesting studies of attachment in the Kibbutz social system in Israel found higher rates of insecure attachment when children lived in communal homes rather than in the home of the parents. These and other studies suggest that culture can play a strong role in how attachment security develops and, therefore, must be sensitively understood when working families. (See Van IJzendoorn et al., 2006, for a full review of this cross-cultural literature.)

SECURE ATTACHMENT IN ADOLESCENCE

In contrast to popular belief, the quality of the parent–child attachment relationship continues to play an important role during adolescence (Ainsworth, 1989). Historically, psychology has promoted a view that adolescence is inherently a time of storm and stress and that the central task of adolescent development is separation and individuation (Erikson, 1950; Hall, 1904). But in the past 30 years, developmental psychology has generated a body of research that challenges this assumption. Research findings have shown that a balance of attachment and autonomy provides the foundation for optimal adolescent development (J. P. Allen et al., 2002; Steinberg, 1990).

This is not to say that adolescence is not a stressful time. Adolescence is a time of rapid change in a child's biological development, social context, and role in the family (Steinberg, 1990). The onset of puberty and sexual maturation ushers in a host of biochemical and physical changes (e.g., weight, height, and hormonal changes; sexual characteristics). Adolescents also experience significant cognitive developments that allow them to think more abstractly and critically. This allows them to question social convention and moral standards, increases their expectation to be included in decision making, and reinforces an emerging sense of autonomy and differentiation from parents. Emerging independence includes adolescents' increased affiliation with peers, which can begin to compete with family time and values. At least in Westernized societies, adolescents experience a loosening of restrictions and increased independence; increased unsupervised time and expectations for self-directed responsibility, especially in school; and more frequent exposure to mass media.

These developmental changes can put stress on a family system. If kept within a moderate range of intensity, however, parent–adolescent conflict helps adolescents learn and practice how to examine and voice their opinion, define themselves separately from their parents, regulate emotions, and exercise problem-solving skills. At the same time, these minor conflicts push parents to recalibrate their perception of their adolescent, themselves, and their parenting as the adolescent moves into a more autonomous stage of life. Family flexibility becomes critical for successfully negotiating new rules and expectations (Walsh, 2006).

A secure base sets the foundation for trust, which provides the context to support the bumpy road of adolescent development. Adolescents with a secure attachment can speak to their parents about topics that are embarrassing or difficult without feeling that they will be rejected, abandoned, ridiculed, or controlled. They can criticize or make explicit demands and feel that they will be taken seriously. Adolescents with a secure attachment may have strong peer networks that increasingly provide support and advice, but they can still turn to their parents in times of need or distress, without being concerned that they will overburden their parents (Kobak, Rosenthal, & Serwik, 2005). In fact, securely attached adolescents show sustained engagement with their parents and respect their parents' values. Thus, they can increasingly consider disagreements from both their own viewpoint and that of their parents. They may not agree with their parents all the time, but they can understand their parents' reasoning and intent. As with research on early attachment, studies consistently show that adolescents with secure attachment have less psychopathology (e.g., depression), do better at school, have more positive social relations, and are less involved in deviant behaviors (e.g., drug use, crime; J. P. Allen et al., 2002; Kobak, Sudler, & Gamble, 1991; K. L. Thompson & Gullone, 2008).

These secure relational conditions also set the foundation for an effective goal-corrected partnership in which each person is willing to compromise to maintain a gratifying relationship (Bowlby, 1988; Kobak & Duemmler, 1994). Bowlby (1988) proposed that if children feel parents are responsive and available, they are more likely to cooperate when resolving problems. When adolescents feel loved, understood, and respected by parents, they are more willing to cooperate in the resolution of day-to-day problems and autonomy negotiation. In a secure adolescent–parent relationship, negotiations over, for instance, curfew, chorus, and homework do not get infused with underlying feelings of anger, distrust, resentment, or fear. Parents and adolescents navigate the normative developmental milestones associated with adolescents' increased need for autonomy (school, work, leaving home), without getting derailed by the parents' or the adolescents' frustrated psychological needs. In fact, when adolescents feel loved, they are motivated to protect their relationship with their parents and thus rein in negative behaviors and emotions. The idea of attachment, or of a secure base, supporting goal-corrected negotiations is reflected in the logical structure of the ABFT model. We avoid problem-solving until we can reestablish the attachment bond. Once trust is on the mend, parents and adolescents can return to the negotiation of the adolescents' autonomy but in the context of a successful goal-corrected partnership.

INSECURE ATTACHMENT IN ADOLESCENCE

Whereas infants' attachment to primary caregivers is categorized as (a) secure, (b) anxious, (c) avoidant, or (d) disorganized, adolescent and adult attachment states of mind are categorized as (a) secure, (b) preoccupied, (c) dismissive, or (d) cannot classify. Adolescents and adults are also categorized on a separate dimension: whether or not they have unresolved feelings with respect to any potential traumatic experiences (both attachment related and nonattachment related; Kobak, Cassidy, Lyons-Ruth, & Ziv, 2006; Main & Goldwyn, 1998). These adult attachment categories are referred to as *states of mind*. This is because attachment style in adolescence and adulthood is measured by how individuals describe their relationships with parents (as captured in the AAI), rather than how they behave (as is done with children based on the Strange Situation task). An adolescent's dismissive (avoidant) attachment state of mind is thought to be associated with childhood experiences of rejection, abandonment, or parental unavailability. As a defense against hurt, the adolescent's desire for, and valuing of, attachment is denied, ignored, or kept out of awareness. At times, dismissive adolescents may idealize their parents, but more often they act as if relationships have little impact on them and/or do not really matter. Minimizing the importance of the relationship with their parents, these adolescents withdraw from involvement and avoid disagreement, thus limiting opportunities for learning emotion regulation, problem solving, and how to negotiate autonomy.

A preoccupied (anxious) attachment state of mind is thought to be associated with childhood experiences of parental inconsistency, guilt induction, and role reversal. Caregiving is largely dependent on the parents' needs and desires rather than responding to the signaling from the adolescent. These teens learn that their parent will not always or consistently respond to their needs, and they believe this inconsistency arises because the teens themselves are not sufficiently worthy of attention. Lacking validation of their own needs, they become more dependent on the approval of others and doubt their own needs and their healthy entitlement to have their needs met. Thus, they may insist on attention but be difficult to soothe (Mackey, 2003). Lacking effective emotion regulation skills, they often ruminate about negative experiences or memories and vacillate between anger and dependency. Often, these adolescents find themselves taking care of the physical or emotional needs of parents, toward which they feel both tremendous responsibility and resentment. Their intense focus on their parents' needs undermines their development of autonomy and emotional, interpersonal, and cognitive skills.

Adolescents whose attachment style cannot be classified and those with unresolved traumatic events are also at elevated risk for psychopathology and poor functioning. Adolescents who fall in the cannot-classify category tend to vacillate between dismissive and preoccupied states of mind and lack overall coherence. Exposure to trauma can also significantly influence adolescent and adult attachment state of mind. These traumas may be related to parental maltreatment, experiences of violence (inside or outside of the family), or the death of someone significant. If parents cause the trauma (e.g., sexual abuse), they can be the source of both comfort and fear, thus significantly complicating the attachment relationship (e.g., love and abuse become entwined). Adolescents with attachment-related trauma may have trouble accurately seeing their parents' strengths and weaknesses, especially when talking about abuse or loss (e.g., "He used to beat me when he was drunk, but it was not really that bad"; Cicchetti & Lynch, 1993; Main & Goldwyn, 1998). Adolescents with insecure attachment are at greater risk for problems with emotion regulation, social relations, interpersonal problem solving, school performance, and psychopathology, including depression (Abela et al., 2005; J. P. Allen, Moore, Kuperminc, & Bell, 1998).

Some have proposed that anxious/ambivalent attachment in childhood and preoccupied attachment state of mind in adolescence convey the greatest risk for depression. It has been theorized (Hesse, 1999; Kobak et al., 1991) that a preoccupied state of mind inhibits reflective exploration and emotional development and contributes to heightened and more frequent fear responses. Others have argued that adolescents who experience disorganized attachment in early childhood and unresolved trauma in childhood or adolescence may feel more helpless and vulnerable in the face of threatening experiences (Groh et al., 2012). Empirical evidence has demonstrated that insecure attachment style, regardless of the classification, conveys higher risk for the development of depression and anxiety, as well as other negative outcomes (K. L. Thompson & Gullone, 2008). Bowlby would not find this surprising, given his belief that attachment security sets the foundation of so many fundamental psychological processes: self-efficacy, emotional development, confidence to explore, trust in others, and feeling worthy of love. Although depression is most certainly multiply determined, attachment insecurity can clearly set in motion risk factors that make youth more vulnerable to depression (Cicchetti & Toth, 1998), whereas attachment security serves to protect against depression.

An individual's attachment style (or state of mind) is not etched in stone (Ainsworth, 1989). Although there is a significant level of attachment stability across the life span, and Bowlby (1969) believed that early childhood experiences profoundly shape one's view of self and other, attachment states of mind remain open to revision. Main (1995) developed the category of *earned security* to describe individuals who reported high levels of relational adversity in childhood but who nonetheless demonstrate a secure state of mind as an adult. Either through therapy or just good relationships in adulthood, these adults develop a more coherent and emotionally honest narrative about their childhood experiences, even if they were negative. Since most studies on earned security are retrospective, maybe these adults never had an insecure attachment style as a child. Maybe they experienced relational adversity but had a resilient personality that allowed them to develop a more positive view of relationships in spite of negative child relationships (Roisman, Padrón, Sroufe, & Egeland, 2002). Siegel (2012) argued that early attachment relations influence the neurological pathways that get established during brain development. Yet neuroscience has also shown that the plasticity of the brain allows neurogenerative growth in adulthood when optimal relational conditions are provided: empathy, emotional attunement, and validation.

In individual adult psychotherapy, it is the therapist who provides the optimal healing, relational environment. In contrast, in ABFT, we teach parents to provide emotional attunement of the type that was missing during their adolescent's childhood, in an effort to promote secure attachment in the present. In this way, parents create an optimal relational environment in the here and now. This not only provides a new experience of safety and trust but also helps to revise adolescents' view and expectation of the parent as available and responsive: their attachment schema. Helping parents recover or learn for the first time the types of behaviors that promote secure attachment (e.g., emotional attunement, responsiveness, protection) can be a challenging task. Therefore, it is essential to have a model of what this process looks like and what barriers may be encountered along the way.

PARENTS' CONTRIBUTION TO ATTACHMENT

Models of Attachment-Promoting Parenting

Despite the fact that parenting plays a large role in shaping children's attachment style (Van IJzendoorn, 1995), surprisingly little has been written about exactly which type of parenting promotes secure attachment (Bronfenbrenner, 1979). Attachment theorists generally describe the need for parents to be sensitive, responsive, and available. Infant research has focused on parents' ability to mirror the infant's emotions, track the infant's needs, and promote the infant's exploration (Izard et al., 2011; Stern, 1985). Well-attuned parents detect what their babies are feeling and reflect those emotions back in their facial expressions, voices, and other behavior. Parents' attention to the infant's verbal and nonverbal expression communicates that the parent understands what the infant is doing, feeling, and eventually thinking. These interactional moments set the foundation for future social interactions. When mother is attuned to the baby, both experience positive emotions. If out of sync, the baby will show signs of distress, including crying, that indicate the need for reattunement (Schore, 2001). These parenting behaviors are frequently associated with the development of a secure attachment relationship with infants and young children.

Parenting behaviors have also been associated with children's emotional development. Eisenberg, Spinrad, Eggum, Silva, and Reiser (2010) argued that although children's and adolescents' capacity for emotion regulation may be rooted in biology and temperament, parenting plays a particularly important role in socializing emotional development. The responsive and available parent accurately assesses their children's emotions, thus improving parents' ability to assist their child with interpersonal challenges. For example, the parent who perceives the sadness beneath the child's expression of anger can better facilitate the child's self-understanding and emotional processing. On the basis of work by Haim Ginott (2009), Gottman and colleagues (Gottman, 2011; Gottman, Katz, & Hooven, 1996) have argued that parents promote healthy emotional development when they (a) believe that emotional expression is important, (b) tolerate difficult emotions, (c) facilitate emotional expression, and (d) validate children's feelings. Children of parents who provide this type of emotional environment are more successful at school and with peers, manage stressful situations more easily, and even have better medical health outcomes.

Attachment-Promoting Parenting in Adolescence

Parenting models for promoting attachment during adolescence are less well developed. J. P. Allen et al. (2003) characterized attachment-promoting parenting during adolescence as being (a) emotionally attuned, (b) supportive of autonomy development, and (c) reaffirming of the relationship, even after conflict. Emotionally attuned parents of adolescents are aware of the adolescent's underlying or primary feelings, such as sadness, disappointment, shame, fear, or assertive anger. These parents are supportive of their adolescent's autonomy strivings. This does not mean being permissive, but rather facilitating and regulating developmental challenges. These parents maintain or reaffirm the relationship, even during or after a disagreement. Such unwavering support and commitment gives the adolescent the freedom to autonomously evaluate himself/herself and the parent without it threatening the foundation of the relationship or evoking dysfunctional anger or hostility. In a healthy, goal-corrected partnership, each member of the relationship works to maintain a positive relationship, even in the face of conflict. In addition to these attachment-promoting parenting parting practices, J. P. Allen et al. (2003) also suggested parents should expect that adolescents will begin to de-idealize them and have a more balanced view of parents' strengths and weaknesses. This partially frees adolescents up to connect to peers and romantic partners that will serve as a broader source of safety and security. Parents must tolerate this transition, as they increasingly become less central figures in the child's life.

Moretti, Holland, Moore, and McKay (2004) proposed essential attachment-promoting parenting practices in their psychoeducational program for delinquent youth. They suggested that parents need to understand the importance of attachment through the adolescent years and view conflict as a learning opportunity rather than as a personal assault. Parents should be able to step back from confrontation, modulate their own emotions, and try to consider the adolescent's perspective. Parents should be more empathic and sensitive and less reactive. Moretti et al. also encouraged parents to be more reflective about themselves, their past, and their relationship with their children. Overall, these parenting practices serve to improve parents' capacity to navigate conflict and set limits without resorting to coercion and aggression. This allows parents to remain authoritative without rupturing the attachment relationship.

Although research on parenting behaviors and attachment remains sparse, extensive developmental research on parenting practices has operationalized what parents do to promote healthy adolescent development (Maccoby, 1992). Developmental research on parenting has primarily focused on two dimensions of parenting: warmth and control. *Warmth* refers to the quality and amount of support, empathy, encouragement, and positive expression. *Control* refers to the quality and type of parents' structure, rules, and expectations for their children. Good parenting consists of both warmth and control. When one is emphasized at the expense of the other, or both are absent, problems emerge. The most effective parenting style is *authoritative*, which uses a balance of warmth and support while also establishing rules and expectations. Authoritative parents have a more collaborative problem-solving style and are more responsive to their child's feelings, needs, and questions. They are assertive but not intrusive, restrictive, or punitive. An authoritative parenting style tends to result in children who are happy, capable, and successful (Baumrind, 1989).

In contrast, *authoritarian* families are high on control and low on warmth. These are rule-driven parents who do not tolerate adolescents' natural inclination to question and challenge authority. For authoritarian parents, obedience is more important than connection. Authoritarian parenting styles generally result in children who are obedient and proficient but who rank lower in happiness, social competence, and self-esteem. *Permissive* parents are high on warmth and low on control. These parents provide limited discipline, have low expectations of maturity, and self-control, and avoid confrontation. Permissive parents are generally nurturing but often communicate more like a friend than a parent. Their children are often *parentified:* pulled in to help take care of the emotional needs of the parent. Permissive parenting often results in children who rank low in happiness and self-regulation, perform poorly in school, and have difficulty with authority. Finally, *uninvolved* parents offer no control or warmth. These parents are detached, and in extreme cases they can be rejecting or neglectful. Children of these parents have the most problems with self-control, self-esteem, social success, and emotional regulation (K. L. Thompson & Gullone, 2008).

Steinberg (1990) and Barber (2002) have made important contributions to better understanding the control dimension of parenting, differentiating between psychological and behavioral control. *Parental psychological control* refers to parents' attempts to coerce their child into thinking, feeling, or behaving in a certain way (Barber, 1996). An example might be scolding (humiliating) an adolescent for not doing well in school but not providing any new structure or guidance to help him succeed. Psychological control undermines children's self-confidence, efforts toward independence and identity formation, and has been associated with onset of adolescent depression.

In contrast, *behavioral control* refers to parents' use of rules, regulations, and restrictions as a means to manage a child's behavior. This includes parental supervision and monitoring (e.g., knowing where your children are and with whom), which has been associated with better school performance and lower deviant peer involvement (Patterson, DeBaryshe, & Ramsey, 1989). Authoritative parents, who have clear rules and expectations for their children's behavior, use more behavioral control and less psychological control. In contrast, permissive parents have fewer behavioral rules and tend to use psychological control to manage their children. Authoritarian parents use both. Some research suggests that these parenting models have cross-cultural validity as well (Barber, 2002).

IMPORTANT FACTORS INFLUENCING PARENTS' BEHAVIORS, ATTITUDES, AND STYLE

A number of factors influence how parents experience and respond to their children and adolescents. These factors include parental stress (both parenting related and external stress), parental psychopathology, and parents' own attachment state of mind.

Parental Stress

Marital quality, availability of social support, physical health, and socioeconomic status have all been shown to impact parental functioning (Belsky, 1984; Smith, 2010). Parents preoccupied with their own problems are less available to focus on the needs of their child. For example, poverty places a heavy burden on families, substantially increasing the risk for parenting-related stress, lack of support, and negative psychosocial outcomes (McLoyd, Aikens, & Burton, 2006).

Parental Psychopathology

Another major obstacle to optimal parenting is parental psychopathology. For example, parents struggling with depression have fewer emotional resources for attending to the needs of their children and are at higher risk for being less responsive and more withdrawn, impatient, and inconsistent (Garber, Ciesla, McCauley, Diamond, & Schloredt, 2011). Depression also leads parents to make negative attributions about themselves (e.g., "I am a failure," "I cause so many problems"), which is associated with children making similar attributions (Radke-Yarrow, Nottelmann, Belmont, & Welsh, 1993). Indeed, this may be one of the reasons that children of depressed parents are 6 times more likely to develop depression themselves. Research also indicates that parents struggling with bipolar disorder or substance abuse can have difficulty sustaining a warm and organized family environment, impacting their ability to be sensitive and consistent with their children (Cicchetti, Toth, & Lynch, 1995). It is important to note that the link between parental psychopathology and children's pathology is multiply determined and involves factors such as genetics, marital conflict, and greater exposure to stressful events (see Goodman & Gotlib, 1999, for a full review).

Parents' Own Attachment Style

An additional factor influencing the attachment environment is parents' own attachment history and style. Attachment can be a generational legacy. Parents were once children seeking protection and comfort themselves. Whether parents' parents were responsive and sensitive to their needs influences, to some degree, whether they themselves developed a secure or insecure attachment style. Because attachment style influences one's capacity for relatedness, it impacts parenting practices. Parents with a secure attachment style are less defended, guarded, or preoccupied (Van IJzendoorn, 1995). This frees up their psychological energy to focus on their children's needs. Less preoccupied with their own unresolved attachment needs, secure parents more accurately read the emotional signals of their children.

In contrast, parents with a dismissive style may experience discomfort with closeness and intimacy and thus rebuff or ignore their child's attachment needs. Investing energy in denying their own attachment needs, they can be uncomfortable with their child's expression of similar needs. Children may experience their parents' avoidance of these emotional needs as rejecting and invalidating or they may feel unworthy of being loved. When parents invalidate their child's attachment needs, the child learns to devalue these needs and consequently has difficulty learning to regulate the emotions associated with them.

Alternatively, parents with a preoccupied style tend to have excessive concern with closeness but strong fears of abandonment. Parents who themselves suffer from unresolved attachment needs tend to be less psychologically available for their child and less sensitive to their child's emotional needs. Though preoccupied parents are more aware of their child's attachment needs than are dismissive parents, preoccupied parents are more inconsistent in their responsiveness: sometimes available, sometimes overwhelmed, and usually needy. These parents may get their own emotional needs met by being overly involved, sometimes intrusively, with their children. Sometimes children of preoccupied parents become parentified, feeling the need to take care of the parent's emotional needs.

Finally, parents with unresolved trauma are at the highest risk for chaotic parenting, and their infants are at the greatest risk for developing disorganized attachment (Van IJzendoorn, 1995). On the AAI, unresolved trauma or loss is scored when a parent is disorganized and disorientated when talking about loss or trauma during the interview (e.g., speaking about a deceased person as if they were still alive, becoming confused or disoriented when discussing fearful experiences with a parent). Unresolved trauma is associated with a greater likelihood that a parent will perpetrate, or not protect his or her child from, more trauma (Neborsky, 2003). This becomes particularly complicated psychologically when the person the child naturally wants to seek comfort from is also the one who is frightening and often the source of emotional, physical, and/or sexual abuse.

Parent's attachment style, as mentioned earlier, is one of many factors that have an impact on parenting and the family environment. We should note, however, that the concordance between parents' attachment style and a child's attachment style is not high (Fraley, 2002): Just because a parent is preoccupied, the child will not necessarily develop that same style. Many child, parent, and contextual factors influence the attachment environment (e.g., the presence of a second parent who is more emotionally available; Brenning, Soenens, Braet, & Bosmans, 2011). We present the above patterns of parental attachment as one of multiple factors related to how parents parent their children.

AN ATTACHMENT THEORY OF ADOLESCENT DEPRESSION

Figure 2.1 summarizes an attachment-based view of adolescent depression. As we have presented, the central premise of attachment theory is that children have a basic evolutionary instinct to seek out parents for care and

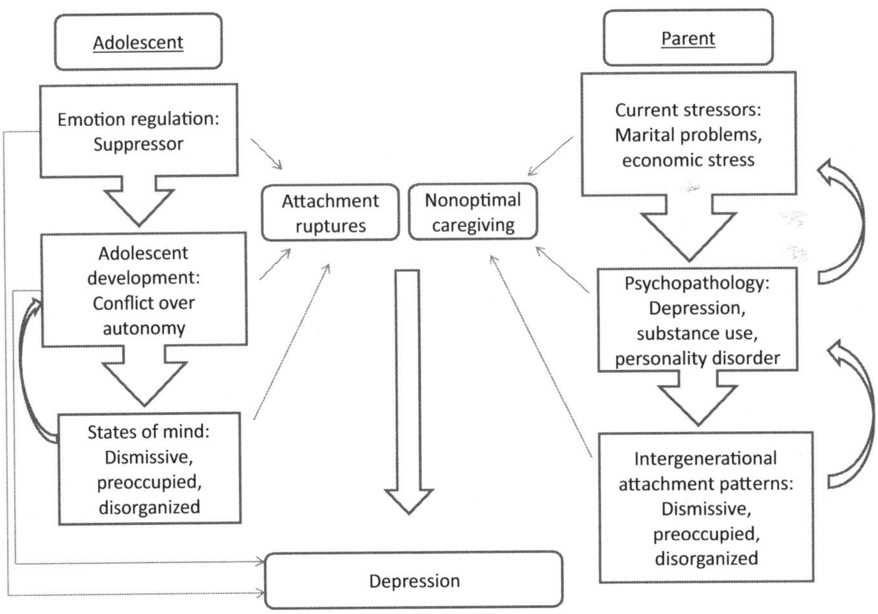

Figure 2.1. Attachment-based theory of adolescent depression. This figure depicts the psychological and interpersonal domains that contribute to adolescent depression and become targets for assessment and intervention in attachment-based family therapy.

protection. Having a secure attachment (i.e., the expectation that one's parents will be available in times of need) is related to healthy adaptive development outcomes. When children do not have a secure base and do not feel parents are sensitive and available, they are at substantially greater risk for having negative developmental outcomes, including depression. Forces determining the development and stability of the secure base include child factors (i.e., temperament, capacity for self-regulation, genetic vulnerability), parent factors (e.g., parenting practices, parental psychopathology, parental attachment history) and environmental factors (e.g., poverty, victimization, peer environment). This multitude of factors continues to influence the context and quality of attachment relationships long into adolescence.

The challenge of preserving attachment during adolescent becomes compounded with the emerging desire for more independence and autonomy. If successfully negotiated, these challenges become growth-promoting opportunities. If, however, parents cannot revise their parenting style and adolescents cannot effectively regulate their emotions, normal developmental struggles become a source of further attachment injury. A history of chronic family dysfunction or traumagenic events such as abuse compounds these conflicts. These adolescents view others as unsafe, untrustworthy, and unreliable, and they view themselves as unworthy of love and comfort.

These adolescents experience more difficulty and yet have no one to go to for help, guidance, and comfort. Combined with possible biological or temperamental vulnerabilities, these children may develop a more negative attributional style, poor affect regulation, weak impulse control, low self-esteem, and more hopelessness about life's opportunities. Instead of learning to be comfortable with appraising, expressing, and working through their negative emotions, depressed adolescents use avoidance, rumination, and suppression as their primary emotional coping strategies. Suppressors avoid conflict, deny emotions, and experience fewer positive emotions and for shorter amounts of time (Grice, 1975). This coping style puts adolescents at risk for depression and reinforces depression once it has developed (Yap et al., 2007).

As the adolescent becomes more depressed, parents often respond with more negative emotions. Rather than being responsive and sensitive, parents of depressed adolescents have been characterized as rejecting, critical, high in affectionless control, and low in support (Restifo & Bogels, 2009). These parenting practices inhibit autonomy development, discourage expression and communication about vulnerable emotions, and undermine negotiation and problem solving (Sheeber, Davis, Leve, Hops, & Tildesley, 2007). Rather than expecting their parents to be responsive, depressed adolescents view their parents as unsupportive and overly controlling or too permissive (e.g., indifferent). In these families, the normative perturbations of adolescence become a source of conflict, rejection, and emotional injury rather than an opportunity to practice individuation. The risk for negative parental behaviors is increased when parents are experiencing psychiatric distress (e.g., depression, substance use) and/or have an insecure attachment style (Essau, 2009).

The framework we propose above supports an interpersonal theory (Gotlib & Hammen, 2009; Joiner & Coyne, 1999) or transactional theory (Cicchetti & Toth, 1998) of adolescent depression. Much like a diathesis–stress framework (Belsky & Pluess, 2009), these models do not ignore biological, temperamental, or cognitive factors of depression but instead view environmental factors, especially family relations, as playing a major role in shaping the developmental course of the child's interpersonal and intrapersonal strengths and vulnerabilities (Cummings & Davies, 2010). In particular, a depleted attachment environment during childhood undermines children's opportunity to develop self-esteem, emotional regulation, and more resilient cognitive strategies. When faced with the stressors of adolescence, these deficits render the adolescent more vulnerable to depression. Given the parents' psychological or environmental stress, they may respond in ways that exacerbate the problem. Thus, the intrapersonal vulnerabilities of the parent and child often collide and reinforce negative family interactional patterns that reinforce negative views of self and other (Sheeber & Sorensen, 1998). This negative symptomatic cycle (Micucci, 1998) causes or fuels the adolescent's depression (Yap et al., 2007).

THE ATTACHMENT-BASED FAMILY THERAPY THEORY OF CHANGE

Given our attachment perspective, how do ABFT therapists think about change? Our primary goal is to move the child from an insecure state of mind to a secure state of mind. This means more confidence in parents' ability to provide a secure base or a better understanding and acceptance of parents' limitations. Again, Main (1995) called this process *earning security*, which refers to those who grew up in a negative family environment and worked through, came to terms with, or resolved their feelings about these negative experiences, perhaps because of positive life experiences (e.g., good marriage, psychotherapy) or a resilient temperament. This resolution of past negative attachment experiences frees the individual to choose more interpersonally satisfying, safe, and secure relationships as an adult. Although the process of earning security is not well articulated by attachment theorists, the concept reflects a process that lies at the heart of many individual psychotherapy models: learning to understand how past events influence current behaviors in order to become freer to act differently and more adaptively in the present.

In ABFT, as in individual therapy, we aim to help adolescents develop a more coherent understanding (e.g., an emotionally complex and accurate appraisal) about their perceived attachment injuries. However, we also do complementary work with the parent. We help parents understand how their current stress and attachment history influence their parenting practices. Aware of attachment needs in self and other, adolescents and parents become better prepared for productive attachment-promoting conversations. Therefore, we bring them together to discuss and work through these attachment ruptures. These conversations not only help resolve past conflicts or current problems but also create a corrective attachment experience in which adolescents express vulnerable feelings and needs and parents respond with sensitivity and availability. These positive, productive transactional interactions between parents and adolescents promote the revision of the parent and adolescent's working models of self and each other. Thus, the transactional model of psychopathology (Cicchetti & Toth, 1998) becomes a transactional model of change, as shown in Figure 2.2.

Restoring secure attachment can, however, be a challenging process. To accomplish this, we use several different change mechanisms and intervention techniques. In ABFT, these include reframing, emotional processing, narrative development, intergenerational exploration, parent education, and enactment. But the techniques are not the unit of focus; they do not organize our treatment plan (e.g., this week this, next week that). These techniques are a means to an end, not the end in and of themselves.

In ABFT, the treatment tasks organize our clinical approach. The five tasks provide the logic, or blueprint, for the ABFT change process. The goal of

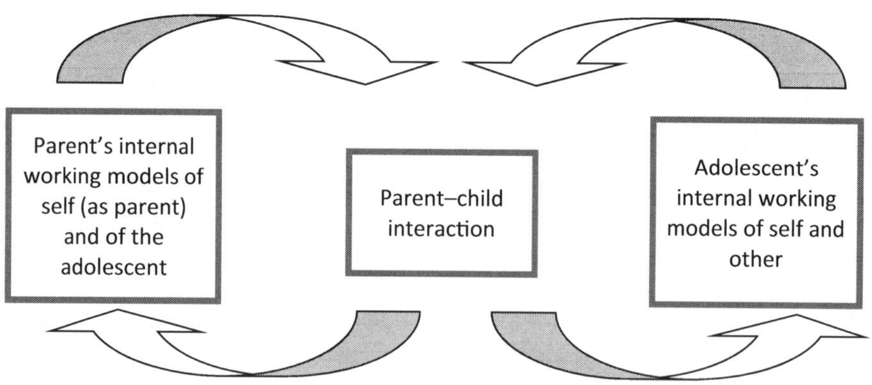

Figure 2.2. Transactional model of change. Parent and adolescent psychological functioning and view of self and other shape their interactional experiences, which reinforce or challenge their psychological functioning (e.g., affect regulation) and confirm or disconfirm their view of self and other.

each task determines what techniques we use or mechanisms we promote, for how long, and to what end. In this regard, ABFT is not a curriculum-based skills training program in which we teach different skills each week. Nor is ABFT an eclectic model in which therapists randomly use a wide range of interventions. Instead, ABFT is, in the true sense, an integrative model in which we organize the use of techniques and strategies on the basis of a coherent and overarching theoretical framework (Palmer & Woolfe, 2003).

Within each task, several techniques or strategies may be used simultaneously and/or sequentially (e.g., deepening emotional awareness, challenging of attributions, teaching new problem solving skills). Although many clinical strategies may be operating in the background, or as facilitators, each task has its own primary process and outcome goal. For example, we always pay attention to the emotional tone and depth of the conversation, but in the reframing task, emotional processing is in the service of setting the treatment contract (i.e., defining relationship building as the primary goal of treatment), not an end in itself. In the attachment task, in contrast, the relational reframe operates in the background and in the support of the primary goal of emotion processing in the service of repairing relational ruptures.

The tasks represent a matrix of independent yet interdependent treatment processes (G. S. Diamond & Diamond, 2002). Each task stands alone but also has logical relations to each other: a logic that builds momentum in the therapy. Without accepting the relational reframe, family members have lingering doubts about the focus of the therapy. If the adolescent alliance task has not revived hope for attachment security, adolescents will not risk being vulnerable in the attachment task. When the parent alliance task has not enhanced parents' appreciation of their adolescent's attachment needs, the parents come to the attachment task with less empathy and responsiveness. Finally, when the attachment task does not create more safety and trust between family members, the process of negotiating normative, adolescent developmental tasks continues to be fraught with suspicion and resentment. In this regard, each task represents a particular piece of the puzzle that must be accomplished and held in place to successfully move forward and accomplish the overall treatment goals.

In Table 2.1, we summarize (although simplistically) the process and outcome goals of each task. The central process goal of the reframing task is to change how the family members define the problem and the solution. They come to the first session focused on depression; they leave that session focused on rebuilding or enhancing the adolescent–parent relationship. This willingness to shift focus requires that we resuscitate the desire for attachment security and the hope that this restorative process is possible. To accomplish this, we place the attachment rupture at the center of the therapeutic conversation. Interpersonal failures and disappointment often fuel the adolescent's

TABLE 2.1
Process and Outcome Goals for Each Task

Task	Process goal	Outcome goal	Approximate no. of sessions
I. Relational reframe	Attributional shift in how family members view the problem and solution	Agree to participate in relational-focused therapy	1
II. Adolescent alliance	Better understanding of attachment narrative (i.e., thoughts, feelings, memories)	Revive adolescent's desire for and willingness to negotiate attachment	2–4
III. Parent alliance	Shift in the parents' working model of the adolescent and their parenting role	Acquire emotion-coaching skills	2–3
IV. Repairing attachment	Engage in conversations that work through attachment ruptures	Revise view of self and other and renew interpersonal trust	1–3
V. Promoting autonomy	Parents effectively help adolescents resolve non–family-based problems (depression, school, emerging self-identity)	Resume negotiation of adolescent development	8–9

anger or distrust and shape their view of attachment security. Acknowledging this level of hurt and disappointment on the part of both the adolescent and his or her parents helps uncover the lost desire for attachment and caregiving. Initially, focusing on the adolescent's sense of felt relational injustice also helps engage the adolescent in the treatment process (Liddle & Diamond, 1991). The reframing task progresses through many domains, but all in the service of leading to the outcome goal: creating a willingness on the part of all family members to participate in a therapy focused on relationship building rather than symptom reduction or behavior management.

To move this agenda forward, we then work with adolescents to deepen and expand their understanding of their attachment needs and ruptures. Adolescents tell the story of the relational experiences that have shaped their expectations from their primary caregivers. Most depressed adolescents have little capacity to explore these attachment ruptures. Their deep-seated feelings of sadness, disappointment, or anger often go unrecognized or are avoided. These adolescents have never been invited, or shown, how to turn their spotlight inward. These conversations with the adolescent alone help uncover more intricate details and memories about relational ruptures; help adolescents connect to, allow, and tolerate the feelings associated with these stories that emerge; and promote a reflective process that helps give these experiences more meaning (Angus, Levitt, & Hardtke, 1999). These conversations also validate and legitimize adolescents' feelings of sadness, hurt, and/or anger. As the stories becomes more coherent (more detail remembered, more comfortable with emotions, more understanding of the impact of these events), these conversations help revive the adolescent's desire for attachment and the hope that it can be repaired.

The primary process goal with the parent alone (Task III) is to resuscitate his or her caregiving instinct—the instinct to provide protection and care to his or her child. To accomplish this, we have parents remember their own attachment disappointments or losses. This process helps parents access their own, more vulnerable emotions and increases their capacity to step back and reflect on how these experiences have shaped who they are as a person, spouse and parent. Through this process, we also heighten parents' appreciation of their adolescent's similar attachment disappointments and needs. This increases parents' degree of remorse, and sometimes guilt, and provides motivation to repair the attachment relationship. The outcome goal of this conversation is that the parent agrees to learn emotion-focused parenting skills to help the adolescent talk about his or her thoughts and feelings about perceived attachment ruptures.

Although Tasks I, II, and III are therapeutic in and of themselves, they also all serve as preparation for the attachment task (Task IV), which is the central change mechanism in ABFT. Using the attachment narrative as the central focus of the therapeutic conversation, we engineer in-session, experiential, emotionally arousing, attachment-promoting interactions in which adolescents disclose vulnerable, private thoughts and feelings, and parents become more supportive, validating, and protective. This conversation deepens emotions about, and understanding of, past or current attachment ruptures. At the content level, this conversation helps the family work through important negative events or processes. At the skill development level, this task improves emotion processing and interpersonal problem solving. At the process level, these conversations serve as experiential moments of secure attachment. When parents are responsive, it disconfirms the adolescent's negative expectations of their parents and begins to create new more positive ones.

The autonomy task (Task V) is the real test of a revived secure base. The process goal is the normative negotiation of autonomy for the adolescent. In these conversations, we return to discussion of the challenges the adolescent faces outside of their relationship with their parents (e.g., rules in the house, siblings, school, peers, romantic relationships, self-identity). With the secure base on the mend, the capacity for a goal-corrected, parent–adolescent partnership has been resuscitated. Adolescents can begin to differentiate from parents without having to sacrifice attachment. Successfully negotiating these normative developmental challenges of adolescent life helps solidify the internal models of each other as connected and cooperative, yet tolerant and supportive of autonomy. As adolescents get older, their parents' role is less about solving their children's problems and increasingly about supporting them as they learn to master the challenges of growing up. The balance and transition between these parental functions greatly depend on the capacity and needs of the adolescents. The desired outcome goal, however, is further consolidation of the adolescent's revised expectations of parents' availability. It is one thing for parents and adolescents to share memories and feelings about past disappointments, but the real consolidation of these new relational skills will come in working through current and future challenges.

EMOTIONS IN ATTACHMENT-BASED FAMILY THERAPY

A discussion of the ABFT theory of change would not be complete without specific attention to the role of emotional processing in therapy. Above, we reviewed some of the literature on emotion regulation and the role it plays in the development of depression. Given the centrality of emotions in depression, ABFT, as does EFT, aims to expand adolescents' and parents' capacity for emotional processing. In ABFT, as in schema therapy (Young, Klosko, & Weishaar, 2003), we initially focus on the emotions bound up with attachment ruptures. Identifying and expressing avoided, primary, vulnerable attachment-related emotions is essential for changing the internal working models and habitual, maladaptive interpersonal relational strategies. To revise internal working models or make more coherent one's narrative of self and other, we need to unpack the complicated emotion structures that have evolved to help defend against or cope with these attachment injuries.

A primary goal in ABFT, therefore, is to improve emotional processing. Productive emotional processing involves arousing and sustaining emotion in the therapy session, helping adolescents put feelings into words, helping adolescents differentiate and accept competing emotions (e.g., anger and longing), and helping them improve their capacity for emotion regulation (e.g., not shutting down or becoming explosive, and expressing needs more directly) (Greenberg, 2002). Emotions linked to attachment ruptures can include loss, anger, sadness, and worthlessness, along with longing for care and connection. Accessing these feelings also may generate fear and anxiety—fear that these vulnerable emotions will not be tolerated or that further rejection is possible. Rachman (1990) suggested that productive processing occurs when the fear–anxiety network is activated and brought into awareness. For the dismissive adolescent, we aim to decrease the use of avoidance as a coping strategy. For the preoccupied adolescent, we aim to build emotional scaffolding that can help the adolescent better understand and contain strong emotions. Productive emotional processing then helps adolescents tolerate their sadness and unmet attachment needs without becoming overwhelmed or withdrawn. Productive emotional processing has been linked to reductions in depression and resolution of unfinished business in studies of individual emotion-focused, experiential therapy (Greenberg, Auszra, & Herrmann, 2007) and decreases in avoidance and other symptoms in cognitive–behavioral therapies for a wide range of fear/anxiety disorders (Foa, Huppert, & Cahill, 2006).

An essential element of emotional processing is emotion arousal. Without sufficient activation of emotion, it becomes more difficult for a client to fully explore its meaning. Sufficient emotion arousal is necessary to activate certain neural systems (e.g., basolateral amygdal and anterior cingulate cortex) associated with the processing and regulation of emotions and emotion–cognitive schema (Izard, 2011). On the other hand, overactivation leads to a failure to incorporate new information (Foa et al., 2006). In this regard, the optimum therapeutic process activates a certain level of emotional arousal and anxiety but should not let the process become overwhelming, unmanageable, or frightening.

As the adolescents become more aware of the "logic" of their internal working models (e.g., what they expect from relationships) and better able to acknowledge and process difficult emotions, they become more capable of incorporating new information about the relationship as the interactions improve. As adolescents come to understand their own needs and motives, they become more aware of parents' needs and motives (e.g., "I guess she is trying to protect me, just not in the ways I want"). This expanded view of their parents' behavior helps adolescents perceive parents' motives in new ways that are more tolerable. As adolescents become more aware and tolerant of their own vulnerable emotions (e.g., sadness, hurt), they become less afraid to seek help and comfort from others (Greenberg, 2011; Greenberg & Watson, 2005). When faced with relational loss and sadness, one's adaptive response is to reach out for support and communicate the need to be loved, cared for, and protected. From a transactional perspective, this new behavior from the adolescent tends to pull for more effective emotionally focused caregiving from the parent.

Unfortunately, we often find that therapists are nervous or uncomfortable talking about core relational ruptures, worried that doing so will be upsetting to or embarrassing for clients. Yet, the opposite is true in our experience: A therapy that does not get to the heart of the matter quickly will be less engaging and perceived as superficial. Attachment is ground zero, where safety and trust are nurtured or betrayed. For many depressed adolescents, everything else is a distraction, a defense, an acting out against these core ruptures in trust. Attachment injuries and desires must become the initial central theme of therapy. By doing this, we invite the evaluation, understanding, and renegotiation of the very fabric of attachment itself.

CONCLUSION

In this chapter, we have provided a theoretical framework for ABFT. The remainder of this book operationalizes this theoretical framework. We provide a step-by-step pathway to facilitate the kinds of corrective attachment experiences we are describing. Again, we provide the ideal performance map with many of its typical challenges and strategies. But every family presents their own story. The therapist will constantly be modifying and adjusting his or her approach. To do this effectively, the therapist must have a deep understanding of the ideas in this chapter so that the moment-by-moment adjustments are guided by theory and with intentionality.

3

TASK I: RELATIONAL REFRAME

Most families with depressed adolescents present for therapy concerned about how to reduce their adolescent's depression and associated negative behaviors (e.g., "My daughter is depressed and constantly argues with us," "She says she hates school and life is not worth living"). Consequently, family members assume that treatment will focus on the adolescent or the symptoms per se. In attachment-based family therapy (ABFT), we too aim to reduce symptoms, but we approach this goal through enhancing the quality of the adolescent–parent attachment relationship. We do this for a number of reasons. Sometimes family conflict or negative family processes (e.g., parental criticism, lack of care) appear to be the primary cause of the depression. In other cases, past family trauma (e.g., abuse, abandonment) has contributed to the depression and needs to be addressed. In yet other cases, the primary cause of the depression is extrafamilial (e.g., being bullied in school), but poor

http://dx.doi.org/10.1037/14296-004
Attachment-Based Family Therapy for Depressed Adolescents, by G. S. Diamond, G. M. Diamond, and S. A. Levy

parent–adolescent communication prevents parents from being a resource to the adolescent as he or she tries to cope with this challenge. Whether or not family events or processes have caused or exacerbate the depression, the first goal of ABFT is to strengthen the family context so it can support the adolescent's recovery. Given this perspective, we aim to help family members accept relationship building as the initial goal of treatment.

The relational reframe helps shift the therapeutic focus from depression to improving the adolescent–parent relationship. The reframe centers on one pivotal question: "When your son or daughter feels so depressed, why doesn't he or she come to you for comfort or help?" This question shifts the content of the conversation from depression to relationships. In many cases, shifting the focus onto the adolescent–parent relationship elicits in both parents and adolescents feelings of remorse and sadness about what is and what could have been. Adolescents are faced with their deep but universally present need to be acknowledged, understood, cared for, and protected by their parents, and parents recognize that they have not sufficiently cared for and protected their adolescents. At the same time, parents' instinctual attachment impulses to care for and protect their adolescent surface and generate motivation for our treatment plan.

The relational reframe does not occur in a vacuum or out of the blue. Instead, we deliver it in the context of a carefully constructed therapeutic task. It begins with joining, symptom assessment, and gathering contextual and historical data. We then focus our assessment on the quality of the attachment relationship itself: "What things have happened that have created distance between you and your daughter?" However, in this task (which almost always occurs in the context of the first session), we do not yet look to fully process past hurts and relational ruptures. Rather, we seek enough information about these ruptures to establish their existence and highlight their consequences: loss of trust and loss of safety. We use these attachment themes to elicit and amplify vulnerable emotions such as sadness, disappointment, and loneliness. In turn, these feelings resuscitate family members' longing for connection and more meaningful relationships.

As the family's desire for a better relationship surfaces, we begin to form a treatment contract focused on this goal. Without a foundation of trust and goodwill, parents cannot provide protection and guidance, and adolescents will not turn to parents for comfort and problem solving. This leaves adolescents isolated and more vulnerable to depression and its consequences. Therefore, we propose relationship building as an initial treatment goal. Focusing the therapy on relationship development sets the fundamental direction of the entire therapy. It defines our basic theory of change: the more your child perceives you as responsive and available, the more freely he or she will turn to you for support, comfort, and problem solving during times of distress, rather than recede into depression. The relational reframe also defines the tasks of this therapy. We aim to enhance the relationship by helping the family engage in conversations about events or processes that have damaged trust in the relationship. This treatment goal circumvents unproductive arguments over behavioral conflicts and management by inviting the family into profound, life-changing conversations about love, trust, and safety.

STRUCTURE OF THE RELATIONAL REFRAME TASK

The relational reframe task, as depicted in Figure 3.1, comprises three phases: (a) joining with the family and understanding the depression, (b) shifting to attachment themes, and (c) making a relational treatment contract. Each phase progresses through an intuitive, logical sequence of processes that lead family members to embrace the reframe. Phase 1 provides a systematic strategy for joining with each family member and conducting a brief, concise assessment of the presenting problems and their consequences. Phase 2 outlines how to shift the conversation from history taking to a focus on attachment themes and more primary, vulnerable emotions. Finally, Phase 3 provides recommendations on how to establish a treatment contract focused on repairing or improving relationships. This task is usually completed in the first session with the parents and adolescent together.

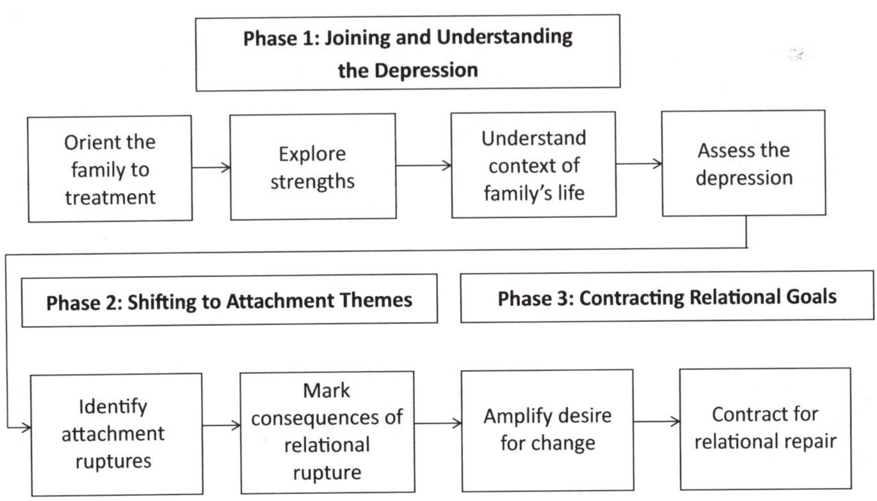

Figure 3.1. Task I: Relational reframe. This figure depicts the therapist performance map for facilitating the relational reframe task.

PHASE 1: JOINING WITH THE FAMILY AND UNDERSTANDING THE DEPRESSION

This phase has many purposes. First, we are trying to help the family settle in and get over the nervousness of coming to therapy. Meeting us for the first time, they may feel cautious or suspicious. For many families, this may be their first time in therapy. They may feel embarrassed or ashamed, and certain family members may feel more resistant or indifferent to treatment. Some parents have to drag their adolescents to therapy and some parents feel burdened by having to attend themselves. In other families, the interpersonal pain at home has been torturous and they are eager for help. In any case, the initial, casual conversation helps to make family members feel more comfortable, socialize the family to treatment, and demystify the therapy process by providing some structure and direction.

We do not want to come across as too informal. Jokes, teasing, and playfulness may easily offend a family member or make us appear flippant. So as a rule, we are upbeat and lighthearted but avoid being too casual. But each therapist has to find his or her own way on this. If humor is your strength, then use it. Just pay attention to the family's feedback. The therapist must be flexible and adapt his or her skills, style, and strategies to meet the needs, culture, and style of the family. As a general principle, the therapist is responsible for reaching out to each family member and helping him or her to feel at ease. This is the therapist's house; the family is the guest. We must make the effort to connect. This may require drawing on different parts of ourselves to connect with different family members. In this way, we begin to model flexibility, compassion, and a sincere desire to develop a relationship with each family member.

Orienting the Family to Treatment

We begin the first session by conveying our leadership and confidence in the model. Families come to therapy looking for help. They are lost and desperate. They cannot solve these problems themselves. They want us to contain their pain and provide a path for growth. Like the mother who provides safety to the child, therapists must provide safety and protection to the family. Although we put tremendous responsibility on family members to make changes, we offer them a clear treatment plan and structure. We have a theoretical framework and a road map for how to achieve our goals. Therefore, we know that repairing attachment will be our first treatment goal. We use this to organize the stories that the families bring to the treatment. Starting like this demonstrates leadership, confidence, and competency. Therefore, the first session typically opens with some kind of statement such as the following:

> Welcome, everyone. I am very glad you could make it today. [Turns to the adolescent] As you know, I talked with your mother on the phone and got some idea of her concerns about you. But today I really want to hear from all of you. My name is Suzanne Levy. I am a psychologist here at the hospital. I have been here for many years working with families like yours. I have a particular interest and expertise in working with adolescents who are feeling depressed so I think I can be helpful. [Allows a moment for reactions or questions]
>
> So before we get started, let me explain a bit about how I work. This is a relatively brief treatment. We will have about 16 weeks together. At the end, we can discuss if we need a bit more time together. I find, however, that if we work hard, and you come every week, we can get a lot done. [Pauses for response or questions] Sometimes we will meet as a whole family, and sometimes I will meet with people individually. Most likely [turns to the adolescent], I will meet with you alone next week and then the following week [turns to the parents], I want to see the two of you together. This way I can get to know everyone better and work on a few things. Then we generally come back together for a few sessions. After that, we will make plans based on what we are working on. When we do meet alone, things we discuss will be confidential. [Says more if necessary] But you should know that my goal is to create more honesty and open conversation among all of you. So I will be encouraging you to discuss with each other things during our sessions all together that I feel are important and should be discussed to get this depression under control. Do you have any questions about this? [Addresses questions and concerns]
>
> So today, I want to spend a few minutes getting to know some things about each of you: what you do, your interests, and hobbies. Then I am going to ask more about how you have been feeling. [Turns to the adolescent] Sounds like you have been pretty sad or depressed lately? [Looks for verbal or nonverbal response] So I want to ask each of you about that and see whether there are other problems I might help you with. Toward the end of the hour, I will summarize a few of the problems as I see them. Then we will come up with a plan about what we might work on here. Do you have any questions about the structure of the treatment? [If the family has questions, gives short, informative answers but blocks launching into any discussions of problems at this point] [Turns to the adolescent] Johnny, tell me something about yourself. What do you enjoy doing?

Exploring Strengths

After our introduction, we begin learning more about each family member. Who to talk with first is sometimes a sensitive decision. We use our best judgment. If no observations suggest otherwise, we often turn to the adolescent first. We do not want to disrespect the parents, but we do want to demonstrate our commitment to engaging the adolescent. In traditional structural family therapy, it was important to begin by supporting the hierarchical position of the parents. However, Liddle (e.g., 2002; Liddle & Diamond, 1991) helped us all understand that with adolescents, joining with them and making them feel there is something in this therapy for them is critical to treatment engagement and progress.

In this phase, we look for positives—strengths, achievements, and activities that make the adolescent proud. We ask about his or her hobbies or talents, friends, or if need be, something as simple as favorite music or movies. To better understand the context of the adolescent's life, we ask what school he or she goes to, or what clubs or groups he or she belongs to. The goal is to remain lighthearted, make the conversation fun or at least comfortable, and avoid getting into descriptions of problems. We aim to identify strengths and unique qualities that have been forgotten or ignored by the family. This is particularly important for the adolescent, for whom the depression has taken control of his or her life, and everyone has understandably begun to overly focus on problems. As Micucci (1998) described it, as the symptoms worsen and the conflicts deepen, the parents increasingly focus on the adolescent's problems and forget or ignore other aspects of her or his life. We want to bring these other parts of that adolescent back into focus. We identify strengths, amplify them, build them, and later use them to facilitate growth.

We often ask the parents about their view of the adolescent's strengths; this has multiple goals. At one level, it may serve to generate a brief positive moment between family members. At another level, we want to observe the process. Can the family enter into a positive conversation and have at least a moment of closeness? Do the parents try harder than the adolescent or vice versa? Can the parents be thoughtful and reflective? Can they disengage from their own anger or frustration long enough to appreciate the positive aspects of the adolescent? How psychologically rigid or flexible are the parents? If the moment does not go well, we redirect the conversation quickly. We do not want to generate negative affect or allow for an empathic failure at this stage of the treatment.

Understanding the Context of the Family's Life

As part of joining, we aim to understand the general context of the parents' life as well: Where do they live? Who lives in the house? What kind of neighborhood do they live in? Is there extended family in the area, and how involved are they in the adolescent's life? What kind of work do the parents do? Do they belong to a church, synagogue, or mosque? When we work with low-income families, we might empathize with the hardships or admire their ability to live a good life in spite of it. When we work with immigrant families, we may ask about country of origin and ask how they or their parents decided to come to America. When we work with biracial families, we acknowledge this, explore it a bit, and punctuate it as something worth returning to in future sessions. When we work with gay or lesbian couples or parents of a gay, lesbian, bisexual, or transgender youth who are out, we might ask how this affects their lives and their relationships. The goal here is not to open up long discussion about these kinds of issues but to demonstrate some sensitivity to these challenges and a willingness to discuss these topics in the therapy. These questions allow each family member to talk about the world in which they live.

In addition to understanding context, we are looking for themes, metaphors, or activities that could assist later in the therapy. Suppose the mother is a seamstress. Using metaphors of a weak stitch or a suit tailored too tight might assist the therapist in clarifying therapeutic themes later in the work. Similarly, we may discover the father owns a garage that could later become a work opportunity for the adolescent. Or we might hear that that the adolescent used to play basketball and still has hopes of getting back on the school team. This goal might direct aspects of the autonomy task later in the therapy.

Observing Interactions

Finally, the joining phase gives us a first opportunity to observe how the family interacts with each other: Can they talk about positive things without quickly digressing to conflict? Does one parent talk for the other? Does the adolescent give in to the parents' interpretation of things too easily, or does the adolescent have a voice of his or her own? Does the adolescent express himself or herself well? Do the parents listen to him or her? Of course, depression can smother an adolescent into silence. Still, it is helpful to note how the family reacts when the adolescent attempts to express himself or herself. Can the family have an organized conversation in which each family member feels his or her opinion is appreciated and respected? Is there a general sense of warmth, caring, and concern between them? How independent or dependent are family members? We may or may not point out these processes at this point, but we will certainly begin to observe them and incorporate this information into our case conceptualization and treatment planning.

Avoiding Surprises

Finally, we identify critical life circumstance that impact the family but that families often forget to tell us. Families may be embarrassed to mention these challenges (e.g., the mother receiving treatment for cancer), or they have habituated to them (e.g., an ill grandparent lives in the home). Family members often underestimate how these stressors contribute to the depression directly or indirectly through causing additional family stress. We want to uncover these kinds of events and circumstances now rather than have them surface later in the sessions during the more emotionally focused reframing process. When deepening the emotions associated with relational ruptures, we do not want to be distracted by suddenly hearing that the adolescent was arrested last month. This would derail our focus. Therefore, we often end the joining phase with a general statement such as, "So are there any other important things I should know about your family? Is everyone in good health? Are there other family stressors I should know about?"

Although joining is critical, it is generally short, lasting approximately 10 or 15 minutes. The content and process are important. As therapists, we want to be asking ourselves, Do I have the general lay of the land? Have I identified the major recent life events? Do family members appear to be more relaxed and less suspicious? All in all, joining is not just about getting people comfortable. It is about getting a broad overview of the context of the family's life before moving onto the next subtask: understanding the presenting problem.

Assessing the Depression

In this subtask, conversation follows a progression from symptoms to systems to relationships. This framework keeps one focused and organized. Obviously, information crosses over these domains, and new information generates new questions. Do not be rigid, but do not be scattered. Remember, one key principle of ABFT is for the therapist to have a plan, even if that plan needs to be modified along the way.

To hit most of the critical points, we use the questions in Exhibit 3.1 as a general guideline for the next 20 to 30 minutes of the session. These questions are not required or set in stone, and others may spontaneously arise. More information might be needed for a full biopsychosocial assessment. These are, however, essential questions to ask when trying to understand the depression in its context.

Understanding the History of Symptoms

To begin this phase, we make an intentional shift and usually say something along the lines of the following:

> OK. Well, I appreciate you sharing things about your life. I hope to get to know you more over the next few weeks. But let's now turn to the

EXHIBIT 3.1
Understanding the Presenting Problem

Symptom level
1. How long has the adolescent been feeling depressed?
2. What symptoms has the adolescent been having?
3. When was the worst period?
4. Has the adolescent ever felt suicidal?
5. How much is the depression impairing the adolescent's life (school, home, peers)?
6. Is the adolescent experiencing other kinds of psychological distress (e.g., anxiety, posttraumatic stress disorder, drug use, attention-deficit/hyperactivity disorder)?
7. What previous treatment has there been, if any?
8. Have medications of any kind ever been used for the depression? If yes, what medications were used and who prescribed them?

Systems level
1. How does the adolescent understand the causes of depression?
2. What cause do the parents attribute to the depression?
3. How has the depression affected the adolescent's school performance, and/or has school performance affected depression?
4. Have the parents been working with the school personnel? Has any previous psychological or psychiatric testing been completed? (If so, request a copy of the report.)
5. Is the juvenile justice or social welfare system involved? If so, what are the names of those involved?
6. Who referred the family to treatment? What is the relationship with that person?
7. Is the adolescent's pediatrician aware of the problem?
8. Have the parents ever struggled with their own psychological problems (e.g., depression, anxiety, alcohol or drug use)?
9. Have any other adults been involved in helping the family with the depression (e.g., family members, neighbors, church members)?

Relational description
1. How has the depression affected the family?
2. How does each family member react to the depression?
3. How has the depression affected the adolescent's peer relations or extrafamilial activities?

To the parents specifically:
1. How has your child's depression impacted the family?
2. How do you feel when you see your child feeling this way?
3. What have you done to try and help him or her? Has it worked?
4. In the family, who deals the best or worst with this problem?
5. Are the responsible adults in agreement about how to handle the problem?
6. Does the adolescent have as much difficulty with all adults and peers (e.g., mother vs. father, parent vs. sibling/teachers)?

problems that brought you to therapy. From what your mother told me on the phone, it sounds like you have been pretty depressed for a while can you tell me more about this?

We have no rule about whom to talk with first, but again, we often begin with the adolescent. We want adolescents to start assuming responsibility for presenting themselves and not perpetuate the idea that parents understand them better than they understand themselves. So, moves to promote maturity in the adolescent support our treatment goals—as long as doing so does not alienate the parents.

Understanding the History of Treatment

After we get a better understanding of the history of the depression, we ask about previous treatment. Many of our adolescents have had multiple courses of treatment, with varying degrees of success. We might ask which therapist they liked and did not like, and why. This can provide clues about how to best join with the adolescent and an opening to invite the adolescent to enter this therapy with a different mind-set.

> So, I want to make this therapy different from the last one. Back then you were only 10, and yes, maybe you did not like Dr. Richmond. But now you are 16, you are not a little kid anymore. You need to have a voice in this treatment if we are going to accomplish anything. OK? Now sometimes I might agree with your mother and seem to take her side. But that does not mean I have lost sight of you. I want to help you solve some problems in your life so you can live life the way you want. Does that make sense? OK? [Discusses if necessary]

This statement reflects several principles of this therapy. First, in family therapy with adolescents, we want to become the adolescent's ally, not a punitive authority figure or a therapist who supports only the parents' agenda and goals. Second, we want the adolescent to help shape the goals and process of this therapy. Depressed adolescents have lost their voice, avoid conflict, and do not feel entitled to address felt injustices. We aim to empower them to speak up and take more responsibility for the direction of treatment. Third, even though some adolescents can speak up, they often do so in an unregulated manner. Consequently, their parents do not listen or take them seriously. We will develop these ideas more in Task II, but these themes guide our approach from these initial moments of the therapy.

Understanding Adolescents' Goals and Expectations for Therapy

We often ask adolescents what they would like to get out of therapy. Their answer can provide important diagnostic information. Can they say anything? Do they have any hopes for themselves? Do they identify the depression as the central problem and express some desire to get over it? Do they immediately blame the family as the problem? Do they deny that they need therapy and say that life is OK? If they do have treatment goals (i.e., more freedom at home), we can incorporate that into our overall treatment frame: "I think if your parents knew you better, if they trusted you more, they would give you more freedom."

Understanding Attributions About the Cause of the Depression

One way to transition from a history-taking focus to an attachment focus is by assessing the family members' explanatory models about what causes the depression. This begins the process of shifting from collecting information to interpreting information. The therapist begins to show more interest in why problems occur rather than what is happening. This is a critical point to understand. How people explain a problem partially determines how they react or respond to a problem (Grych & Fincham, 1990). Explanatory models also impact one's theory of change (e.g., a biological problem requires a biological response).

Family members' causal attributions regarding the depression may vary greatly. Some parents think it is the result of genetics or biology, an inheritance from a family member: for instance, "His father was depressed . . . he is just like his father." Some parents think it is stress, resulting from a history of circumstantial events: for instance, "His problems with schoolwork and being bullied; it has just taken a toll on him." Other parents view it as normative or at least an inevitable part of adolescent life: for instance, "Aren't all adolescents a little moody? She will grow out of this." Adolescents will have a similar range of explanations but are more likely to also attribute depression to family problems (conflict, overcontrolling or rejecting parents). Obviously, each family member may have multiple explanations for the depression. As therapists, we have to ask ourselves which attributions will inhibit or promote our relational reframe.

For example, some parents use the genetic or biological view to avoid responsibility for the problems; a biological problem needs a biological solution. On the other hand, the medical model can generate patience and support from parents. A "sick" child often receives more compassion and support than a "bad" child. Parents with a developmental or stress-based view of depression more readily accept that change in circumstances or context could contribute to recovery. On the other hand, parents might also use this perspective to blame others or circumstances (e.g., her friends at school) and deny any personal contribution to the depression. In this regard, parents' and the adolescent's attributions about what causes the depression can be an asset or a barrier to our treatment goals. Therefore, we must understand family members' explanatory models as we move closer to the reframing process.

> We have been talking a lot about the problems that have been going on in your family. I think I have a pretty good beginning idea of how hard things have been. Let me change the focus a bit. I am curious about what you think is causing the depression. When you [turns to the parents] sit and talk together about this, how do you understand why it is happening? How do you explain it to yourself?

Initially, we avoid challenging or changing these attributions. We just want to understand them so we know what we are up against: Do the parents believe they play any role in causing or buffering against the depression? Does the adolescent view the depression as insurmountable or unchangeable, or hold him- or herself or others completely to blame? What follows is an example of how a part of this conversation might go.

Therapist: So, Mr. Jones, tell me how you see this. How do you understand why your daughter is having problems?

Father: Well, like you said, I think she is very depressed, has been for many years.

Therapist: Yes, I agree. Based on what we have been discussing. And I can see how worried you are about her. But tell me, how do you explain this? What do you think is causing her to be depressed?

Father: Well . . . ah . . . I suppose the doctors have said she is like me. I have struggled with depression and now she is.

Therapist: What do you mean by that?

Father: Well . . . she has some of my genes and now has depression herself.

Therapist: OK, so one reason she might be depressed is because of her biological predisposition. She inherited your depressive genes.

Father: Well, yes. . . . Don't you think so?

Therapist: That certainly can contribute. Anything else seem to cause or contribute to the depression?

Father: I suppose the divorce did not help.

Therapist: What do you mean?

Father: Well, when I divorced her mother, things got very difficult and I think this upset her a lot.

Therapist: Is that around the time the depression started?

Father: Let's just say it got a lot worse.

Therapist: So you think that the divorce and maybe some of the conflicts between you and your ex-wife have contributed to her depression along with some of her biological vulnerabilities.

Father: Yes, I guess that sounds right.

Therapist: Yes, sometimes depression can be complex. Sometimes children have an underlying vulnerability to depression, but as long as things go well in life, it is contained. But then under stress, like the divorce, it starts to creep through. Does that make sense?

Father: Well, you had better ask her that. She blames me for the entire problem.

Explanatory models get even more complicated in a multiperson therapy because different family members might have different attributions. For example, parents and adolescents often have different points of view. Sometimes parents think the depression's cause is biological (internal to the adolescent) while the adolescent believes it has been caused by circumstances (external to the adolescent). Not infrequently, parents themselves will disagree on their explanatory models. One parent may say his or her son is just lazy or in a phase, whereas the other one may say he gets it from his grandmother, who was also very depressed. Because attributions about a problem often guide one's theory of change—what needs to happen to change the situation—these parental differences can present potential conflicts between the parents that show up in the therapy.

In our work, we challenge or expand family members' explanatory models, as demonstrated in the dialogue above. Sometimes we flesh out the conflicting points of view as a way to both identify points of tension and/or to help defuse arguments:

> Look, Mr. and Mrs. Miller, it is clear you both love your son. That is not what you are fighting about. You just have different explanations for the depression and that leads to different ideas on how to help your son.

Typically, we eventually provide some brief psychoeducation about depression, generally presenting a diathesis stress model that incorporates biology, development, and environmental factors (see Chapter 2). This allows us to propose interventions directed toward any and all of these domains, when appropriate.

Our main goal during this segment, however, is to understand whether the family members' attributional models will support or undermine the relational reframing process. We want to understand if their causal model of the depression is biological, temperamental, social, or relational. We then have to sort out whether their explanation can coexist with a relational theory of change. Some parents want only medication and refuse to be part of the treatment. Some parents think the child needs medication, but they agree that family conflicts contribute to the depression. The degree to which family members adopt a more environmental/interpersonal theory of depression increases the likelihood they will accept the relational solution. At this point in the session, we do not hard-sell this point of view. We have stronger tools coming. However, we do highlight some relational struggles and strengths as a foreshadowing of things to come.

Observing the Process of the Conversation

Thus far, we have focused on the content of the assessment phase. Observing the process of this conversation may, however, be as important. Is the conversation among family members respectful and civil or harsh and tense? Are the parents interested in the adolescent's point of view or critical, controlling, intrusive, and/or dismissive? Can the adolescent speak up for him- or herself, or is he or she immature, irrational, shut down, or easily flooded with feelings? Are there shared or conflicting views of the problem and solutions? Does the adolescent become disengaged as the parent speaks? Does the parent try to take over the conversation? The tracking of both content and process has been the hallmark of family therapy and is more fully articulated in many basic family textbooks. We refer beginning family therapists to the Recommended Additional Readings (see pp. 245–251).

Maintaining a Polite, Yet Directive, Stance

At this phase of the therapy, therapists can easily get pulled into the details of the family's stories. Some details are critical and essential to gather, but stories can go on for too long, with too much repetition. For example, although we need to understand the adolescent's overall school performance, we do not need to hear every episode of school failure. This can be humiliating for the adolescent and reinforce the view that therapy will focus on behavioral problems. Similarly, adolescents might go on a tirade about their parents. This can alienate parents and give the impression that the therapist cannot provide a safe, controlled therapeutic environment. Therefore, we look for common themes across the stories, punctuate them with a summary that conveys our understanding of the problems, and empathize with the person's frustration. This punctuation process (Minuchin & Fishman, 1981) allows therapists to keep the session moving forward, as illustrated here:

> Ms. Taylor, with all due respect, let me stop you here. . . . It sounds like from the few examples you have already given that school has been very

difficult for your son. He has not gotten along with teachers and has been absent a lot this year, and you feel the school has not responded to your request for help. Is that what you are saying? You sound very frustrated about this. . . . It must be hard. . . . I need to understand this more so I can help you with this. . . . But for now, I want to better understand a few other things. Tell me more about his previous experience with therapy and medication.

In that statement, the therapist punctuates the seriousness of the problem area, empathizes with the parent's frustration, and recognizes this as an area for further work. The therapist is polite but directive. In a multiperson therapy, we have to control the flow and pace of information or the sessions can quickly spin out of control. More important, if discussion of behavioral problems dominates the entire therapy hour, there is no opportunity to build a relationship-focused frame for the therapy. Therefore, being overly polite and passive can undermine the direction of the therapy and our ability to introduce new, core, emotional, relational themes. There will be more time in future individual sessions to make sure important details are not lost. Being helpful and creating new experiences will go further to building trust and an alliance than being polite but accomplishing little in the session.

Punctuating the Impact of the Depression on the Family

To continue laying the ground for the relational reframe, we move on to punctuate the shared impact of the depression on the entire family. As we argue above, depression must be front and center. It is the driving motivation for treatment—the reason that family members came. Whenever the going gets rough in the treatment, we come back to the fundamental reason for the therapy: Parents want to protect their child from the devastating effects of depression, and adolescents are miserable and are looking for a way out of their depression. Therefore, at this juncture, we might make an empathic summary statement and garner agreement on it.

So I am sure there is more to learn, but I am starting to understand how devastating this depression has been for Abby: missing school, missing friends, often irritable, and the medicine does not seem to be helping. Sounds pretty horrible, Abby. You must be really unhappy [looks to Abby for agreement]. But it is also clear that this depression affects everyone in the family. Mr. and Mrs. Exton, I can see how hard this is for you and I can see that you are suffering right along with your daughter. And you have tried so hard to help and feel like nothing is working. I can see how painful this is for the both of you [looks for agreement]. This situation is very hard, but I think I can be helpful.

PHASE 2: SHIFTING TO ATTACHMENT THEMES

So, it is a little more than halfway through the first interview. The therapist has joined with the family and gained an initial understanding of the depression, its course, consequences, treatment history, and some of the factors family members perceive as contributing to it. Future sessions alone with the adolescent and parents will be used to gather needed details. But now, the conversation must shift to a different level—one more interpersonally focused and more existentially meaningful. Rather than stay at the level of history taking and fact finding, the therapist needs to orchestrate an emotionally meaningful, experiential moment that pulls for attachment longing. To accomplish this, we aim to refocus the conversation onto fundamental attachment needs of love and protection and access emotions of disappointment and longing for connection. This requires that the therapist sit up, lean forward, express deep empathy and admiration of family members and their efforts, and then guide the family away from anger and indifference and into the territory of love and longing. This phase of the conversation often increases anxiety but tends to be intimate and profound. The therapist will feel the intensity in the room increase. Therapists must use their own personal strengths and sensibility to guide the family into this land of attachment themes and vulnerable emotions. This reframing moment requires a clear shift in the therapist's intention. In our early study of these transitions from problem focus to relationship focus, we found that such shifts often happened spontaneously and unexpectedly (G. Diamond & Liddle, 1996). However, we now know that these good moments can be planned and engineered. Key therapist questions promote this transition. On the one hand, these questions should map onto the culture or story of each family. On the other hand, these questions address universal attachment themes: trust, abandonment, loss of love, and desire for connection. Such themes are not culture bound and touch the hearts of anyone struggling to love or be loved. Therefore, we encourage therapists to use our generic phrases as a starting point. As Howard Liddle used to say to us,

> I am going to call you on the supervision phone and tell you what to say. Sit back down and say it exactly as I told you. That will get you into the right conversation. After that, you are on your own.

These questions—relational reframes summarized in Exhibit 3.2—mark the pivotal moment in this therapy. They shift the focus from behaviors to relationships, from problem solving to relationship mending. They close the door on depression as the focus and open the door on relationship as the focus. The entire therapy is built around acknowledging, understanding, and repairing these ruptures; what has damaged trust; and attachment security.

EXHIBIT 3.2
Questions Addressing Attachment Themes

To the adolescent:

- When you feel so depressed, so miserable and alone, why don't you go to your parents for comfort and support?
- It appears that you want your parents to support you, but you do not trust that they will be there when you need them. Is that true? Why have you lost trust in your parents?
- It seems like the door of love is closed. That you have no interest in letting your parents in. Why not? What has happened that keeps that door locked?

To the parents:

- When your son feels so depressed, so miserable, sitting in his room, alone, and you're worried to death over him, why doesn't he come to you for help?
- I get the impression that your daughter does not trust that you will be there for her if she turns to you for support. That must break your heart. Why would she think this?
- What gets in the way of your daughter using you as a resource to support her and help her solve some of these problems?

Identifying Attachment Ruptures

To develop and facilitate a conversation focused on attachment, the therapist must manage the content. Until now, the therapist has been asking about depression: its severity, its consequences, and its causes. But now the content shifts. Instead of asking about behaviors and symptoms, we ask about parent–adolescent attachment ruptures: "When did you stop feeling loved?" and "When did he stop letting you in?" We do not wait for these themes to surface; we ask about them. We assess and diagnose the attachment fabric just like we would diagnose the depressive symptoms.

Family members may feel uncomfortable with these topics and want to regress back to discussing problems or behaviors. We resist this pull. By now, we should have enough understanding of the presenting problems and their context. So we have to gently guide the family and hold them in this new zone. We are polite but directive, as follows:

> We have talked a lot about school, Ms. Myers, and I see how upsetting it is for you. We will get back to that. But right now, I want to understand what you mean when you say that you and your son are no longer close. Tell me more about that.

If family members feel sufficiently admired, empathically understood, and not judged, they will accept this redirection and begin to talk about attachment ruptures. They will begin to tell stories of relational traumas or long-standing resentments or disappointments. Adolescents might complain that parents have neglected them or are overcontrolling. Parents might complain that the adolescent has rejected them and has scorned their attempts to be helpful or close.

These attachment ruptures exist on a continuum of severity. Adolescents often attribute the ruptures to experiences of neglect, abuse, or abandonment. We call these experiences "trauma with a big *T*." Other adolescents complain that parents are critical, rejecting, overcontrolling, and/or indifferent. We refer to this as "trauma with a little *t*." Although maybe not as insidious, these kinds of deleterious family environments/processes rupture the attachment bond and, as we know, confer a high risk factor for depression (Sheeber, Hops, & Davis, 2001). Attachment ruptures can also result from parental psychopathology, marital conflict, or parents' negative reaction to the stress of parenting a depressed adolescent. Parents often perceive ruptures as resulting from (a) the adolescent's withdrawn and irritable behavior, (b) the adolescent's lack of interest in closeness, or (c) preoccupations with peers and adolescent life.

The power in this moment in the session is the breaking of the silence. We help adolescents say things that they have kept hidden from parents and often from themselves (e.g., "I hate you for divorcing mom," "You did not protect me when dad was abusing me"). Experiences, feelings, and memories that have been avoided for fear of reprisal or causing parents' pain are suddenly given voice and expressed in the open.

Sometimes, adolescents do not disclose the trauma specifically or directly but, instead, merely show discomfort. They may become tearful, defensive, or just more withdrawn. Even though they do not describe the rupture, it becomes clear to everyone that they have things on their mind. Often this shift in mood is enough evidence to support the need for further conversation. Regardless of how much they disclose, this is a courageous moment for adolescents. Whether they express their pain verbally or nonverbally, they express a need or hurt that speaks to the core of the relationship. The therapist will feel the shift in the room. The conversation slows down, anxiety and pain increase, and the therapist suddenly feels he or she is at the heart of things. Every therapist has been in this moment and knows it when it comes; our goal is to sustain it.

This moment can become derailed if the disclosure sounds too much like blaming the parent and the parent becomes defensive. We amplify the parent's desire to understand and help the adolescent: "I know this is hard to hear, Mr. Bianchi, but your daughter is talking to you for the first time about what bothers her. Maybe we should hear her out." Framed this way, parents can often increase their tolerance for hearing difficult stories from their adolescent. Many parents are desperate to understand their depressed adolescent, and we amplify that desire as a means to decrease parents' defensiveness. They might not be happy to hear their child's accusations, but they do feel some relief that the silence has been broken. As the adolescent becomes more honest and vulnerable, the parents become more sympathetic and attentive, activating the parents' natural instinct to love and protect. When we interviewed parents after the first session, they reported feeling relieved to hear their adolescent talk, even though they felt a bit blamed. They understood the need to engage the adolescent and were willing to trust the therapist's treatment plan (G. S. Diamond, Siqueland, & Diamond, 2003). The most important tool in orchestrating this complicated dialogue is managing the emotional quality of this conversation.

Deepening Vulnerable Emotions

A shift in content (to attachment ruptures) constitutes one aspect of the relational reframe process. The right content is necessary but not sufficient. An effective shift to attachment themes must be accompanied by a simultaneous shift to softer, more vulnerable primary affect. In the beginning of the session, the tone is light, comfortable, and even jovial, as the therapist pulls for strengths. In the middle of the task, feelings of frustration, anger, blame, and impatience are minimized or circumvented to keep the history gathering on track. In this phase, the relational reframe itself, we aim to activate more vulnerable, softer primary emotions that will deepen the exploration of attachment disappointment and longing. The challenge here is deciding which emotions to pull for and process.

Greenberg and Paivio's (2003) framework about primary and secondary emotions described in our theory chapter (see Chapter 2, this volume) guides us in this process. Remember, secondary emotions serve as a defense against the more vulnerable primary emotions. For example, adolescents often express anger as a means to cover up their hurt and disappointment. Alternatively, they withdraw, become self-critical and hopeless, and/or show indifference when in fact they are angry. In the reframing process, we aim to amplify the primary emotions and minimize the secondary or maladaptive primary emotions. Specifically, we aim to identify adaptive primary emotions that accompany the attachment ruptures. To the adolescent, we might say,

> You say you do not care anymore. But I do not believe you. I think you feel abandoned by your father [attachment rupture] and feel very hurt and disappointed [primary emotion]. Is that possible? Could you share those feelings with your parents?

To the parent, we might say, "Ms. Knight, I know you are angry and frustrated, but I think you are also scared [primary emotion]—scared you might have lost your son [attachment loss]. I wonder if you could share those feelings with him." When we can access these softer emotions in the adolescent, it reduces the parents' defensives and pulls for empathy and caring. This process transforms the adolescent message from "I hate you" or "you ruined my life" to "I miss you and wish we were closer." The therapist may have to help the parent see his or her child's pain and need: "Mr. Knight, I know this is not an easy conversation, but I think your son really misses you!"

Anger is a complicated emotion. In some cases, adolescents use it to keep people at a distance and to protect themselves from being hurt again. In other instances, the anger has become a familiar, habitual but maladaptive response, blocking the surfacing of avoided primary adaptive vulnerable emotions and unmet attachment needs (i.e., loneliness, longing for connection). When adolescents express excessive anger over daily interactions (chores, homework, curfew), most likely the anger is maladaptive. Faced with this, the therapist might say, "I hear that you are angry about these things, but I think it is bigger than this. What are you really so angry about? What has your father done to you to deserve such hatred?" Often, such questions often unearth themes about attachment ruptures (e.g., being violated, neglected). This can lead to the expression of primary adaptive emotions associated with these injuries. The elicitation of these more vulnerable emotions help transform negative interactions (e.g., anger and defensiveness) into more authentic—although often painful—productive conversation.

For many depressed adolescents, the problem is different—instead of suffering from easily triggered, underregulated anger, they disavowal or overregulate their anger. These adolescents avoid experiencing and expressing primary adaptive anger associated with parental neglect or injury (e.g., criticism, abuse, abandonment). Greenberg and Paivio (2003) referred to this direction expression of legitimate anger as "assertive anger." Adolescents do not express their anger because they feel (a) protective of their parents (e.g., "I do not want to hurt their feelings"), (b) feel no one will care (e.g., "I have expressed this before and no one listened, or it did not make a difference"), and/or (c) feel unworthy of being heard (e.g., "I do not want to burden them"). Helping a depressed adolescent directly express legitimate anger about attachment ruptures breaks through their avoidance or self-protective stance.

One question facing the therapist is how long we want anger to be the main emotion in the room, even if it is primary. When adolescents are angry, parents eventually withdraw or become defensive. It is a natural instinct when one feels emotionally attacked. In contrast, when an adolescent shares sadness, disappointment, or loneliness, parents are more likely to offer comfort and protection (Johnson, 2004). Thus, vulnerable emotions, even if uncomfortable, promote conversation, exploration, and self-reflection. Therefore, although we may want to elicit primary anger, eventually we use it to activate the associated primary vulnerable emotions of sadness, disappointment, or fear. To accomplish this, the therapist cannot be dismissive of the anger but has to identify or access more vulnerable emotions that are rooted in attachment needs:

> Johnny, you have a right to be angry. These were hurtful events. I am glad you can say this to your parents. But I also wonder if your anger is so strong because you also felt hurt or disappointed. Disappointed that they did not protect you more?

This statement does not deny the secondary or primary assertive anger but seeks to elicit associated primary vulnerable emotions as well (e.g., sadness, longing, disappointment, fear).

The power of these softer emotions comes from their link to attachment (adolescent) and caregiving (parent) instincts. The innate, positive impulse is to love and protect (parent), and to be loved and supported (adolescent). These needs have been lost in the emotional chaos of family conflict. The therapist brings these instincts back into focus and the emotions associated with these unmet needs. If the therapist asks about anger, she or he will get anger. If the therapist asks about core ruptures, and softer, more vulnerable emotions, the likelihood of hearing about those increases.

Marking the Consequences of the Relational Rupture

Critical to the working of the relational reframe is judging how much processing of this newly touched upon attachment rupture should be attempted in this first session. Occasionally, families identify, feel, discuss, and even start to resolve these attachment ruptures in the first session. In other families, adolescents will acknowledge that they do not feel comfortable turning to parents for help, but they do not say why. Still, in other families, adolescents deny there is a problem, but the adolescent's discomfort with even talking about this sometimes reflects the emotional distance that has emerged between family members. Regardless of whether or not the adolescent identifies the rupture or its causes, we do not try to resolve these ruptures in this first session. Family members do not yet feel safe. The alliance with the therapists has not fully formed. Family members have no new interpersonal skills to address their problems in a productive way. In fact, to fully launch a discussion of the ruptures would most likely generate the anger, antagonism, hostility, impatience, and/or breakdown in communication that brought the family to therapy in the first place.

So, we take a turn in the conversation. We go up to the door of the ruptures, maybe we knock, but we do not usually go in, yet. Instead, we focus on the consequences of the rupture—the pain, loneliness, and sense of loss. Regardless of the reason for, or nature of, the rupture, the consequences are the same: The adolescent cannot turn to his or her parents for support, and parents' attempts to protect and care for their child are rebuffed. This sad reality—each family member longing for connection but alone in his or her pain—becomes the focus of the conversation. All family members can agree this is a tragedy and not what they had hoped for in their relationship. Focusing on the disconnection, loneliness, and disappointment, regardless of the cause or who is to blame, redirects the family from a focus of blame to a focus on regret and longing. Focusing on these softer vulnerable emotions amplifies the parents' desire for love and connection. The therapist uses this mood to engineer a moment where the family members acknowledge what they miss (connection) and recognize what they want (to repair the relationship). This becomes the foundation for acceptance of the reframe.

The transcript and commentary below help exemplify this process. This 14-year-old girl was referred to our program. This first session included the daughter and mother; the transcript begins after about 45 minutes have elapsed. The therapist has been gathering information about the course of the depression, including her history of learning problems and struggles with peers. When it becomes clear that the daughter does not talk to her mother about these problems, the therapist uses this as segue into the relational reframe.

The session we present is not an easy one. The daughter is a typical depressed, withdrawn, noncommunicative adolescent who gives the therapist little information and remains emotionally withdrawn for most of the session. But the segment exemplifies three important ABFT principles. First is the therapist's intentionality and persistence. Even when blocked by the adolescent, the therapist remains focused on the parent–adolescent relationship and uses a variety of pathways to identify attachment content. Second, the therapist aims to access softer emotions that might facilitate a more honest and less defensive or guarded conversation. Finally, although the therapist wants to discover what specific events or processes have eroded the trust between adolescent and parent, the daughter denies any problems in the relationships. Her nonverbal expression, however, indicated a rupture in the secure attachment base. The primary goal guiding the conversation is to activate the attachment and caregiving instincts that will in turn motivate family members to accept relationship building (i.e., identify what has undermined trust and commitment) as the first and primary treatment goal.

Therapist: Is that typical . . . that you don't talk to mom about yourself, your thoughts and feelings?

Adolescent: Yes. [Looks down and plays with hands]

Therapist: How come?

Adolescent: 'Cause I don't want to.

Therapist: You don't trust her?

Adolescent: I trust her. I just don't like telling her things about me.

Therapist: You don't like talking about yourself to anybody?

Adolescent: To anybody. I don't have anything that personal to talk about . . .

Therapist: [Turns to evidence of unhappiness that adolescent identified earlier] But when you're feeling frustrated about things at school and your problems with reading and not feeling smart, and you start feeling depressed and moody . . . does your mother know that you are upset about these things?

Adolescent: [Holds head down, playing with hands, shakes head] No.

Therapist: How come?

Adolescent: 'Cause I don't tell her. [Gets teary eyed]

Therapist: This topic seems hard for you. You seem upset just by me asking? [Long pause, girl hanging her head and sniffling; therapist turns to the mother] Why do you think she doesn't come to you?

Mother: Well, she will say, "I don't like school. . . . I don't wanna go to school anymore."

[As the girl becomes more visibly upset, the therapist realizes that the daughter's shift in mood is more important at this point than the questions he just asked. He politely interrupts the mother to direct her attention to the daughter's tears, trying to use the affect that has emerged in the room as the focus of the conversation.]

Therapist: Your daughter is getting a little teary eyed. Could you find out why?

Mother: [Turns to daughter] What's wrong, Cindy?

Adolescent: [Continues to hold her head down, then grabs the jean vest that she is wearing to wipe tears from her face] Nothing!

[The daughter is very withdrawn and depressed. Faced with the girl's resistance, the therapist decides to try a nonverbal strategy by seeking to move the mother physically closer to her daughter, hoping the daughter will allow mother to comfort her. Even without the content of the relational rupture identified, the therapist hopes to engineer a corrective attachment sequence whereby the mother can comfort and the daughter seeks, or at least accepts, comfort.]

Therapist: [To mother] Does your daughter let you comfort her when she's upset like that?

Mother: [Shakes head] No.

Therapist: Would she stop you from moving over next to her and putting your arm around her?

Mother: She doesn't want anybody touching her. You know, she just does not like that.

[An attempt to have the mother provide physical comfort and protection is blocked. The therapist decides to intensify the mother's sadness about the relational breach, hoping it will build some momentum in the session.]

Therapist: [To mother] Do you see her crying like this very often?

Mother: Not lately; last year she did a lot. But then, she hardly talked to me back then.

Therapist: You seem upset by this too.

Mother: Sure. Seeing her upset makes me upset. And then I am trying all the time to figure out what is wrong. [Starts to cry]

Therapist: That must be very hard on you . . . and very disappointing. [Mother gets more tearful. Hoping the mother's sadness might touch a soft spot in the girl, the therapist turns back to the daughter.]

Therapist: Do you know that mom's upset that she can't be there for you?

Adolescent: She can talk to me. I just don't want her to touch me.

Therapist: But it sounds like when she tries to talk to you, tries to understand what's going on, you shut the door on her.

Adolescent: [Holds her head down, sniffling] Sometimes, but not always.

[The therapist tries to further explore daughter's tearfulness by suggesting that maybe she misses her mother and that even though she sees her every day, they do not connect. The mother resonates with this, but the girl remains guarded. So the therapist returns to his original questions in a soft and empathic voice.]

Therapist: Why don't you talk to your mom?

Adolescent: I don't feel comfortable talking to her.

Therapist: [Sees this as a little opening] Oh, OK. So there are things to say, but you are not comfortable saying them?

Adolescent: I guess.

Therapist: Have you tried before, and it has gone badly?

Adolescent: [Shrugs her shoulders]

[After 20 minutes of trying to find the right content, the ruptures that have created this distance, the therapist shifts to consequences.]

Therapist: Look, Cindy, we have been talking for a long time here. It remains unclear to me what has gotten in the way of you trusting your mother. Maybe she hurt you or betrayed you in some way, or maybe you are just protecting her from your worries. But one thing is clear to me, you cannot go to her for help and that is tearing you and your mother up. I see a young woman overwhelmed with depression, worries, and fears. But that girl is very alone and lonely. And that makes the pain worse. And I see a mother who cares about you deeply. Who loves you and wants to be there for you. And I see how much she is suffering, and how afraid she is for you. This for me is tragic. A girl in pain and a mom that wants to help, but so much distance between you.

This segment shows the type of the maneuvering sometimes needed to get through to a depressed teen. The therapist persists with the theme, keeps the conversation focused on attachment ruptures and their consequences, and looks for content that might help explain the emotional distance between them. The therapist also blocks anger and indifference and keeps focused on sadness. Emotions such as sadness and loss in the adolescent pull for feelings of empathy and caring in the parent. This moment of tenderness helps motivate family members to accept the relational reframe.

Not all adolescents are as difficult as the one in the example above, nor are all parents this cooperative. Many adolescents are quicker to show their emotions and are more forthcoming with what bothers them. In some instances, adolescents report that it was a traumatic event or series of traumatic events that ruptured the relationship. More often, adolescents report that it is their experience of not being heard, understood, or taken seriously by parents that has led them to give up on trying to reach their parents. The most common complaints are

- "I have tried to talk to you but you do not listen."
- "You will get mad if I tell you what is on my mind."
- "I do not want to burden you. You have enough going on in your own life."
- "When I have told you things in the past, you tell others. I cannot trust you keep my private thoughts private."

Not all parents are as willing and compliant as Cindy's mother. Parents respond in a variety of ways at this juncture. Some are defensive: "I have tried to listen to her, I want her to talk to me, but she never does"; "You had it much better than I did; you have no grounds to complain"; "Are you telling me that it is my fault, that I am to blame here?" Each type of parental response requires a different response from the therapist. At this juncture, we want to block parents' automatic reflex to blame and defend themselves and, instead, focus on the issue of loss and disconnection. When this goes well, parents are able to say, "For whatever reasons, we do not communicate, and I want to make this better."

PHASE 3: CONTRACTING FOR THE RELATIONAL GOALS OF THERAPY

Amplifying the Desire for Change

So, here is the final critical step. The foundation has been set. We have helped family members identify and acknowledge the ruptures and the disappointment, sadness, and grief they feel about the distance that has emerged. Now we must amplify the desire for change. We begin to craft the main goal of the therapy as an opportunity for relational repair. We empathically punctuate how tragic it is that so much distance has emerged between them—that each is left alone to deal with their loss of connection. Then we begin to try generating and amplifying the motivation and willingness to change:

> If things could be different . . . if you felt like you could trust each other again . . . if you could feel that love was given and received, would that interest you? [Looks for agreement and explores hesitations] Good, because this is what I want to work on for the first few weeks of therapy. Is that a goal you would be willing to work on in therapy with me?

If you have laid the foundation of identifying relational ruptures and relational consequences of these ruptures (e.g., loss, withdrawal, disengagement) and have deepened vulnerable emotions, agreement on this goal is not hard to get. Remember, deep down, adolescents want and need their parents to love, admire, and protect them and parents want the respect of, and closeness with, their children. Many family members, however, feel hopeless about this possibility. But if one person is hopeful, that is enough to build on. If no one is hopeful, then the therapist serves as the harbinger of hope, the keeper of the flame.

The motivation here is not just to rebuild love. The goal of relational repair has to be linked to protection, specifically against depression. Maybe there is too much damage and distrust between parents and adolescents. Maybe talk of love seems sappy and melodramatic. But protection! Protection is an instinct, a drive, a biologically wired force that propels people to action even in the face of danger. If love will not motivate parents and adolescents, protection will (in most cases). But the therapist has to make this link, connect the dots, so that parents and adolescent view relational repair as a worthy goal.

There are at least three different ways we explain this to parents. First, repairing ruptures can help reduce tension in the family. Whether conflict is causing or maintaining the depression, relational ruptures fuel tension, distrust, animosity, and/or withdrawal. Consequently, mending these ruptures can help improve family cohesion. As a result, adolescents will distance themselves less and allow parents to resume their role as a resource to them. In this regard, reducing tension allows the family to feel more like a team again, allowing parents to serve a more protective function (e.g., comfort, support, problem solving).

A second strategy, usually aimed at the parents, is to argue that the adolescent is trapped by depression and having a hard time growing up. The adolescent needs help to manage emotions, handle conflict, and solve problems. In this way, resolving these family problems can serve as learning opportunities; opportunities for the adolescent to try new skills in a safe and loving environment. Helping the adolescent solve the problems within the family helps him or her build the skills she or he needs to solve interpersonal problems outside the family. We might say the following to a parent:

> You are right. She is overwhelmed by her emotions and sometimes out of control. She is immature and needs to grow up. We agree with you on this. But we think she needs your help. She needs you to teach her how to talk about problems without blowing up or retreating into isolation. You need to teach her to be honest about what she is feeling. But to do this, she needs to feel safe, and feel that you are on her side. She needs to trust you, so you can be her parent again.

This strategy may be helpful when a parent is a bit defensive. No parent wants to be blamed, but most parents want to help. We amplify that instinct.

Finally, we might take a more pragmatic approach with parents, one that leverages the urgency inherent to depression and suicidal ideation.

> Your child is at high risk! He is very depressed. He has active thoughts of suicide. I cannot be there all the time, but you can. Your child needs you, needs you to protect him. But right now, he does not trust you. He does not want your help. We have to work through this barrier. You have to help me to help him get these things off his chest, even if you feel as though they are selfish or inaccurate. Until he feels you can listen to him, he will not let go of his anger and distrust. We just need to hear him out, so you can be on his team again. It is imperative! Will you work with me on this? I know it will not be easy. And I am going to work with him so whatever he has to say is reasonable. But if we do not repair this relationship, I worry that your son is adrift and in danger.

We also need to motivate the adolescent's desire for change so he or she will agree to work on the relationship. Here again, many pathways are possible.

First, we find that many depressed adolescents welcome this relational focus of therapy. They often come to therapy attributing their depression to negative family interactions (e.g., overly critical or controlling parents) or negative family events (e.g., divorce, marital problems) and want some relief. Often these teens have felt blamed for the depression and its problematic consequences. They see the relational reframe as a chance to get their side of the story heard, to be listened to and understood. This takes some of the blame off of them and makes everyone in the family more responsible for change. But more important, many depressed adolescents deeply miss being close to their parents. They do not want their parents to be overly involved in their private matters, but they do want their parents to be more interested in them and sensitive to their needs. Consequently, we often find that the adolescent is more accepting of the relational reframe than are the parents.

Still, some adolescents are hesitant, resistant, indifferent, and hopeless about change. They might feel like they have tried to address problems but that their parents are not really interested. Often these adolescents have adopted a dismissive posture and have walled off their needs for love and comfort to protect themselves from being hurt again. With these adolescents, we lend them hope that change is possible and that things can improve between them and their parents. Without making false promises, we express confidence in our ability to improve family relationships. When appropriate, we affirm their perception that they have been treated unjustly and present treatment as an opportunity to finally be heard and acknowledged. Most of all, however, we speak to their grief, their loneliness, and their buried desire for love.

> Rosa, I hear how hurt you feel and how hopeless you feel about things ever getting better. But I see it in your tears. I hear it in your voice. You would not be so angry if you really did not care anymore. I see how scary it is to want your mother's love. You feel you have been so disappointed before.

Contracting for Relationship Repair

What are we trying to accomplish by the end of Task I? What is the task outcome? We want to persuade the family that rebuilding the adolescent–parent relationship is the first and most urgent goal of the therapy. This is the treatment plan, and we work to reach agreement on it. So, at a certain point, we stop exploring, uncovering, deepening, and cajoling. We have laid all the groundwork we could at this time. Ideally, each family member has connected deeply to their loneliness, sadness, frustration, and pain. At this point we pause. We take a breath. We look each family member in the eye. With great conviction and intentionality, we then ask each of them for a commitment:

"Are you willing to make relationship building the first goal of therapy?" We wait for an answer. We do not get distracted. We ask again, in softer and more hopeful ways. We acknowledge that there are other problems to work on, but we believe this has to happen first before we can work on the depression and its associated problems. We lend them hope by expressing confidence in this approach and our ability to help. We do not waiver from our conviction. We stay steady. The relational reframe is the center, the pillar of the conversation, and we want the family conversation to organize it (Brendler, Silver, Haber, & Sargent, 1991). If we need to, we ask again, "Can we agree that working on relationship building, finding out what is getting in the way of you turning to your parents for help, will be our first goal of therapy?"

Without agreement on this goal and tasks, therapists will be battling over the definition of treatment in every session. The therapist however, cannot, nor does she or he want to, beat the family into submission. That is not the goal. However, we do not give up easily. We continue to suggest that transforming the relationship is the best path out of the forest. We continue to believe in the goodness of the family members and their ability, no matter how buried, to have more honest and trustworthy relationships. We acknowledge the good in them. We compliment them. We admire the adolescent's willingness to engage in this kind of conversation and attribute their maturity to the good parenting they must have received. We assure them that this is not about blame or taking sides. This kind of conviction, commitment to our goal, coupled with our admiration and support of family members, confidence in our approach and our desire to protect each of the family members from harm, is powerful. By the end, many families say to us, "No therapist has ever asked this of us before." They often feel relieved and inspired. They begin to believe there is a way out, a pathway of tenderness and connection.

Sometimes one or more family members say "no." They are ambivalent or even clear about not being ready to commit to relationship building. Perhaps the resentment or hopelessness are still too great at that moment. So, we start to scale back our expectations and accept that fully embracing this approach may take more time. We acknowledge that we have just met and they have no reason to trust us yet. All we ask is that they consider this as a possible treatment goal and come back for a next session alone so that we get to know them and discuss this more. But most of all, we make an empathic, affect-focused, straight-to-the-heart offer of help:

> Look, Yolanda, I see you are angry. I see you are hurt. And I understand why you feel the need to protect yourself. But I do not believe for a second that you do not miss your mother's love. It may take some time, but I think I can help you . . . help you feel loved again. How about you and I meet next week and we can just talk about this some more?

So in the face of their reluctance, from the teen or the parents, we may scale back the treatment contract to an acceptable level, knowing that we will revisit their commitment to this treatment goal in the upcoming alliance tasks. As Bugental (1992), one of the great existential therapists, used to say, "Resistance does not get in the way of the therapy; it is the therapy" (p. 184). Where they are stuck or hesitant, we need to go and make that the focus of the conversation. The therapy has to stay honest and have integrity. We are not tricking anyone, or forcing anyone, or pretending anyone is further along than they are.

Two caveats should be mentioned at this time. First, many parents feel blamed or guilty to some degree during the relational reframe process. Although these feelings might be warranted and actually motivate parents to change, too much guilt can generate defensiveness, self-criticism, or hopelessness. Therefore, the therapist attempts to leverage feelings of responsibility or even guilt into action. We emphasize that, no matter what happened in the past, parents can become a great resource to their adolescent now. The main goal of the session is to get family members interested in repairing trust and connection. Therefore, we might say,

> I do not know what caused this distance. There might be a lot that we have to sort through, and I have only just met you all. But what I do know is that you both miss each other and would like to feel close once again. And that even though Janice is mad [or withdrawn], I think she still wants a relationship with you. Let's keep that as our goal and then we can see what we have to understand or work through to accomplish this.

Second, some parents equate being more emotionally available with losing authority. Sometimes parents believe that if they listen and empathize with their kid's pain or desires, it is equivalent to agreeing and then they have to acquiesce. They interpret our treatment plan as a request to drop expectations, rules, and consequences and just let their adolescent do whatever he or she wants. Nothing could be further from the truth. We promote a balance of warmth and structure. However, we do advocate that therapy start with a focus on relationships' rebuilding rather than on problem solving. If nothing else, this strategy helps engage an otherwise disengaged and withdrawn adolescent. We tell parents that our first goal is to get the adolescent more engaged and active in the treatment. To do this, we need to put some of the adolescent's complaints front and center and help the parents listen and understand these concerns. But being a better listener does not mean agreeing with the adolescent's view or having no rules and expectations. We are just trying to help parents find a better balance. We also believe, and often tell the parents, that when adolescents are angry about interpersonal problems, they often express their anger through problem behavior. We suggest that if we can solve some of these bigger issues of trust and betrayal, if adolescents finally feel they have been heard and validated, that this often diffuses a great deal of family tension. Once tension has been diffused, adolescents are more cooperative in problem-solving conversations and more willing to let their parents help in autonomy development. Below, we provide an extended excerpt from the final moments of the reframing process to better demonstrate what we have been discussing. The excerpt starts late in the first session.

Therapist: So, why don't you talk to your parents about your problems?

Adolescent: [Looks nervously at mother, who tries to look supportive]

Father: Go ahead, say what you want. We told you to be honest here.

Therapist: [Responds to the observed process] You look nervous. Do you feel safe sharing your concerns and feelings with your parents?

Mother: Dr. Diamond, I think it is hard for Tammy. . . . You see, she and Allen [father] butt heads a lot about schoolwork. I have encouraged him to let me help her, but he insists . . .

Therapist: Mrs. Williams, let me interrupt you a minute. We talked a bit about schoolwork. There are clearly frustrating problems there. We will come back to that . . . but why . . . why can't Tammy share her feelings with either of you? As we know, she is very depressed and very distraught. Why can't she come to either of you for support?

[Tammy hangs her head. Mother looks nervously at father. Father stares blankly at his daughter.]

Mother: Well, she does talk to me more than to Allen. . . . He is a bit harsh with her.

Father: I do not agree with that. We are very close. You are just too easy on her, so she comes to you knowing that she can get what she wants. [Conflict begins to escalate.]

Therapist: Hold on here. Let's slow this down. We know there are some differences between the two of you. And sometimes these differences lead to arguments. You both feel right, but neither of you feel heard. Is that sort of how it goes?

Mother and Father: [Hesitantly nod in agreement]

Therapist: I know this is frustrating for both of you, for all of you. But I bet it is disappointing that Tammy cannot come to you for emotional support.

Clearly, this is a family with conflicts. The daughter is angry and withdrawn. The mother is close to the daughter but also a bit overprotective. The father is a bit more harsh and disengaged but clearly committed to his daughter. The parents are deeply at odds with each other and are likely having marital problems. The challenge for the therapist is where to go from here. Remember, the goal is the reframe, not the working through of problems. Does the therapist have enough information about the rupture and its consequences so they can move to the reframe, or is a bit more information needed? From earlier in the conversation, the therapist has evidence that the daughter does not trust her parents; she does not feel safe. That might be enough to elicit empathy and concern from the parents. But if the therapist remains in the domain of conflicts too long, the hostility could dominate the session and inhibit the shift to a relational-focused therapy. The mood must be softer. This can be achieved by further exploring the consequences of the conflicts for the adolescent, and the cost of the adolescent–parent ruptures.

Father: What do you mean? I think the kids are happy. We do not fight in front of them.

Mother: [Rolls her eyes]

Therapist: You know, Mr. Williams, kids are pretty smart. They pick up on these things. [Turns to the daughter] Tammy, you clearly are angry when they start to fight. But I also see some fear in you. Are you worried about your parents?

Adolescent: I am not worried. I couldn't give a shit about them. They fight all the time; there is nothing I can do about it.

The therapist asks about worry. It is a relevant question, especially if the therapist wants to explore the daughter's fears about the parents getting a divorce. That is an important theme but is premature at this stage of the therapy. Moreover, a vague question about worry is likely to just pull for more anger. The daughter is actually more concerned that the parents are not taking care of her, that they will abandon her. The therapist regroups and looks for better words and a more accurate, precise definition of what the girl is feeling—one that will help the daughter express her fear and hurt, which might activate softer parental caregiving behaviors and feelings in the parents.

Therapist: So, you have given up?

Adolescent: What do you mean? [Looks irritated]

Therapist:	Well, you say you have given up caring about them . . . but I think you have given up hoping that they can care about you, given up hoping that they can love you.
Adolescent:	It's just that [starts to cry] I mean . . . oh, what's the difference . . . ? They don't care about me!
Mother:	[Talks softly] That is not true. Of course we care about you.
Father:	Tammy, how could we not care about you?
Adolescent:	[Turns away, crying and rejecting the parents' comfort]

Now the mood has shifted. The therapist has helped the girl express a core fear or unmet need. As she becomes more vulnerable, the parents soften and focus more on comforting their daughter than on fighting with each other. Is it perfect? Maybe not. But an opening exists, and the therapist will try to build on it.

Therapist:	Mr. and Mrs. Williams, It is clear how much you love and care about your daughter. [Both nod their heads.] It must be painful to see her suffering like this and disappointing that she will not let you comfort her. [These observations are not exactly accurate, but the therapist creates opportunity for feelings of love and protection to emerge.]
Mother:	We want to love her, but she just does not let us in!
Therapist:	I can see how much you want to reach out and comfort her.
Mother:	[Becomes teary]
Therapist:	[Turns to the daughter] Is that true, Tammy? That you do not want to let them in?
Adolescent:	[Keeps head turned away and does not respond]
Therapist:	[Lets the silence linger] You are so angry at them. But I also see sadness You wanted their comfort so much. But they let you down. They disappointed you.
Adolescent:	[Cries more]
Therapist:	[Allows a long pause] Do you think this hurt between you can ever be repaired?

The therapist is crafting a very specific conversation: blocking tangential themes that might derail the conversation and directing family members to focus on attachment and longing. Now the content, process, and affect are right. The content is not on the parents' conflicts and pending divorce but on the lack of safety, trust, and shared love in the family. The affect is not hostility and anger, but sadness (daughter) and regret and hope (parents). The therapist could continue exploring these themes, but again our goal is not to work through these conflicts. We save that for the attachment task. Instead, our goal is to punctuate the rupture, the longing for love; motivate the family for change; and galvanize a commitment to repairing these ruptures as the initial goal of the therapy.

Therapist: Tammy, is there any hope left in you? Hope that things could be better?

Adolescent: [Sniffles; mother hands her a tissue. Darts a series of looks of anger, fear, and longing at her parents but takes the tissue.]

Therapist: Oh, I can see how hard this is for you. [Turns to the parents] What do you think, Mr. and Mrs. Williams? Do you think there is any hope, any chance?

Mother and Father: Of course we do. . . . We really want . . .

Therapist: I know you want this. And Tammy knows you want it. But she is worried that things will not change.

Mother: I think I do a pretty good job.

Father: Oh come on, Betty. We fight like we hate each other. How can you expect her to trust us? [Starts to cry] I know, Tammy. . . . I know how hard this has been on you. Mom and I have to make it better. We will make it better. Maybe Dr. Diamond can help with this.

Therapist: Do you believe him, Tammy?

Adolescent: [Shrugs shoulders but clearly has been touched]

Therapist: So, look. Clearly, there has been a lot of hurt here and a lot of lost love. I want to help you get that back. [To Tammy] No matter what happens with your parent's marriage, they can both love you. I want to help that happen. [To the family] But I think Tammy has to find her voice. Find a way to say how angry she is and how scared she is rather than cutting herself. That is my first goal for us. Mr. and Mrs. Williams, can we work on this first and then later solve some of these school problems?

Mother and Father: [Nod in agreement]

Therapist: Tammy, will you work with me on this? On finding your voice and being more honest about how you feel?

Adolescent: [Shrugs] I guess.

Therapist: [Lets the silence linger for a few moments as a way to punctuate the moment] Good. OK. You are a very impressive young woman, Tammy. [Turns to the parents] That is a testament to your good parenting. I feel very hopeful that we can get some good work done here. So, Tammy, can you and I meet alone next week? There is so much more I need to know about you.

Adolescent: Sure.

CONCLUSION

We do not always get this far in the first session. But more often than not, we get very close. We accomplish this because the therapist has a plan. The therapist has intentionality. The therapist believes that cutting to the heart of the problem will actually provide the family some relief and hope. A therapeutic process has begun in the first session, and the family members get a feeling that this therapy may be different from other therapies. Many therapists we train initially feel they need more time to build an alliance before they can be this direct, challenging, or focused. We believe that alliance emerges from being helpful, not from being nice. John Brendler used to tell us to stake out a position and let the family narrative begin to organize around it (see Brendler et al., 1991). In ABFT, we make attachment rupture and attachment longing the centers of the conversation. With that topic as the organizing theme, we invite the adolescent and the parent to sessions alone to further build alliance and to focus on repairing or strengthening attachment.

4

TASK II: ADOLESCENT ALLIANCE

Attachment-based family therapy (ABFT) contrasts with traditional structural family therapy, which has historically focused on parental hierarchy and boundary making as the initial goal of therapy. Although sometimes this focus is necessary (e.g., in a crisis or for adolescent safety), generally this is not an effective approach with adolescents (Liddle & Diamond, 1991). First, adolescents can more easily resist coming to treatment or engaging in treatment. Second, this approach collides with the adolescents' emerging sense of self, new ideas about justice and fairness, and their cognitive capacity to question authority. Therefore, we aim to capitalize on these developmental processes by placing adolescents' concerns at the center of the therapy. We accomplish this not by supporting their complaints about daily problems but rather by identifying and validating more fundamental feelings of betrayal, disappointment, or sadness about perceived attachment injuries (e.g., parent's unavailability, overcontrolling, frightening behavior). We present treatment as an opportunity to gain a voice—to say, often for the first time, why they

http://dx.doi.org/10.1037/14296-005
Attachment-Based Family Therapy for Depressed Adolescents, by G. S. Diamond, G. M. Diamond, and S. A. Levy

are so angry, afraid, or hurt or have lost trust in the relationship. We help them connect with and articulate their unmet attachment needs: the desire to be loved, admired and protected by their parent. This process can help the adolescent once again value their attachment needs or at least understand how these unmet needs drive self-destructive behavior. Thus, Task II focuses on forming an alliance with the adolescent.

This task includes three phases, as shown in Figure 4.1. We begin with the bond. We want to make the adolescent more comfortable, build up some trust, and help them begin to engage in the therapy. We always look for strengths, competency, and avenues for autonomy. We then turn to the second phase: treatment goals. We need to locate the central motivation for treatment within the adolescents. Therefore, we merge their desire for change with our strategies for achieving it. We begin by exploring their unhappiness and their past efforts to change it. This helps adolescents take ownership of their struggles and thus motivates them to engage in the therapeutic process. We then begin to link their depression to attachment ruptures, either as a cause of the depression or as a barrier to gaining support from parents. We want them to agree to our treatment goal—that working through these ruptures with their parents may alleviate some of the depression. If they accept the logic of this perspective, we move on to the third phase, the task.

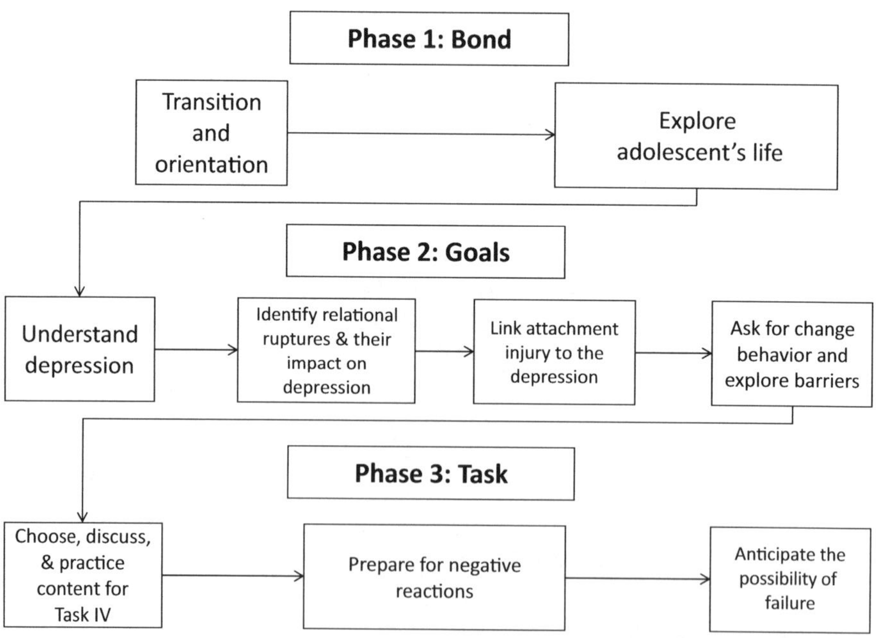

Figure 4.1. Task II: Adolescent alliance. This figure depicts the therapist performance map for facilitating the adolescent alliance task.

We begin to prepare them for productive conversation with their parents about these past felt injustices. Typically, this requires two sessions but can take up to four, depending on the adolescent and the family circumstances.

The three phases of the adolescent alliance task build on Bordin's (1979) tripartite working alliance framework. Bordin proposed that alliance comprised three dimensions: bond, goals, and tasks. *Bond* refers to whether the client feels liked, respected, and supported by the therapist. *Goals* refer to whether the client and therapist agree on the aims of therapy (e.g., reducing depression, reducing family conflict, getting back to school). *Tasks* refer to whether the client and therapist agree on how to achieve these goals: Will we meet together as a family or meet alone? Will we teach the adolescent social skills or talk together in sessions about painful past experiences? Whereas goals determine our target outcomes, tasks determine how we will do it. Alliance increases when clients agree with the therapist about what to work on and how to do it. Thus, this task strengthens alliance by building the bond and getting clear agreement on the goals and tasks of this therapy.

Without agreement on the therapy goal, getting agreement on tasks can be difficult. The relational reframe aims to make improving the parent–child relationship the initial and central goal of this therapy. If family members accept this, they will more likely accept the direction and process of the therapy, specifically, the attachment task. If they do not accept this goal, family members will resist the treatment process. The ABFT model works so effectively and rapidly because we intentionally focus our early efforts on establishing a shared treatment goal. In this regard, we think of alliance not as a nonspecific or common factor in the background of therapy but rather as a specific topic to be directly negotiated early in treatment.

Although agreement to repair relationships is the goal of the relational reframe (Task I), agreement to participate in the attachment task (Task IV) is the end point of the adolescent alliance task (Task II). By the end of the task, the adolescent should say, "Yes, I will meet with my parents and talk directly to them about why I don't go to them for help." With this in mind, the therapist monitors all session content, affect, and process for whether they support or distract from the mission of this task. The remainder of the chapter describes how this process unfolds.

PHASE 1: BOND

Transition and Orientation

In the opening moments of the task, we have a few small goals. First, we ask how the adolescent felt about the initial session and the proposed relational focus of therapy. This gives some idea of how well the relational reframe resonated with the adolescent. Second, we establish some clarity about confidentiality, both in general and in relation to these individual and family sessions. Finally, we give an overview of the goals and process for this task, thus showing we have a plan for the sessions and demonstrating our confidence and the fact that we know what we are doing. What follows is one example of how this conversation might unfold.

Therapist: So, thanks for meeting alone with me today. I wanted a chance to get to know you a bit more without your parents here. It is important that you and I develop a good working relationship so I can support you in this program. So I am curious what you thought about our first session?

Adolescent: It was OK.

Therapist: What did you think about my suggested goals of treatment—that you and your parents figure out what is getting in the way of you trusting them?

Adolescent: It doesn't matter to me. They don't care, and they are not my problem . . . that's not why I am depressed.

Therapist: Well, OK . . . that is why we are here today: You and I, just sorting out what is making you depressed and some ideas about how to improve it.

Adolescent: Sure. OK.

Therapist: So let me say a bit about what is private here between you and me. You know, this family treatment is a bit tricky. I am seeing you alone, and then I will see your parents alone. And I want you to feel free to speak your mind and say what you want. The only things I am obligated to tell them or someone is if you are thinking of hurting yourself or someone else or if you are being hurt by someone. [Provides more detail if needed] Do you know what I mean by that?

Adolescent: Yeah. I have heard that before.

Therapist: Good. But there will be other things you might want to talk about and do not want your parents to know. Here is my take on this. My initial goal is that you trust me. And together we will figure out what has got you so upset and why you can't go to your parents. And that will stay between us. OK? But my main goal is that eventually you feel safe enough to tell your parents these things yourself.

Adolescent: Yeah, sure, like that's going to happen.

Therapist: Well we will sort this out. But I just want you to know where I stand. OK?

Adolescent:	Sure.
Therapist:	OK, good. So let me find out a bit more about you. You told me last week that you like rap music . . . tell me more about that . . . who do you listen to?

This is a simple and clear beginning to the session. We check in about the previous session. We define confidentiality. We state our goals for today's session and the task. The therapist effectively sidesteps the adolescent's negativity for now, knowing that this entire session is focused on winning him or her over to the ABFT treatment goal and tasks. The therapist is matter of fact about the goals and accepts the adolescent's hesitation. If the resistance arises from bravado, the therapist can just let it go. If the resistance emerges because the adolescent feels hurt or betrayed, the therapist might choose to discuss this a bit more but still not linger on this too long at this stage of the session. We have to trust in the game plan of the task.

Exploring the Adolescent's Life

We next explore the landscape of the adolescent's life (Liddle, 1995). The conversation focuses on topics like strengths, hobbies, music, neighborhood, friends, school, romantic relationships, sex, and drugs. Therapists familiar with contemporary adolescent culture (e.g., movies, music) can use this knowledge to demonstrate some shared interests. Although this segment repeats the joining moments of the initial sessions, this conversation alone with the adolescent allows for more depth and focus on the adolescent's life. Initially the conversation might be lighthearted and fun. As the bond builds, however, the therapist can ask more meaningful and challenging questions about values, beliefs, desires, longings, hopes, and dreams.

Several principles guide this conversation. First, the therapist aims to make the adolescent feel at ease. Adolescents who are depressed can be nervous, shy, avoidant, and suspicious. They may have never been in therapy before or may have had bad experiences in previous therapies. Therefore, this conversation helps the adolescent relax and the therapist demonstrates sincerity, curiosity, and support. This sets the foundation for more difficult topics to come. Second, the therapist looks for stories, interests, and content that represents strengths in the adolescent's life. Too often, therapists focus on problems and ignore strengths and competencies. Identification of strengths shows interest in often ignored aspects of the adolescent's life (Micucci, 1998). This may be the first time a professional (or any adult for that matter) shows interest in their music, hair braiding, skateboarding, or movie making. Besides serving to build a bond, this demonstrates our willingness to view the adolescent as competent and capable.

Third, the therapist uses the adolescent's experiences of success to formulate motivational metaphors. Such metaphors can help adolescents fight the depression or overcome therapeutic hurdles. For example, when preparing the adolescent to talk with his or her parents, the therapist might say, "Remember when you were in that play? How nervous you were talking in public? But then your voice came out loud and strong! It will be the same here, only this time you will write your own script." Fourth, the therapist identifies any talents and activities that the adolescent has lost interest in because of the depression. We may want to revisit these activities later in the treatment, in the autonomy-building task, in the hopes of getting the adolescent motivated and reengaged in the productive, enjoyable aspects of his or her life.

Finally, we encourage the adolescent to see the therapist as an ally rather than as an authority figure (Liddle & Diamond, 1991). Too often, adolescents enter therapy with suspicion and distrust of adult figures, expecting them to be controlling and dismissive. We want to challenge this belief. We want to be viewed as an *authoritative* figure they respect, trust, and turn to for advice and guidance, rather than as an authority figure to react against. Minuchin is credited with saying that a therapist should be like an aunt or uncle: "Close enough to care, but distant enough to keep perspective." From an attachment perspective, we want to be supportive and caring, yet protective and demanding. We serve as a transitional object (Winnicott, 1953), helping rekindle hope and trust with us, and then redirecting those needs to the parents.

Thus, with an eye for strengths and competency, we explore the details of adolescents' lives. Although we began this conversation in the reframe task, we now go back and do this in more depth. We ask adolescents about domains that they are often uncomfortable talking about with their parents, such as sexuality and the use of substances. We display curiosity and interest in their life in a nonjudgmental manner. This further helps build trust and sometimes leads the adolescent to reveal important content to be addressed later, in the autonomy task.

Making Meaning

Making meaning out of this bonding conversation requires the therapist to be attentive and focused. We are not just making small talk or chitchat. The therapist has to be thoughtful about what he or she asks about: What topics are important to the adolescent, and what themes will facilitate the treatment goals? If the conversation is just random, jumping from topic to topic, or overly detailed on nonessential content area, therapy remains flat, with no depth or meaning. The therapist must listen and respond to content that can bring depth and focus to the conversation, either now or by planting seeds for later work.

Therapist: Tell me a little bit about school.

Adolescent: I hate school.

Therapist: Really. How come?

Adolescent: The teachers are mean, the kids all gossip behind your back, and the work is stupid. Should I say more?

Therapist: Is there anything you do enjoy there? Any class at all that you like?

Adolescent: I like art class. My teacher is cool and she likes me a lot, but that's about it.

Therapist: Have you always liked art?

Adolescent: I guess. I used to draw pictures for the school newspaper. They would bring me a story and I would make up a picture to go with it. Some of them were pretty funny. One time I did this picture. . . . Oh, well, it doesn't matter anymore. I wasn't very good. And I don't even think I am going to finish school anyway. Are we done soon?

Therapist: But it sounds like you enjoyed making the drawings!

Adolescent: Yeah, I suppose . . .

Therapist: Do you ever imagine doing that again . . . drawing pictures?

Adolescent: No. Not really.

Therapist: Do you have any drawings at home that you can bring in and show me?

Adolescent: Well, I have this stupid portfolio at home. I was supposed to submit it to some contest. But I never did.

Therapist: I would love to see that sometime. Do you think you could bring them in?

Adolescent: You want to see them? Sure, I guess.

This short excerpt shows the therapist searching to hold on to the adolescent's strength even though the pull of depression and hopelessness threatens to bury it. The therapist avoids being enticed into discussing problems and experiences of failure. That can come later. During this bonding phase, the therapist wants to bring forgotten strengths into the conversation. The therapist can get a lot of mileage out of the theme of the "adolescent as artist." It offers an expanded identity: "You're not just a troubled youth, you're also an artist." It provides a plethora of metaphors that can be used throughout the therapy and some concrete activities to focus on in future autonomy-building sessions. We might even say to the adolescent, "OK, I think we can use this as an indication of our success. The day you get back to drawing pictures for the school newspaper, we will know you are feeling better."

One common question is, How long should we stay on a given topic? At what point has the topic been developed sufficiently to achieve the desired goal? If therapists leave the topic too soon, they might miss an opportunity to develop a meaningful topic or they might not seem genuinely interested. If they stay too long, the conversation can feel like an interrogation. For guidance, therapists can ask themselves the following questions: What is my goal in this exchange and has that goal been met? Am I just gathering more details or promoting depth and meaning? Is the adolescent appropriately engaged in the topic or is he or she getting annoyed? Have I made it meaningful to them? Has the adolescent's emotional response indicated more engagement in the topic? How much is this conversation facilitating the identification of treatment goals or my relationship with the adolescent (i.e., intimacy, closeness, trust)? The reflective practitioner constantly makes decisions about the value of each and every moment of conversation.

Ultimately, the therapist must decide when to end the bond phase and start the goal-focused conversation. This is a clinical judgment based on the process and content of the conversation. The therapist has to ask himself or herself the following types of questions: Have I covered the major important areas? Have I found a few good themes or metaphors to help with the story line of the case? Does the family member seem more relaxed, comfortable, and/or talkative? Is he or she looking bored and thinking I am wasting his or her time with this chitchat? In general, this segment should not be too long—perhaps 15 to 20 minutes; there is a lot more to accomplish. Remember, we want to establish the bond, goals, and tasks and end the session or task with some concrete direction and buy-in to the therapeutic goal of relationship building and the utility of attachment sessions.

Sometimes, however, the conversation during the bond phase can be uniquely meaningful. In such instances, therapists may be compelled to linger here longer. For example, one female adolescent had originally been resistant to attending family therapy. In the first alliance-building session she wanted to tell us about her social life, including boyfriends, sex, and drugs. In part, this topic was important to her. She had a miserable social experience in middle school and was quite proud that she now had a successful social life in high school. In part, she was testing the therapist: Could he hear about her outrageous exploits without becoming judgmental and controlling? Could he really be trusted? In part, she wanted to know whether he could help her with these kinds of challenges and not just with family relationships.

Given these perceived tests, the therapist listened, asked questions, became curious, and tried to clarify her views and values about her "druggy" friends and her reported promiscuous sex. As the conversation progressed, she admitted that although she liked being in with the cool crowd, she was sometimes bored and wanted more challenges. The therapist punctuated her ambivalence and empathized with her dilemma. He also decided not to move on to discuss the adolescent's depression, the family's contributions to the depression (goals), and her willingness to talk to her parents about this (tasks). Instead, he spent nearly the entire first session of the alliance task on the bond phase. The therapist passed many tests that day, which gave him the credibility to move to more challenging problems in the next sessions: her depression, suicide attempt, and eventually, her relationship with her parents. Although with this adolescent, not moving too fast was the right decision, many therapists move slower than necessary. Remember: Aim to get a sufficient amount of detail to better understand the adolescent, help him or her feel comfortable, and strive to build one or two meaningful therapeutic themes that capture something important about the adolescent. We do not need to explore every aspect of the adolescent's life in great depth. This is the tension of conducting a therapy that not only sees value in reflective conversation but also has an agenda and goals that move the conversation forward.

PHASE 2: GOALS

Once we have deepened the bond with adolescents, we return to discussing the reason that they came for therapy: their depression. We ask more about that experience, such as how bad it has been and how they have tried to overcome their depression. We want to document their despair and amplify their longing for relief. We also begin to better understand their view of the attachment relationship with his or her parents. Developing this narrative can be therapeutic and sets a foundation for the attachment task.

Understanding the Depression

We begin this sequence with a transition statement. We want to clearly mark that we are leaving this more casual phase of the conversation about life and strengths and starting to focus on problems. Even if the conversation has not gone that well, we praise and admire whatever the adolescent gave us. Depressed youth rarely receive praise and have little capacity to sustain a positive self-image. Therefore, we try to infuse them with confidence and optimism whenever we can. We might say something like the following:

> So, look. I am very impressed with you. You have a lot going on, a lot of strengths and hopes and dreams. Some you have given up on, but some you still hold on to. In the face of what you have been through, you still remember and believe in these parts of yourself. That impresses me. I am

> particularly struck by your interest in art. That is a part of you we can build on, recover, and bring back to life. Sounds like you got a lot out of that. Can we work on this together? [Looks for agreement from the adolescent] Great! So, I want to talk now about some harder things. I want to better understand your depression and the impact it is having on your life. Is that OK?

Unlike old-style family therapy, symptoms (e.g., depression) remain front and center in this therapy. Depression is something both parents and adolescents want to resolve; it is the reason and motive for everyone to engage in treatment. Therefore, we never lose sight of it. In fact, we use it as leverage to work on underlying relational themes and interactions. We begin this sequence with a short reassessment of the depression. Although this segment repeats the assessment moments of the initial session, this conversation alone with the adolescent will ground the conversation in the presenting problem. We then expand on what we previously learned by asking some of the following questions: What kinds of depressive symptoms does the adolescent experience, when did they start, and how long have they lasted? How bad has it been? What additional problems (i.e., comorbid disorders) might be contributing to or resulting from the depression: substance use, anxiety, attention-deficit/hyperactivity disorder, medical conditions? How much functional impairment has it caused? What circumstantial factors might be contributing to the depression (e.g., school failure, social problems, abuse/neglect, victimization, identity confusion, racial/ethnic/religious prejudice)? This sequence is not a diagnostic interview; rather, it is a strategy to amplify and make undeniable the depth of the adolescent's misery and the urgent need for change. At this point in the conversation, we block any exploration of how family processes contribute to the depression; we save that for later.

The primary goal of this sequence is to acknowledge, validate, empathize with, and punctuate the adolescent's suffering. We want adolescents to know we understand their pain. More important, we want the adolescents themselves to acknowledge their unhappiness. Many adolescents come to treatment denying problems or minimizing the depression and its impact. This undermines their motivation to engage in treatment: If problems are not really that bad, adolescents will feel less motivated to work hard in the therapy. They might say a version of "Things are not that bad, really. I'm not sure it is worth getting into all of that." We anticipate this possibility. For that reason, we try to get adolescents to acknowledge, recognize, or admit the severity of the depression and its impact on their life. Howard Liddle used to say, "Take them into their own hell." We want the adolescent to make a statement like the following: "Yes, the depression is bad. Yes, it has created problems in my life. Yes, I am unhappy." These sorts of statements set the foundation for the remainder of this conversation.

When adolescents acknowledge their own depression, they begin taking ownership of the problem. Many adolescents come to us feeling like passive victims of negative circumstances that they can do nothing about. We want to challenge that mind-set. Developing an identity, a sense of self-efficacy, and a capacity for goal directedness are core tasks of adolescence. Depression undermines these tasks. When adolescents acknowledge their unhappiness, however, it is the beginning of them taking the problem more seriously. Regardless of what is causing the depression, the depression begins to become a problem they want to solve. In this moment, we begin moving the locus of control for the treatment from the parents or us, to the adolescent. We want him or her to take ownership of and have an investment in this process. Developmentally, we want him or her to find his or her voice and feel entitled to be heard and taken seriously. Therapeutically, we want him or her to rise out of the gloom and despair of depression and to want something meaningful again. Fighting for something counters the hopelessness and helplessness of depression.

The success of this conversation about the depression depends on the degree to which the adolescent acknowledges his or her pain and suffering and desire for change. Once enough evidence has been gathered, the therapist must punctuate the themes of this discussion. Look and ask for confirmation from the adolescent. Make sure he or she understands and agrees with you before moving to the next step. Empathic summary statements like the following punctuate these themes and serve as building block for subsequent tasks:

> Wow, Cassandra, you have really been unhappy. This depression has been going on for years. It must feel like you are missing out on your adolescence. Instead of doing all things you used to do, you are home, suffering, fighting with mom, and having a hard time at school. Is that how it feels?

Helping adolescents acknowledge their suffering also helps us challenge them to remain engaged in the therapeutic process when they become ambivalent or scared. Howard Liddle used to call this "getting them on record" as being miserable so that the therapist can go back later and use this when it is needed. When adolescents retreat from conflict, we remind them of this conversation.

> Wait a minute, Billy. You told me 3 weeks ago that you were miserable, unhappy, and tired of being depressed, that you wanted your life back . . . remember? This is your chance to start that! You need to turn to your parents and tell them what we have been talking about.

Using Vulnerable Emotions to Motivate Change

Next, we typically ask about previous attempts to improve things. We usually ask adolescents what they have done, if anything, to try and improve the depression. If they have tried, we ask for details and assess how well it worked. If they have not, we ask them why not. We always use empathy and admiration to punctuate these efforts and to deepen their felt need for help.

> Wow, so it sounds like you have made several attempts to feel better. You tried to talk to your mom, tried to get some help in school, tried to get back with your boyfriend. . . . That is impressive that you have made such efforts. But it must be [painful, sad, frustrating, etc.] that none of these things helped [or that you still feel this way even though some of it helped].

Softening their mood, focusing on sadness, even pulling for tears at this juncture can help break through indifference or dismissiveness. This moment in the conversation may be the deepest, most painful, or most hopeless spot to which you take them. We do not want to worsen their depression, but we do want to talk about the depression in the most candid, real manner possible, getting past the denial or avoidance. We want them to feel their pain so they will be more motivated to accept our (and in turn, their parents') help.

Once the adolescent acknowledges the depression and his or her need for help, the therapist can begin to talk about motivation for change. We begin by asking if he or she would like things to be different or to improve. We could assume it, but again we want him or her on the record saying it. Thus, we might ask, "You know, Cassandra, this depression really seems to be ruining your life. Would you like to feel better, to feel less depressed?" We usually get an affirmative response, to which we respond with optimism, hope and commitment:

> OK, good. I can help you with this. We can do some good work here to help you feel better. Would that be good? [Adolescent responds with "Yes."] OK. You will have to do a lot of the work, but I can guide you.

This moment is a new starting point. It is not the sulky, withdrawn, angry, passive, resentful adolescent that often comes in the first session. This is an adolescent who recognizes that she or he has problems and welcomes help to overcome them.

Establishing motivation for change before asking for change behavior is critical to our success and is the underlying methodology of this entire task. If the adolescent does not want to change and we ignore that, moving forward with skills and strategies will inevitably be met with resistance. Some adolescents want to change (goal) but do not know what to do (task). That is easier for us because we have a lot of ideas on how to help. Most of the time, they want to get over the depression (goal), but we have to win them over on the strategies (resolving attachment ruptures) to accomplish it. Here is how we might focus on motivation for change.

Therapist: If things could change, would you like that?

Adolescent: What do you mean?

Therapist: I mean that if I could help you clear up some of these problems with your school and your parents and your boyfriend, and you started to feel better. . . . Would you like that?

Adolescent: Sure . . . but how?

Therapist: I have some ideas. I have worked with a lot of adolescents like you, young people depressed, lonely, and I have helped them out.

Adolescent: What do I have to do?

Therapist: Well, we will get to that today. But what I need to know is that you want it—that you want to get through this.

This kind of dialogue is not meant to be tricky or strategic. This is not the old devil's pact "If I give you what you want, will you do what I say (without me saying what I want you to do)?" It is just a short but incredibly important, essential moment in a conversation that tries to anchor the adolescent's commitment and investment in change. We can then go back to this moment (or acknowledgment) in future sessions and use it as leverage when things get difficult and the adolescent withdraws.

> But wait, Cassandra, you told me last week you were unhappy and that you wanted things to change. Remember? I know you want out of this darkness. This is why we are here today. I know how unhappy you are and how much you want to feel better. Right? So you can do better than this, I need you to be direct and tell your mother what you think.

Identifying Relational Ruptures and Their Impact on Depression

Once the depression is better understood and firmly established as a problem, and the adolescent's motivation for change has been amplified (as much as possible), the therapist begins to explore how attachment ruptures contribute to the depression. This is still not asking for change ("Would you be willing to resolve these issues?"). This step focuses on assessing to what extent the adolescent sees family problems as causing the depression or inhibiting the parents from being a resource/support to the adolescent. We have established the adolescent's motivation to change the depression. Now we want to understand his or her theory of depression (e.g., what contributes to the depression). Their theory of cause impacts their strategy for change. We want the adolescent to see family relations as causing or contributing to the depression so that the only logical solution is to improve these relationships.

We begin this phase of the conversation by exploring relational ruptures and highlighting how alone the adolescent is with her or his depression/frustration. We might say,

> So you have told me how unhappy you are when things are so bad. Last week when we were here with your parents, you also made it clear that you didn't go to them for help. I want to better understand why you don't go to them.

Most depressed adolescents have complaints about their parents. They identify past experiences of neglect, abandonment, or abuse or point to past negative events (e.g., divorce, parents' depression) or to frustrating interactions (e.g., parents are overcontrolling, overwhelmed, or intrusive) as the causes of friction or detachment.

In this conversation, we are interested in the content and consequences of these conflicts/processes. At the content level, adolescents bring up very important problems that need to be addressed: "My mother is too critical. . . . My father won't accept that I am gay. . . . I cannot stand my parents fighting all the time." These content areas need to be elaborated upon, fleshed out, and understood, as they may become the focus of future family conversations. We are also looking for the consequences of these problems:

> How have these problems affected your relationship with your parents? Do you still trust them? Do you feel more disconnected? How have these problems affected the way you see yourself and your parents? What does it mean to you that your parents did X?

These kinds of questions will further our case that family problems need to be addressed. But the importance and therapeutic power of these stories grow when we frame these conflicts as attachment ruptures.

Understanding Family Conflict/Processes From an Attachment Perspective

Attachment and Cognitions

Framing problems as attachment ruptures moves conversation beyond the details of day-to-day struggles and misunderstandings and onto more profound interpersonal injuries, such as betrayal, abandonment, mistrust, or lack of protection. Focusing on attachment ruptures shifts the conversation from behavioral details to interpersonal themes that have come to organize family relationships: "I cannot trust you," "You don't love me," "You are never there for me," "You don't listen to me or take me seriously." These overarching themes help the adolescent construct a more complex cognitive and emotional understanding of his or her experiences. Instead of adolescents complaining about curfew, we help them think about autonomy and independence. Instead of them complaining about parents being too busy, we focus on the adolescents' feelings of abandonment. Instead of them complaining about parents fighting, we help adolescents articulate how unsafe and unprotected they feel. Liddle (2000) taught us to look for larger organizing themes that would bring more meaning to conversations about conflict. Luborsky (1984) taught us all to think about the *core conflict:* the primary dilemma that underlies many of the client's problems.

In ABFT, we always seek to organize these themes around the adolescent's attachment injuries and unmet attachment needs. These experiences and interpersonal failures shape people's internal working models of self and other: their narratives about who they are and what they can expect from relationships. To bring these themes into conversation in the therapy creates a profound opportunity for adolescents to better understand themselves and to begin reworking the very foundation of emotional narratives about themselves and their relationships.

The attachment frame also legitimizes the adolescents' often-unacknowledged felt emotional injustice. When parents and adolescents fight about behavioral conflicts (e.g., chores), adolescents cannot articulate why these conflicts hurt so deeply. Parents either belittle these complaints or see them as a power struggle (i.e., who is going to be in charge). This discounts the adolescent's felt reality. This "crazy making" (Laing, 1998) reinforces depressed adolescents' distrust of their own feelings and their ability to express themselves more directly. But when a complaint becomes characterized or understood as an attachment injury (e.g., abandonment, rejection, unprotected, unloved), it takes on new meaning. It helps the adolescent (and eventually the parents) understand why these problems hurt so deeply: "This is not just about mom's hypercontrol; this is about feeling invisible and ignored most of your life." Here are some examples of statements that try to use attachment themes to understand behavioral problems:

- "I understand that you think your mom's rules are unfair. But it sounds to me like bad things have happened to you, and your mother was not there to protect you? And you have not forgiven her for this. Is that right?"
- "So, all these problems—the divorce, the change in school, dad moving to Boston—tell a similar story; a story of a child who feels unloved and lonely. Is that right?"

- "So, it sounds like you have tried to talk to your parents several times. But you feel like they have not listened—not taken you seriously. And so you have given up trying, given up hoping they could be there for you. In fact, you will not even let them try. Is that right?"

Each of the above statements takes bad events or negative family processes and frames them as core relational attachment ruptures, ruptures that organize the adolescent's view of self and other. As indicated by the question at the end of each statement, such interpretations are offered as possibilities. The therapist checks in to confirm whether this thematic summary resonates with the adolescent. Sometimes the adolescent endorses such themes explicitly (e.g., "Yes, exactly . . . I don't really trust her to be there for me"). In other cases, the adolescent may be silent but tears well up in his or her eyes. When the relational reframe does not seem to resonate, the therapist works with the adolescent to find a better attachment framework that fits with his or her experience. Good therapy is thematic therapy, where overarching themes or core conflicts help us understand the motivation that drives conflict and the pathway to better communication (Liddle, 2002; Luborsky, 1984). In ABFT, attachment theory provides this framework.

Attachment and Emotions

In addition to providing better content, focusing on attachment ruptures also helps deepen the adolescent's emotional experience during the conversation. Many depressed adolescents start therapy angry or withdrawn. Adolescents with an ambivalent attachment style will be more angry and preoccupied with their parents. Adolescents with an avoidant attachment style will be more indifferent and dismissive (Mackey, 2003). We view these maladaptive responses as secondary emotions used as a defense against more painful and vulnerable primary emotions (Greenberg, 2002). The attachment framework helps the therapist identify more primary emotions associated with unmet attachment needs that have been unacknowledged but that may drive adolescents' behavior. Angry adolescents usually also feel hurt and disappointed. Their anger, at least in part, defends against their underlying vulnerable feelings of hurt. These adolescents want to be loved but may undermine or block the parents' attempts to offer it, fearing that their parents cannot or will not follow through. This is how the ambivalence plays out.

Avoidant adolescents also want to be loved but may use indifference to protect themselves from being hurt again. They lack the confidence that their parents will provide sustained love and protection. Rather than gamble on being hurt or disappointed, they repress or deny their attachment needs. The therapist, however, wants to increase adolescents' awareness of these primary emotional states. This opportunity for more effective emotional processing creates a therapeutic moment and helps build skills that can be used in future conversations in and out of the therapy room. The therapist also needs access to the adolescents' primary vulnerable emotions during the attachment task to activate the parents' empathy and caregiving instincts.

Therapist: Mary, I am not surprised you have stopped caring about your mother. . . . But it is not that you are too old to care . . . that you are just a teenager now. I think you feel very hurt and rejected by her, like she has abandoned you, given up on you. I think you are afraid to reach out to her again . . . afraid she will not listen.

Adolescent: Oh, I stopped hoping for that a long time ago.

Therapist: Maybe . . . but I can still see the hurt in your eyes. I can still see in your face how much you long for her love but are afraid to feel that longing.

This dialogue aims to move the adolescent away from defensive secondary emotions by helping her acknowledge underlying, avoided primary vulnerable emotions. As Greenberg (2002) articulated so well, emotional processing involves connecting with previously avoided emotions, tolerating intense feelings, exploring and reflecting on these emotions, and creating new meaning to better help manage and understand these feelings. For some adolescents, this means moving them from anger to sadness. For others, the sadness may be a defense against legitimate, unacknowledged anger, or what Greenberg called *assertive anger*. So, at the individual level, we are improving emotion regulation by helping adolescents experience strong emotions; feel more comfortable with previously avoided feelings; making meaning of emotions; helping them move past maladaptive, self-destructive feelings; and allowing more adaptive primary emotions to take the forefront. Some adolescents are overregulated, and we want to increase their arousal and tolerance for emotional expression. Some adolescents are underregulated, and we want to give them an emotional and cognitive framework that will help them better manage their feelings.

On an interpersonal level, acknowledging primary emotions and unmet attachment needs helps motivate adolescents to engage in relationship repairing with their parents. Secondary emotions protect the adolescent from feeling hurt and thus discourage them from expressing their need for love, caring, and protection. But when adolescents begin to identify more vulnerable emotions, they are more likely to acknowledge denied attachment needs. In this way, relabeling negative experiences as attachment injuries helps penetrate the affective armor that many adolescents use as protection from further hurt and increases the motivation to engage in the attachment task. We often say something along the lines of the following:

> I can see you have some very confusing and mixed feelings in you. Part of you is very angry with your father. You feel like he abandoned you, and you do not want to forgive him. But I can also see that part of you still loves him and wishes you could let him back into your life. This is such a painful dilemma for you.

Coherence

The concept of coherence also helps us think about this therapeutic sequence. *Coherence* implies that a person can tell a story about attachment relationships or ruptures that contain appropriately detailed memories, associated primary emotions, the valuing of attachment needs (even if they were not met), and the psychological freedom to be self-reflective and curious about self and others (Hesse, 1999). Not unlike the explorative process outlined by Angus, Levitt, and Hardtke (1999) in their narrative model of emotion-focused therapy, in our process we want adolescents to explore painful memories and experience in enough detail to immerse them into the reflective experience. Then, we excavate the emotions adolescents were feeling during these events, ideally identifying and accessing vulnerable primary emotions. These emotions are not only important to work through but they also provide the appropriate level of emotion arousal needed for a more effective therapeutic process (Foa, Huppert, & Cahill, 2006; Greenberg, 2011). Finally, we ask adolescents to reflect on how these experiences may have affected them as people and in their relationships with their parents. This more cognitive explorative process helps create new meaning about past events and a new understanding about current family relationships.

Take, for example, an upper-middle-class, 15-year-old girl and her mother we treated in one of our studies. The two of them constantly fought about grades, chores, school performance, and the girl's disrespect. These arguments were constant and intense, with no resolution or behavioral change. It was unfortunate that the daughter had lived through the parents' violent marriage, a nasty divorce, financial decline, and the family disorganization. Although both mother and daughter could superficially acknowledge the destructiveness of this family history, they could never discuss these events without it erupting into an argument. The daughter, protecting the absent father, blamed the mother for most of these problems, thus fueling her resentment and disrespect, while overidealizing the violent father.

In the adolescent alliance task, we helped the daughter piece together the details of this family history. The daughter told her version of the family history: the fighting, the divorce, and its aftermath. She talked about watching her father beat her mother and how she used to take the younger children upstairs to shield them from this violence. For the first time, the daughter acknowledged to herself that she has never forgiven her mother for divorcing the father and has continued to punish her for this loss. Initially, the daughter told these stories like she was reading from a teen magazine. With sensitive probing from us, however, she began to allow feelings of sadness and loneliness to come into awareness. As her emotions softened and deepened, she could allow herself to feel some guilt about being so hard on her mother. She also began to acknowledge how angry she was at her father, but afraid to express that for fear that he would further abandon her. We did a lot of listening, asking questions, displaying empathy, and accessing primary emotions of disappointment and abandonment beneath her defensive secondary emotions of anger and indifference. We also began linking these traumatic relational ruptures to her acting-out behavior with her mother. In this way, her attachment rupture narrative became more coherent: clear, complex, and flexible enough to integrate new information.

In a sequence such as this, the therapist essentially could do individual, explorative therapy, focused on attachment ruptures. During the course of the conversation, the therapist might use techniques from psychodynamic, cognitive–behavioral therapy, emotion focused, interpersonal psychotherapy, or other therapies aimed at increasing the adolescent's awareness of her emotions and schemas, thus amplifying her curiosity and willingness to honestly reflect about herself and life's disappointments and joys. We are less concerned about which technique is used but are very concerned that the exploration has the goal of making the attachment rupture more coherent and the adolescent ready for the attachment task.

Sometimes the adolescent does not engage deeply in telling his or her story during Task II. Some adolescents remain guarded or merely rehash old familiar thoughts and feelings. If we cannot help them connect to primary emotions, we may merely look to punctuate themes that will support engagement in the attachment task:

> Look, it seems you do not want to feel that hurt again or you are actually over it like you say. But it certainly is clear that back then you felt like your mother really did not protect you. Can we agree on that?

In this way, the adolescent's resistance does not deter us. We know that adolescents can talk indifferently to a therapist about parents. But when we get them in front of their parents and ask them to discuss attachment ruptures, the emotional intensity emerges. This is a basic premise of exposure therapy: Direct exposure activates emotional arousal (Foa, Hembree, & Rothbaum, 2007). So the guarded adolescent who says, "Yeah, sure I was hurt and disappointed, but not anymore" is less likely to remain composed and indifferent when telling his father about how he felt when his father walked out on the family.

Linking the Attachment Injury to the Depression

Before asking adolescents to actually begin thinking about talking to their parents about these ruptures, a small but helpful next step is to make sure they see these attachment ruptures as linked to their depression or linked to their parents' inability to support them in their management or recovery from depression. To do this, we briefly summarize all that has been explored thus far:

> So, Cooper, you have told me that you are pretty depressed and that makes you very unhappy, right? And you are saying that these conflicts with your parents are really making you mad and that makes it hard to go to them for help, right? So I wonder, then, if you see these ruptures as contributing to, or even to some extent causing, your depression? I am not saying that is the whole story, but maybe a part of it. What do you think?

Obviously, this link may have unfolded as part of the conversation above, or the adolescent may already blame the depression on these negative family processes. But it is essential to clearly and succinctly verbalize or nail down his or her commitment to our change strategies (e.g., attachment task). We aim to reduce the depression by addressing and, to some degree, resolving family problems. Therefore, we have to make sure the adolescent sees how family problems contribute to the depression, exacerbate the depression, or at the least, prevent parents from being a resource. If the adolescent agrees the depression is bad and agrees that family processes contribute to it, then asking him or her to work on improving family relationships is a solution that is hard to ignore.

If adolescents do not see the depression as linked to family problems, we do not argue with them about it. We scale back our goals (as Howard Liddle used to say) and find a different framework that might help achieve the same goal. We are always flexible and light on our feet, ready to try a different pathway to get a theme to stick, for example:

> Well, look, even if you do not agree with me that these problems contribute to the depression, we still agree that these are problems that are frustrating for you and cause you some misery. What is more, these conflicts with your parents get in the way of you turning to them for help when you do feel depressed or suicidal. That is a problem for me. That means we have no safety net for you. I need to know that you are safe and have someone to turn to for help.

Asking for Change Behavior

Now we cross a critical juncture. We have gained an understanding of the depression, its consequences, and the adolescent's desire to overcome it. We have also gained an understanding of how attachment ruptures and negative family processes contribute to the depression or prevent parents from being a source of support. We have helped the adolescent have a more coherent and complex understanding of how these events or processes impact how he or she views himself or herself and his or her parents. The obvious implication of this becomes clear whether it has yet been stated directly or not: "If we could resolve some of the feelings about these ruptures, maybe the depression would decrease or at least you would be able to use your parents for support."

If the progression of this conversation has gone well, the adolescent generally feels understood, respected, and supported by the therapist. Building on this goodwill and new understanding, the therapist can clearly cross over into behavioral change talk: "Are you willing to try talking to your parents about these problems?" Some adolescents readily respond positively to this request, others equivocate, and a few straight out refuse. Most of the teens agree because they feel our sincerity, sense our competence, and see this as an opportunity for their side of the story to be told.

Assessing Past Efforts to Talk to the Parents

Sometimes we enter the domain of change talk by asking if the adolescent has ever attempted to talk to his parents about these struggles. Understanding how these past conversations have gone helps us identify and address potential barriers and negative expectations that may impact future conversations. We generally ask, "Do your parents have any idea that you feel this way . . . not just about the depression but about how these conflicts with your parents make it hard to go to them for help with other problems as well?" If adolescents say no, we ask them why not. What keeps them from telling their parents? What do they expect will happen? We usually hear one or many of the three following responses:

1. *They don't care about me or what I have to say.* Sometimes adolescents fear that the parent does not care and will not listen to them. This worry often derives from past experiences of parents' empathic failures or their lack of attention to their adolescent's needs. Sometimes, however, adolescents' depression makes them hypersensitive to the slightest mistake or miscue from the parents. Therefore, we often counter this set of negative expectations/interpretations by saying something along the lines of the following:

> I am not so sure that they do not care. I know your mother gets impatient sometimes. And I know your father is not a good listener. But I am not at all convinced that they do not care. I see them here struggling to help you, struggling to figure out what they can do to make you feel happier. They love you; that is clear. They just show it in ways that are not working for you.

We might add as needed: "And sometimes you are very sensitive. You expect to get rejected, and so I think it might make it hard for them to support you."

2. *My parents have too much going on; I can't put another thing on them.* Sometimes adolescents worry they will burden their parents. Sometimes this is the depression talking: "Oh, I do not deserve any attention or help." But sometimes this may be accurate. Many parents have multiple stressors, which might include depression, anxiety, marital conflicts, working, and being single parents. Adolescents experience their parents' stress and do not want to hurt their parents' feelings or put more pressure on them. Regardless of whether parents are stressed or not, this perspective of "I do not deserve it" and "my parents can't take it" has to be challenged. Faced with this concern, we say something like the following:

   > So, you think telling them how you feel will burden them? You are very protective of them. Well, I actually think that not telling them what upsets you puts more of a burden on them. They do not know what is going on with you and they constantly worry that you might hurt yourself again: That is a burden. Yes, they might feel hurt by what you have to say, but that is a pain they can live with. Your silence creates a constant dread that they cannot shake off.

   We also discuss the lack of entitlement as a safety issue.

   > Look, these feelings you are having, these problems you are describing, they are eating you up inside. They are causing you to feel depressed, and sometimes you are even thinking about hurting yourself. And this is getting in the way of school, your friends, and even causing problems with your boyfriend. This is a serious problem for you. You deserve to get this off your chest so you can get out of this fog of depression.

3. *I tried before and it did not make a difference.* Sometimes adolescents say they have discussed these problems with their parents in the past and it has not helped. When we hear this, we can be fairly confident that the process of the conversation was not optimal. If these themes were discussed, they were most likely blurted out during an argument or raised years ago before adolescents had the interpersonal skills to effectively talk about these things or the parents lacked the skills. Some adolescents even say, "Oh, we talked about this in the last therapy. It did

not change anything." So, regarding this barrier, we always say something like the following:

> Look, Aisha, maybe you have tried in the past and these conversations have gone bad. But one thing I know, you have never done this with me in the room. You see, I am an expert in getting parents to listen to kids. My entire career has been devoted to this. I am going to meet alone with your mother before we all meet and prepare her. I will help her understand why she has to listen to you and teach her how to listen better. And if I feel she is not ready, we will wait until she is. I have no interest in getting you in that room and things turning bad. And in fact if they did, I would stop the conversation immediately. I will not let you get hurt again. You can trust me on that.

In this sequence, we offer the adolescent the promise of being heard, perhaps for the first time. We acknowledge past failures but promise future success. We present ourselves as experts with the skills needed to help parents be more available. We also offer the adolescent protection. We promise not to initiate the conversation if the parents are not ready. We also promise to stop the conversation if the parents become abusive. We might punctuate the process by asking the adolescent, "Do you feel you can trust me on this?"

Although sometimes a bit ambivalent, by this point the adolescent feels safe, understood, and protected. We confidently challenge these three barriers because we believe the spark of desire for closer connection to their parents lives in these teens, even if buried very deep. We do not make false promises, but we do raise hope—hope that attachment needs can be met. We lend them this hope. We offer to protect them from hurt. This helps carry them forward into Task IV.

But what if we cannot find hope? If we cannot uncover the suppressed attachment needs? What if there has been too much pain, too many failures, too many disappointments? What if the adolescent persists in his or her contention that it is too late and he or she wants distance and separation? (Sometimes adolescents truly feel this way, and sometimes they are just stubborn and will not budge.) Faced with this challenge, we might change our strategy. We might scale back our push for attachment and instead support their goals for separation. We shift focus from a goal about getting closer to their family to a goal of liberating themselves from the ghosts of the past so they can move on with their life:

> So, look, Lidia . . . maybe getting closer to your mother is not your goal, too much hurt has occurred. Maybe your desire to feel loved by her is gone. I am not sure I believe that, but I can see why you are saying that. But you have a dilemma. Even though you do not want to reconnect

> with her, it is clear how painful this continues to be. What I worry is that you will carry this pain, this confusion, with you into your adulthood and future relationships and end up in therapy when you are 35, still struggling with your mother's rejection of you. It is just the way the mind works. We have bad experiences and unless we work through them, we carry them forward. We leave home with one suitcase of clothes and one suitcase of unresolved conflicts and unexpressed pain: the things we never worked out or said to our parents. How many movies have you seen or books have you read where this is the central dilemma? This is an epic challenge, the stuff of great myths and stories. What I want to offer you is freedom now. To enter into that room, sort these things out with your mother, and be free. Even if she does not respond the way you want, even if you do not hear what you want from her, you will know that you did your best to work this out. Then you can leave home knowing that it was not you. It was your parents' limitations.

Sometimes even this fallback strategy does not work. If the adolescent continues to resist the task, we further scale back our expectations and see what we can get. At a minimum, we ask that he or she at least attend the session. We think the parent will have things to say, and we want the adolescent to at least hear them. So, we ask if he or she will at least come to the next family session (the attachment task) and listen. If the adolescent continues to say no, we may slow down the process more and ask to meet with him or her alone again. We may wait to see what unfolds in the parent alliance task. Maybe the parent will get on board enough to invite the adolescent to the family meeting. We just stay open, flexible, creative, and compassionate. We know how hard it is to compromise or cross a line that one has drawn. But if we are clear about our goal and our mission, most of the time we win the adolescent over, at least enough to attend the sessions.

PHASE 3: TASK

Once the adolescent agrees to participate in the attachment task with his or her parents, the therapist begins the task: preparing the adolescent for the conversation. Typically, this is the focus of a second or third session with the adolescent alone. But this new session picks up from where we left off. We bring forward the themes of the last conversation to reset the foundation for the preparation phase. Here we see the full arch of the task. We began with an explorative, open-ended, supportive, and expressive style. We then focused on deepening the adolescent's awareness of, and feelings about, these struggles, specifically with her or his parents. We clearly framed these problems as attachment ruptures. Then we became more directive, aiming to win the adolescent over to a specific goal: participation in the attachment task. Now our stance or strategy changes one more time as we develop a more psychoeducational approach, with the aim of giving the adolescent the skills necessary to make the attachment task go well.

Choosing, Discussing, and Practicing Content for Task IV

We often begin this process by helping the adolescent identify, reconnect with, and elaborate on the specific attachment ruptures. We then help her or him decide which ruptures are most important to talk about or might be the best place to start. Sometimes we encourage the adolescent to initially focus on process rather than content, a sort of metaconversation about the relationship before trying to take on specific issues. So we prepare him or her to talk about trust and respect, support, and communication. Discussion of these topics helps the family renegotiate the very fabric and ground rules of the relationship: Can they listen to each other? Can they trust each other? Will the parent allow the adolescent to express himself or herself without being hurt? Can the parent keep this conversation private from others? Can the parents agree to not get in an argument? Discussing these process issues can be quite intense because these questions often represent the very attachment breaches that have broken the trust. Discussing the process and the adolescent's fears about what might go wrong in the conversation is a necessary precursor to actually beginning the conversation about the content per se (e.g., the divorce, mother's depression, the sexual abuse).

In one case, the daughter began talking to her mother about how she felt the latter was overcontrolling and dismissive of her feelings. Once the parent better understood that, the adolescent began to feel more hopeful that the parent could listen to other, more difficult material. In a later session, the daughter talked about the divorce and how much she misses her father.

Once the topics are identified, we help adolescents think about how they want to present it, what details they want to cover, and what they are hoping to get from the conversation. With that content developed, we ask them to think about how they might feel during the conversation: Will they be angry, sad, shut down, or indifferent? Will they get nervous and lose track of their thoughts? Will they worry about hurting the parent's feelings? We then try to help adolescents gain some perspective on how they overregulate or underregulate their own emotions and how it might affect their parents' capacity to listen and understand. We try to think about how this has gone in the past and what might work better in the future, as in the following examples:

- "I wonder if we could think about you for a minute . . . your feelings and how you talk about them or share them. Your style of self-expression might affect how your parents react to you.

We have seen that when you scream, your parents don't take you seriously. They just see you as a spoiled child having a temper tantrum. You actually undermine your goal. You give them an excuse not to listen to you."

- "I have seen you do this before. When you just blame and criticize them, they become defensive and do not listen to you. Then you feel angry and abandoned. But when you talk about feeling hurt or abandoned or lonely, then they seem to listen more. The more you talk about your sad feelings, rather than your anger, the more they will listen to you. I know that is hard for you, but I think when you are more honest with them, they have to take you more seriously."
- "Sometimes when talking with your parents, you get quiet and withdrawn. They ask you questions and you do not respond. I know you feel uncomfortable at these times. You described it as feeling shut down and stiff. But this is what we have to overcome. You need to find your voice. You need to let them know what you are thinking. When you are silent, they start to ask you more questions. And then you feel like they are interrogating you. I will help them slow down, but you have to give them more information. They will then feel less anxious and seem less controlling."

As these examples show, we want to challenge the adolescent about how his or her indirect and unregulated expression of anger, frustration, and sadness contributes to the negative interactions. Now that we have honored the adolescent's felt injustice, we can challenge him or her to accept some responsibility for his or her contribution to the negative interactions. We do not blame him or her, but in fact argue that his or her expression of rage or indifference lets the parents off the hook: "If you really want to be heard, to be taken seriously, they you have to express yourself in a way that people will listen."

In this regard, we promote adolescents' entitlement to fairness but also challenge them to find more regulated ways to communicate their feelings and needs. We are not, however, at this juncture fostering perspective taking about the parent (e.g., helping adolescents see their parents' point of view or underlying vulnerabilities, or how the parents' past contributes to their current functioning). Instead, we are focused on channeling their vulnerable or rage filled feelings into a more assertive anger.

Preparing for Negative Reactions

Once the adolescent has reflected on his or her own communication style and its impact on their parents, we discuss how we can help him or her regulate their emotions. We might help the adolescent rely on internal resources or techniques. For example, we teach diaphragmatic breathing, progressive muscle relaxation, or positive imagery or mindfulness exercises. These techniques are compatible with ABFT when used in the service of promoting more effective conversation.

In addition to internal resources, the therapist can offer to assist the adolescent during the attachment task. The therapist will monitor the adolescent's thoughts and mood, and offer gentle guidance and support when the adolescent gets off track or emotionally distracted (e.g., too angry, too withdrawn). Obviously, the adolescent needs to agree to such a strategy and give the therapist permission to shape and guide his or her responses during the attachment task. Sorting out together how the therapist will support the adolescent prepares the teen to enter the attachment task knowing what to expect from the therapist.

Therapist: Look, I am glad we are working on these relaxation skills. They can really help you when you start to get upset. But I know this conversation could get complicated. There will be a lot to talk about and a lot of different emotions you might feel. So I want to know if you will let me help you during this conversation. Let me be your guide. Let me assist you when I think you need help?

Adolescent: What do you mean?

Therapist: Well, most of all, I want to protect you. Keep you from getting hurt again. But I know how easy it is for you to withdraw, and I really think you need to tell them about the things we have been discussing. So I want your permission to jump in and push you a bit, challenge you to be honest and speak up. Also, if you are getting too upset and angry, I want to help you calm down. Will you let me help you with this?

In preparing for the attachment task, we also plan for the adolescent's worst fears about how the parent may react. Adolescents typically worry that their parents will be critical, angry, withdrawn, or retaliate once they get home. We need to understand these fears and take them seriously. However, we counter them as well. We often argue that what they fear might not be much different from the current situation and that this task has the possibility of improving the situation. In that sense, they do not really have much to lose but have a lot to gain. We also say it would be unrealistic to expect parents to respond optimally at first. We explain that this process is often two steps forward, one step backward, and they have to be patient. Even if their parents' hearts are in the right place and they have agreed to try to listen better, this is not always easy for them. They have a lifelong history of being reactive, and it will take time and patience to help them be different.

If parents have their own history of emotional or physical abuse, we obviously think more cautiously about the safety of this overall strategy. We assess and explore this in the sessions alone with the parents and then make a decision on how to proceed. Sometimes we bring up both the adolescent's and parent's fears at the beginning of the attachment task. We discuss the family members' fears and have them discuss how they can have more honest conversations without hurting each other or fearing retaliation. The therapist might offer to be available by phone that week in case the conversation brings up difficult feelings. If we cannot negotiate a fair and safe conversation, we think about alternative strategies.

Anticipating the Possibility of Failure

It is unfortunate, but planning, preparation, and hard work do not always guarantee success. There may be times when the adolescent is prepared, ready, and seemingly capable of participating in the attachment task, but in the end, the parent does not respond accordingly. Parents' depression, personality disorders, unresolved trauma, or own attachment histories limit their capacity to provide normative, attachment-promoting caregiving. Sometimes a parent's strong religious beliefs or cultural background make it difficult to adopt a parenting style that allows adolescent psychological autonomy and emotional expression. We do not easily give up on these parents, but we also eventually have to accept their limitations and values. Most often, during Task II with the adolescent, we do not yet fully know the capabilities of the parent. We have not met alone with the parent, nor have we tried to facilitate an attachment conversation. So we remain hopeful and try to keep moving forward, preparing for possible challenges. But the adolescent may express doubts regarding their parents' willingness or ability to do this, and we have to address that concern, as we have described.

Still, we try to convince the adolescent it is worth trying. We make several points in this argument. First, we want the adolescent to find a mature, regulated voice that can clearly express concerns and complaints. So even if the parent cannot respond, this is an opportunity to learn and practice a new set of interpersonal problem-solving skills. Second, if the parent does not respond well, the adolescent can go away feeling that at least he or she did the best he or she could. With our help, the adolescent can begin to see the parents' strengths and weakness with a new perspective. Adolescents can then recalibrate or revise their expectations of their parents. If they can better understand their parents' limitations, they can better protect themselves from disappointment and from self-blame. In this regard, we tell the adolescent that even if the parents do not respond in the way we both hope, he or she can grow from this conversation.

CONCLUSION

The adolescent alliance task can be difficult and frustrating. We find, however, that if we can identify and acknowledge their attachment ruptures, adolescents usually buy into the treatment plan and are willing to prepare for the attachment task. Adolescents are still young enough to want and need attachment security from their parents, thus making it easier to dredge up these issues and use them as motivation for facing other problems. We often find the parent alliance task more complicated and unpredictable. So, let us turn to that now and see how that can unfold.

5

TASK III: PARENT ALLIANCE

It is a well-known fact that alliance is associated with treatment retention and outcome in both individual therapy (Horvath, 2006) and family therapy (Friedlander, Escudero, Heatherington, & Diamond, 2011; Shelef, Diamond, Diamond, & Liddle, 2005). In family therapy, however, establishing and maintaining alliances with multiple family members is inherently more complicated. For this reason, in attachment-based family therapy (ABFT) we devote individual sessions to working alone with each key family member or subsystem (adolescent, mother, father, and others if appropriate) to establish a sufficiently strong alliance. Without a strong alliance with the parents, as well as the adolescent, family members would not trust us enough to venture into the difficult emotional and interpersonal territories that we want them to explore.

As we argued in the adolescent alliance session, in ABFT we do not think about alliance emerging simply from the therapist being nice or providing

http://dx.doi.org/10.1037/14296-006
Attachment-Based Family Therapy for Depressed Adolescents, by G. S. Diamond, G. M. Diamond, and S. A. Levy

unconditional positive regard. In ABFT, alliance also rests on the foundation of an agreement on the therapy goals and on the tasks necessary to achieve them. If the therapist is focused on parent–child relationship building as the primary goal of therapy, but the parents are focused on getting the adolescent to be more obedient, parents will resist the therapist's suggestions and direction. If the therapist wants to prepare for and engineer in-session family conversations (task), but the parents want the therapist to meet alone with the adolescent and "fix" him or her, then the parents are less likely to productively participate in attachment conversation. Therefore, agreement on goals and tasks becomes essential for facilitating the process of therapy. In the reframe task, we aimed to establish repairing relational ruptures as the goal of therapy. In the parent alliance task, we set up the conditions so that parents will agree on the method to achieve it (i.e., attachment sessions).

The success of Task III rests on our ability to access and amplify parents' caregiving instincts. We leverage this instinct to increase parents' appreciation of, and empathy for, their adolescent's attachment needs. Accessing these instincts, however, can be complicated. Although many parents come to treatment interested in and willing to work on rebuilding a connection with their adolescent, others are not. Parents often feel frustrated, angry, rejected, hopeless or helpless about their relationship with their adolescent. These parents may feel demoralized, fragile, and cautious, making them hesitant to move into the territory of relationship building. Helping them revive hope and commitment becomes a critical goal.

In addition to parent–adolescent conflict, we think about three other domains that can undermine parents' motivation and capacity to engage in relationship repair work: life stressors, psychopathology, and insecure attachment. Rather than ignore these issues/obstacles, we view the parents as our clients. Sometimes we work to help parents reduce stress in their own life, offering case management services to help build more resources. Sometimes we assess and empathize with their psychiatric distress and, when appropriate, refer them to services. In all cases, we explore parents' own attachment wounds and how they impact their relational and parenting style. Parents with an insecure attachment style have difficultly sustaining emotional attention on their children's need. Work in this domain is an essential aspect of reawakening parents' instinctual capacity for parental caregiving and emotional attunement. We do not launch into a year of individual or marital therapy, but we do reach deep enough into these problem areas to partially process them and leverage them to help parents better understand and help their adolescent.

With two-parent families, this task can be structured in several ways. It can be a joint conversation that includes both parents, with a mutual sharing of ideas, commiseration, and support. In other cases, for either clinical reasons (e.g., a nonsupportive relationship between parents) or logistical reasons (e.g., one spouse cannot attend), we meet alone with each parent to have this conversation. Family therapists make these clinical judgments every day. The therapist can consider several questions before deciding who to meet with first. How well do the parents get along? Can they support each other in this kind of conversation or will conflict erupt? Is one parent more distressed or defensive? Would an individual meeting with that parent facilitate the treatment agenda? Answers to these questions are partially driven by individual and marital functioning and by the degree to which parents accept the relational reframe. This is a basic strategy in ABFT. We take the individual, try to join with him or her, understand him or her better, explore his or her schemas or working models of relationships or behaviors, guide him or her to accept our treatment goal, and prepare for behavioral change with others. We then bring the family members back together to create new, positive interactional experiences. With this as our pathway to change, each parent is usually seen alone at some time during the course of treatment.

Throughout this chapter, we address some of the variations involved in working with single-parent and two-parent families. Regardless of the family structure, the general goals of the task remain the same: resuscitate parental empathy for the adolescent and get parents committed to and prepared for the attachment task. In single-parent families, we think together with the parent about who else should be part of the therapy (e.g., father, grandmother, siblings). If we bring in a second important adult, we may meet alone with him or her (or with the primary caregiver) first and replicate elements of Tasks I and II procedures to ensure he or she will support the treatment goals and strategies.

As with the adolescent alliance task, the parent alliance task consists of three phases: bond, goal, and task. Figure 5.1 summarizes these phases. With parents, the *bond* phase focuses on understanding parents' strengths, their current stressors, and their own history of attachment and relational ruptures. Exploring these domains allows for a deeper understanding of the parent, conveys empathy and concern, and identifies challenges that might complicate or impact parenting. This work also softens the parents by helping them grieve their own attachment losses, thus helping them become more sensitive to their child's attachment needs. The *goal* phase focuses on getting clear agreement and commitment to work on building a closer relationship with the adolescent. Finally, the *task* phase focuses on preparing the parents for the upcoming attachment task—conjoint conversations designed to work through the hurt and anger causing distress and alienation in the relationship. This preparation helps parents understand the purpose of the attachment task and learn some simple emotion-focused parenting skills that will increase the likelihood of its success. Generally, the bond and goal phases can together be accomplished in one or two sessions and the task phase can be accomplished in a third session.

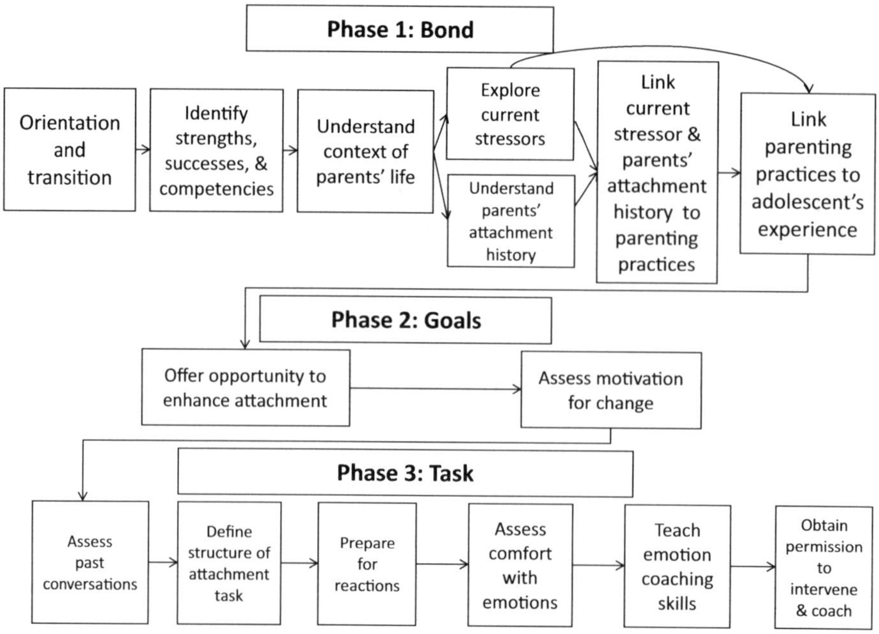

Figure 5.1. Task III: Parent alliance. This figure depicts the therapist performance map for facilitating the parent alliance task.

PHASE 1: BOND

After an initial orientation and transition, the bond phase has three primary subtasks: (a) identify strengths, successes, and competencies; (b) understand current stressors and context of parents' lives (which might include marital distress); and (c) understand the parents' own attachment history. The first two subtasks help us understand the parents' life as an adult, distinct from being a parent. The third subtask, understanding the parent's own attachment history, is meant to enhance parents' capacity to understand and acknowledge the thoughts and feelings of their child, what Fonagy, Gyorgy, Jurist, and Target (2005) might call *reflective functioning*.

Orientation and Transition

Asking parents to come to a session without their child can raise suspicion or concerns. Some parents enter this session (if not the therapy) believing they will be blamed for their children's problems. This fear may emerge from parents' own guilt; accusation from a spouse; or comments from the school, prior therapists, or other social service providers. This fear should be addressed sensitively but directly. We want to empower parents, not humiliate them. Supporting parents, however, can be complicated. Some parents clearly contribute to the adolescent's depression. Parents can be critical, controlling, unavailable, and rejecting. They can be embroiled in marital conflict or disabled by depression or distracted by drugs or alcohol. We are not here to pass judgment. Our goal is to find and amplify that part of them that still wants to be a good parent, that part that still feels deep pangs of love, guilt, or the urge to protect their child when he or she is in distress. We have to believe in the parents we work with and help them resuscitate their desire and ability to be a good parent. Therefore, we do not blame them or ignore their problems but rather empathically and compassionately help them better understand how these problems are getting in their way of being the kind of parent they want to be.

Whether parents worry about being blamed or not, we need to provide a rationale for meeting alone with them. Our approach is simple and straightforward. We explain that we want to get to know them better, including their strengths and vulnerabilities, their challenges and resources, so we can more effectively help them with their adolescent:

> You know, Mr. and Ms. Gibson, I am really glad we are meeting today. I find it very helpful to meet alone with the parents so I can better understand the context of your life: what your resources are, what your stressors are, and what it has been like trying to raise a depressed daughter. I find the more I know you two, the better I am able to help you achieve your goals here. OK? I should add that I am not here to do individual or marital therapy, though I will say, sometimes I may need to understand your marriage a bit so I can know best how to help you. Does that sound OK with you? [Discusses] OK. So before we get started, I'd like to find out how you felt about our first session last week.

Similar to the adolescent alliance task, we often begin this session with checking in on how the parents felt about the first session. The relational reframe task can be upsetting or confusing for some parents. Therefore, we need to acknowledge, if not address, any possible concerns. We do not want to be interrupted in the middle of this task with unacknowledged concerns about the last session. Therefore, we briefly check in regarding their feelings/experience of the first session and get approval to move forward. In some cases, however, parents remain hesitant, ambivalent, or resistant. This excerpt exemplifies how this might go:

Therapist: So, did you have any thoughts about our conversation in our first session?

Mother: Well, I am not quite sure you fully understand the kinds of problems I am dealing with at the school.

Therapist: [Lets this go on for half a minute, then politely interrupts] Yes, I see. We certainly need to spend more time on that. . . . And we will soon, if not today. But what I really meant was, What do you think about my proposal about the goals of the therapy: that we initially focus on strengthening your relationship with your daughter as a means to help her with her depression?

Mother: Well . . . ah . . . I appreciate that you wanted to take her side a bit to help her get more comfortable with you. God knows, she has had a hard time liking any other therapist. She did seem to like you . . . But I am still a little unsure how this will help. My relationships with her, I mean . . . she has been depressed a long time . . . and it is not because of me.

Therapist: I am glad you brought all this up. You are very insightful [compliments mother]. I am trying to make sure she feels a part of this therapy. I find when adolescents feel their needs are being taken seriously, they are more responsive to some of their parents' concerns.

Mother: Well, ah . . . what are you saying . . . that I do not take her concerns seriously?

Therapist: No, not at all, in fact the opposite. I see you as a mother who is very concerned and wants to be helpful. But for some reason she is not turning to you for help, not letting you in. We want to figure out why. She needs you, needs your help . . . so you can help protect her! I do not see you as the problem—I see you as the solution! She needs someone to turn to and it should be you. Does that make sense?

Mother: Yes.

Therapist: OK. Well that is my goal. To help figure out how you two can be closer. OK?

Mother: Sure.

Therapist: And getting to know you a bit better usually helps me think about how to accomplish this. OK?

Mother: Yes. I guess I see your point.

Therapist: Good. Let's get started. We can discuss this more as we talk today.

In the excerpt above, the therapist has walked into a minefield of resistance, suspicion, and defensiveness. Had the therapist not explored the parent's reactions from the first session, the mother's reservations and ambivalence might have lingered in the background and undermined work on Task III. The therapist must address these concerns but not let them derail the session. Therefore, the therapist restates the relational reframe and its goal and plays to the mother's strengths and attachment desires. The therapist speaks to basic caregiving instincts (e.g., "You love her," "You are worried about her," "You want to be closer to her") to engage this mother in the treatment contract. These comments honor the best in the parent and help to assuage her suspicions. Couched in empathy and admiration, this message can soften even the most defensive parent. The therapist does, however, keep this conversation short, knowing that this entire task aims to deepen the parent's commitment to the reframe goal and prepare them for the attachment task.

Identifying Strengths, Successes, and Competencies

As a general rule, we always lead with competency before delving into difficult or demanding work. This support and admiration establishes a baseline of goodwill, conveys respect, and reconfirms our interests in their strengths. It also provides the parents a subtle injection of pride and self-esteem, thus shoring up their confidence to more freely examine difficult and complicated aspects of their psychological and relational life. We also find that when conversations get difficult, returning to these strengths helps firm up the alliance, which provides a foundation with which to more effectively challenge parents.

We often begin this conversation with an exploration of successes. We might ask parents about successes at work, talents, activities, and positive social supports. The conversation can be short or extended. Our goal is to inject positive energy into the conversation and the relationship and demonstrate our interest in them as individuals, above and beyond their roles as parents.

Understanding the Context of Parents' Life and Current Stressors

Once a positive relationship has begun to form, the therapist begins exploring current stressors in the parent's life and how such stressors affect their parenting and the adolescent. This conversation focuses on the parents as adults, not as parents. We want to recognize the broader challenges, demands, hopes, and dreams that make up the context of the parents' life. This focus increases the therapist's sensitivity to the pressures, constraints, and distractions that impact parenting. A parent with depression, multiple children, an ailing grandmother, marital conflict, or no job may have less time, patience, and attention for a depressed adolescent.

At the content level, we might ask about work, finances, marriage, elderly parents, neighborhood, health, or other children. We also ask about things such as mental health, drug use, domestic violence, and marital conflict. The therapist must assess these domains, given the impact they can have on parenting. Sometimes parents welcome this personal attention because they often have no one to talk with about these challenges. Other times parents may feel guarded or embarrassed. More defensive parents will either block the conversation or revert back to talking about their adolescent and his or her problems. During this subtask, we politely redirect the conversation about parenting or the kids, to remain focused on the parent as an adult.

As an example, let us think about parental depression. It is unfortunate, but there is a high concordance between adolescent depression and parental depression (Goodman & Gotlib, 1999). Therefore, many of the parents we see have or have had depression. Faced with this, we may do a brief clinical screening: "Have you ever struggled with depression? Are you currently? How bad has it been? How has it impacted your life? Have you received treatment? Did it help?" If parents are currently in treatment, we typically ask for a release of information and permission to talk with the treating therapist.

During this conversation, the therapist primarily provides a supportive psychotherapy approach: being curious, asking questions, and seeking to understand. Most important, the therapist offers empathy and admiration. Whether parents have high or low income, good or bad marriages, they often come to us praise-deprived and have little support and comfort in their lives. We momentarily serve as the good, nurturing, protective parent. In each story the parent tells, we acknowledge the pain and injustice but also recognize the parent's courage and try to find the strengths that motivated their actions (e.g., "You were doing the best you could at the time"). Many parents cry during these conversations. They have usually felt blamed for being a "bad parent," and few providers have understood their actions in the larger context of their lives. Parents feel they have tried so hard to be a good parent, but no one understands the pressure they are under or the disappointments they have felt. So, we see in them their good intentions and empathize with their frustration or disappointment. Usually, parents are not in their own therapy but could benefit from it. So this little moment of personal attention gives them the comfort and support they rarely experience. It may also plant a seed of motivation to seek therapy for themselves (discussed later).

Mother: I am now a single divorced parent, working two jobs, trying to hang on to the house, while my ex-husband goes to Europe with his new 24-year-old girlfriend. And then my daughter gets mad because I did not come to all her soccer games. [Starts to cry] I just cannot do this anymore. Everyone expects me to hold it all together. . . . Well, I can't!

Therapist: My god, I can see how hard you are trying, but also how much pressure you are under. And no one seems to understand what it is like for you or offers to help.

At this point, we typically explore the parent's support system: "To whom do you turn for help and support when facing these challenges?" If the parent has someone, we explore that relationship and think together about how it could be strengthened and better used. If the parent has no one, we empathize with their loneliness and/or isolation. We explore whether he or she has a desire to reach out, to rely on someone, and how helpful that might be. In this phase of the conversation, we do not focus on the adolescent. We want to understand the parent's life. Bringing in discussion of the teen too soon can complicate this topic.

Linking Current Stressors and Parenting Practices

Once we have gained enough understanding of the stressors faced by the parent, the therapist may shift the focus to parenting: "So tell me, these challenges have been so big, how do you think they have affected your parenting?" Notice here that we do not yet ask how these problems have affected the adolescent themselves; that could pull for guilt and the parent feeling blamed. We just take a small step. If the parents feel supported and acknowledged, they are more likely to talk nondefensively about their struggles, if not failings, as parents. The main themes of this transitional moment are captured in the following statement:

> Ms. Stewart, there is so much going on for you; so many stressors in your life. I am amazed you do as well as you do. But raising teenagers is hard enough, let alone a depressed one. Add to that all that you are doing, and it is clear why you may not be as available or patient with your son as you would like.

This message shifts the narrative from "I am a bad parent" to "I am an overwhelmed parent." With this kind of support and empathy, parents become more willing to honestly appraise their own parenting failures. The parents might say, for example, "I am sometimes impatient with him when I should be more helpful"; "When my husband and I fight, I have no energy for my daughter"; "I am just not around enough. When my daughter gets home from school, I have just left for work." These statements demonstrate the parents' small steps toward openly evaluating their parenting. The power of this moment increases to the extent that the parents are able and willing to identify their own shortcomings rather than the therapist having to point them out. It is important to note that the aim here is not to start problem solving. Instead, the therapist looks for moments of honest self-evaluation and a desire to do better. At this point in the task, we are looking for motivation to change, not change behavior.

Linking Parenting Practices to the Adolescent's Experience

Once parents can reflect on how their stress affects their parenting, we then focus on how their compromised parenting or the stressors themselves affect the adolescent. For example, divorce creates stressors for parents (e.g., a parent has to go back to work or work longer hours), which can affect parenting (e.g., a parent is unavailable, is exhausted when she comes home) which in turn affects the adolescent (e.g., the adolescent feels like the parent does not have time or does not want to burden the parent, or the parent does not respond well to the adolescent's needs because of exhaustion and stress). Alternatively, parental divorce directly affects adolescents, who may have to move, switch schools, or manage parents who do not get along. To explore these links we ask such things as, "How do you think the fighting between you and your husband affects your daughter?" "You mentioned that you aren't able to be at home as much as you'd like because of your job. How does that impact your son?" We find that when stressors and their impact are explored in this order, rather than feeling blamed or at fault for what has occurred, parents are motivated to make changes. (A little guilt, however, can be a helpful motivator as well.)

Sometimes we go from stressor to the goal phase directly (e.g., "Have these stressors affected your adolescent and would you like to change that?") Sometimes, however, we know we are going to explore intergenerational themes as well and do not want to start discussing how parents might want to change. Therefore, we can finish the conversation about stressors in many different ways. One option is merely to summarize and punctuate what has been said. With this goal in mind, the therapist might say something along the lines of the following:

> Ms. Patel, I am really impressed with you. You have a lot on your plate, more than most, yet still you have vision for yourself and your family. That is admirable. And I agree, these kinds of burdens make it hard to be the kind of parent you want to be and that has impacted your son. Still, your son is quite respectful, thoughtful, and well mannered. This is a testament to what you are doing right.

Another common option at this juncture is to discuss with the parent the option of him or her seeking therapy for himself or herself (if warranted). Many parents reject this idea or feel they do not have the time or resources. Still, we make a pitch, knowing that if they did, it would help the adolescent immensely. The conversation might unfold like the following.

> Ms. Park, I know you said that you had been in therapy with your child a lot over these years. But I wonder if you have ever had your own therapy? You know, someone to talk with about the kinds of things we

have explored here today. [The answer is usually "no."] Well, obviously I am a strong believer in therapy and feel confident that you could get some help with these problems, especially your depression. You do not have to suffer like this. There are some very good treatments for adults who are depressed. Also, when you feel better, it will be easier for you to be there for your daughter when she is feeling down. As you said earlier, when you are depressed, it is hard to help her and that is upsetting to your daughter. When you are strong, you have more patience. . . . What do you think of this? [Engages in conversation] Do you think you would be interested in even exploring this idea? Maybe meeting a therapist just to check her out and see what she has to offer? I know a few good ones!

Another possible ending to this sequence is to plant a seed for a future conversation about some of these issues with the adolescent. Again, using the example of the depressed parent, we might tell parents about the extensive research suggesting that children of depressed parents often feel confused by their parents' mood changes and unavailability (Beardslee, 2003). Many children might even blame themselves for their parents' anger or withdrawal. Even adolescents who know of a parent's struggles with depression have often never spoken about their anger, frustration, and confusion regarding that parent's disorder. We explain to parents that helping their adolescent better understand how depression (or other major stressors) has affected their parent's life, parenting practices, and availability, and helping the adolescent to talk about their experience of this with their parent, often brings relief and opportunities for closeness. Although we discourage a premature or full disclosure of all of the parent's struggles or experience, offering the adolescent the opportunity to talk with their parent about the parent's depression or other specific stressors can be a potent and fruitful discussion. Below is an example of how we might suggest this:

I wonder if your daughter knows that you have been depressed for so long? Does she understand it and how it might affect you and her? Have you ever asked her about it? You know, sometimes kids develop a lot of ideas about why a parent is struggling? I bet at times she is scared and confused. Do you think this is something that might be worth a conversation with her, just you and her, here, with me? Maybe she might have a better understanding of you.

Working through this content might be important. But as important as this is, the process of engaging the adolescent in an authentic, nondefensive, heart-to-heart talk about these family challenges creates a context for the adolescent to self-reflect, better understand his or her parents, expand his or her perspective taking, and practice affect regulation. Conversations about a parent's struggles (e.g., psychopathology, why she divorced dad, her relationship with her own parents) can help transform the relationship into one that is more authentic and respectful. Furthermore, when the time is right (see the latter part of the attachment task), helping adolescents de-idealize their parents and see them more accurately can help increase adolescents' understanding of, and empathy for, their parents. The therapist just has to think strategically about when this conversation should occur and how much should be said.

Assessing Parental Teamwork and Marital Conflict

When working with two-parent families, the bond phase needs to include an assessment of parental teamwork and marital conflict. Fifty percent of family therapy work focuses on parenting skills. Improving parenting skills will often make the single largest contribution to helping manage an adolescent's depression. If parents cannot agree on how to support, guide, encourage, and nurture their children, then children get inconsistent messages, which can undermine the stability of the secure base of family life. Even if parents do agree on parenting skills but use a more authoritarian or laissez-faire approach, their parenting will be less than optimal for the adolescent (Baumrind, 1989). This premise drives Task III and much of the work with parents in general.

When the timing is right, we always ask the question in a very direct manner: "So, Mr. and Ms. Thomas, how is your parental teamwork? Are you both on the same page with things or are there disagreements about how to challenge and support your son?" Inevitably, parents have different styles or practices. Usually, one parent is more lenient and empathic and the other is more strict and harsh. Healthy marriages can tolerate these differences and/or negotiate a common ground. In more conflicted marriages, parenting becomes a domain where resentment and distrust can easily play out. At this stage of the conversation, we do not launch into psychoeducation about parenting. Instead, we want to understand the nature of these conflicts, the motivation behind them, and the consequences they have for the child. We also want to be very clear that this domain needs to be explored:

> You know, I can see you are both parents that love your daughter and want the best for her. And for the most part, you share a common parenting approach. But raising a depressed adolescent can be difficult. We need to think together about your cooperation and support of each other as parents. Are you up for that?

At times, or with some cases, we even need to be more direct and challenging: "The conflicts you two have about parenting are very destructive for your child. We have to change how you support each other on this or progress will be very slow here." Initially, however, we do not focus on "changing" the parents. Instead, we want to assess their understanding, motivation, willingness, and barriers to accomplishing this goal. Put another way, we want agreement on the goal before we focus on the task. We often say, "I have plenty of good ideas to help the two of you parent better, but until you two agree that you really want to make a change, my ideas are useless."

In two-parent families, we also have the added complicating factor of marital conflict. We know that marital conflict itself is a strong risk factor for child externalizing and internalizing problems (Cummings & Davies, 2010). Children's exposure to emotionally intense, unresolved parental conflict often predicts poor adjustment. We also know that marital conflict can undermine parental teamwork. The question then for the family therapist is how to manage the marital conflict so it neither undermines or sabotages the parenting team nor negatively impacts directly on the adolescent's welfare. Many great writers (e.g., Framo, 1976; Haley, 1997; Nichols & Schwartz, 1984) have explored this challenge in far more depth than we can here. The most classic model (Haley, 1987) is to block marital conflicts until the identified adolescent recovers. Therapists might even ask the parents not to discuss or plan divorce until the child is out of the hospital or stable again.

We have a similar but less rigid division between these domains. We enter into couples' conflicts just enough to see if we can diffuse its negative impact on parenting and the child. If we can, we try to move forward. If not, we decide whether a few couples sessions might accomplish our goal or whether a referral to couples therapy is needed. Although many couples resist this suggestion, they are more receptive when it is framed as helpful to the child. Regardless of the path we take, our focus on marital issues is always in the service of improving parents' ability to effectively parent.

We often find ourselves helping the parents talk openly, not about the content of marital conflicts but about the impact of the conflicts. Adolescents are frequently preoccupied with worries, disappointments, and fears when parents fight. This fuels depression and anger. In fact, marital conflict often lies at the heart of the adolescent's perceived attachment ruptures. Therefore, these fears and worries need to be brought out in the open, to make the unspoken spoken. As they do with parental depression, adolescents observe marital conflicts and have ideas, fears, and are confused about them, and often become involved unwillingly in these conflicts. Parents, however, rarely ask children how they feel about this fighting, even though children are often victimized by it daily. Parents think they fight behind closed doors, or that things are not that bad. And yet children vigilantly observe parents, often fearing the worst—particularly when there is violence involved. Some children choose sides; some try to mediate and/or feel they have to protect one of the parents. The permutations are endless and not unfamiliar to any therapist reading this book. Although therapists' behavioral injunctions help parents "hide" these conflicts better, this might provide only temporary relief. Adolescents are still left with turbulent and emotionally ridden fantasies about what is and what will be. Marital conflict directly affects a child's felt security, thus leaving them more vulnerable to depression (Cummings & Davies, 2010). In ABFT, we aim to help the parents invite the adolescent to express these fears in order to improve how the adolescent copes with this stress and hopefully motivate the parents to resolve these marital differences in a new way.

Understanding the Parents' Own Attachment History

The therapist next turns to the parent's own attachment history. This is a critical and powerful part of the alliance building with the parent and is designed to increase parents' sensitivity to their children's attachment needs, activate their caregiving instincts, and promote new emotionally attuned parenting behaviors. This sequence typically begins with the therapist asking the parents about their current relationship with their own parents. During the current stressors phase, we should have explored to what extent their parents are a resource and whether they support or undermine their parenting. If needed, we might revisit this with more pointed questions that go to the heart of the parent's attachment security. Assuming that the parent's parents are alive, we often ask if the parent can turn to them now for emotional support. Does he or she trust his or her parents, and can they rely on them for comfort and understanding? Questions like this focus the conversation on themes of love, safety, support, and admiration. A short conversation about this becomes a stepping stone for asking about parents' relationships with their own parents when they were children. "So were you close to them when you were a child?"

Why do we explore parents' experience of attachment in their own childhood rather than focus on current attachment security? Maybe family relations are the same now; maybe they have gotten better or worse. More important, people experience their relationships with their parents differently as children than as adults. Unlike children, adults are more self-sufficient and able to defend themselves or get their needs met elsewhere. As adults, people can protect themselves against current attachment disappointments by finding alternatives or by distancing ourselves: "Oh, my father is still a jerk, but it does not bother me anymore. I just don't see him much," or "I can tell him to shut up now." As children, however, people are more dependent on their parents, more powerless and vulnerable, and have a stronger need for support and protection. As children, people also have few defenses against bad parenting and cannot easily escape these relationships. Therefore, in childhood, and maybe in people's memories of childhood, the conflict of hoping for love and fearing rejection is more raw and unfiltered, defenses are underdeveloped, and they are less protected from disappointment.

Helping parents reconnect with their memories of attachment needs disarms current defenses, thus giving the parent and therapist access to more primary feelings of disappointment, sadness, anger, and/or longing for love. The therapist's use of empathy and emotion-focused questions helps sustain or deepen this exploration and evocative moment. In this vulnerable state, parents begin to remember their own attachment needs and struggles as a child or adolescent.

In the excerpt below, we see a therapist begin to focus on intergenerational themes. At first, the mother presents a positive view of her current relationships with her parents and siblings. As the therapist asks about relationships during childhood, the story begins to change, but the mother's affect remains indifferent and/or inconsistent with the trauma of the story.

Therapist: So, tell me, how well do you get along with your parents?

Mother: We're very close. My mom and dad are still alive and doing well. I talk to them every day. I have one brother and one sister. As I said, my relationship with my sister right now is not so good, but we used to be very close. But we are all fine now . . . really.

Therapist: Has it always been that way with your parents? What were things like when you were young?

Mother: Oh, terrible when I was a child, there was so much fighting! My father was a very dominant man who drank a lot.

Therapist: Your father?

Mother: Yeah. When you heard a car come into the driveway, everyone got up off the couch and went to find something to do. He's mellowed a lot since then, although I learned how to say, "Look, Dad, knock it off."

Therapist: [Wants to keep the mother focused on the past] So, what about when you were young, a teenager?

Mother: Oh, I was scared to death of him. Scared to death! [Laughs] He used to beat the crap out of us, especially my sister.

Therapist: So what was that like for you?

Mother: It was horrible! I'd be screaming, "Stop hitting her!" My mom would get involved [pauses, begins to feel uncomfortable]. But that was a long time ago. My dad still rages, but nothing like he used to. [Comes back to the present, dismissing the severity of the abuse and her feelings of fear]

In this excerpt, the mother recounts her story but quickly argues that it is something in the past that no longer affects her. In attachment terms, she is dismissive and has a hard time telling a coherent story, one where she allows into her awareness the intense feelings of fear she felt as a child. We want to bring these experiences and feelings into alignment. We help the parent to have a more honest understanding of how horrific these experiences were and how they affected her. We want her storyline to match her affect, not laugh when talking about violence or be indifferent when talking about neglect. The disconnection between thoughts and feelings is indicative of people with insecure attachments and associated with psychological distress (Yap, Allen, & Sheeber, 2007). Therefore, we encourage a more complex narrative about these attachment ruptures—a narrative that incorporates both positive and negative memories and feelings.

Although the goal of this conversation is to ultimately help the parent discover a deeper appreciation of his or her child's longing for protection and comfort, we do not rush to link the parent's experience (the current topic of conversation) to his or her adolescent's attachment needs. Rather, we linger in his or her reminiscence and try to "thicken" the details of the story and excavate and amplify the avoided emotions (White & Epston, 1990). Facilitating and sustaining this conversation can be complicated.

The therapist can get lost in the myriad of stories and details that arise when parents tell their stories. Exhibit 5.1 summarizes a strategy for singling out one story and using it to access the parent's attachment history. Essentially, we focus this conversation tightly on one paradigmatic story of attachment rupture. Telling too many different stories can keep the conversation superficial. In contrast, focusing on one episodic memory, immersing the parent in the details of one significant event, can better evoke strong memories and feelings. The therapist helps develop the memory by asking for specific times, places, sequences, and outcomes. The details help immerse the parent

EXHIBIT 5.1
A Pathway to Attachment Ruptures

Find one good paradigmatic story.
Elaborate and elicit sufficient detail to evoke strong memories.
Identify core, primary emotions experienced at that time.
Frame these experiences as attachment ruptures: Highlight the sense of abandonment, neglect, lack of protection, or betrayal.
Look for an opening when the parent's affect softens, and try to amplify primary adaptive feelings and memories.
Use strong emotional language to punctuate the story (e.g., lonely, sad, scared).
Express empathy for their pain and suffering.
Punctuate the parent's own unmet attachment needs.

into the autobiographical memory. This creates a context for identifying and amplifying primary emotions that the parent felt or guarded against back then: fear, longing, sadness, abandonment, or anger. The therapist wants to remain focused on the thwarted attachment need. This is the potent center of the conversation.

To get at these primary emotions, we use words like *sadness*, *abandonment*, *rejection*, and *loneliness*. The therapist must lead the parent into the emotional landscape of these memories and not let the parent divert his or her attention to distractions.

We use a series of questions to increase the likelihood that the conversation remains focused on desired and unmet attachment needs. We often begin by asking about the quality of the parent–child relationship. We might say something along the lines of, "So, I am sure there are a lot of things you could tell me about your parents, but I am most interested in your relationship with them. How close did you feel to your mom and dad?" This question puts the conversation into the desired domain. Then we pointedly ask, "Could you go to them when you needed support or help? Did you go to them when you needed support or help? Was your parent able to respond to those needs?" These questions target the parent's expectations and experiences of support, protection, and comfort.

We often ask, "What got in the way of trusting them or turning to them?" Some parents will blame their parents, some will protect them, and others will have a more complex perspective, a more coherent narrative on their parents' strengths, weaknesses, and environmental factors. We try to understand their perspective and join with them around their felt experience. But if they still are protective of, or idealize, their parents, denying anger or dismissing hurt, we try to penetrate these defenses. We use empathy to bring out primary affect and acknowledge their protectiveness but also the pain that must underlie these stories. So although we attend to the content, we always ask about the affect: "So how did it make you feel back then? What was that little child feeling?" or "Yes, you were angry, but you must have been so scared as well." These kinds of emotion-focused questions move the conversation from an intellectual recounting of details to a more emotional and experiential encounter with deep, often forgotten or ignored, unmet needs. Besides using emotion-laden language, the therapist looks for nonverbal cues (e.g., a tear, tightly folded arms) that provide access to deeper attachment feelings: "It seems hard to talk about these stories. Even the way you are sitting, with your arms so tightly crossed over your chest, suggests how difficult it is to remember these events." At the bottom of this emotional ocean, the therapist is looking to punctuate the core attachment rupture experienced by parents in their own childhood, "So you really had no one to turn to . . . no one to protect you. . . . You were all alone in this sea of chaos and danger."

Then, the therapist adds the emotional anchor, "This must have been so _____ [scary, lonely, disappointing] for you. No wonder you never trusted your mother." These statements or interpretations move parents out of their comfort zone and help them, if even just momentarily, feel their own pain and disappointment as well as their longing for parental love and protection. Therapist's empathy and acknowledgment provide the holding environment, making it safe for parents to venture into these emotional memories and confront their own history of attachment failures. The more uncomfortable the parent becomes, the more the therapist has to offer himself or herself as support. We have to emotionally hold them long enough to allow them to connect with their own pain and needs and, thus, help them remember their desire for a secure base.

Therapist: What was it like when you heard your father pull up in the driveway?

Mother: I was scared every time, never knowing what his mood would be like. . . . I wanted to be able to do something, but what could I do?

Therapist: You felt helpless, unable to stop him, and unable to protect yourself and your family.

Mother: Yes.

Therapist: That's quite a burden for a young child to bear, feeling like you have to stop your father's rage.

Mother: Well, I felt really angry and could not understand why he was doing this to my mom. But speaking up made it worse. So after a while, I got quiet and tried not to get him mad.

Therapist: So you gave up your voice . . . and went silent hoping it would help. [Mother does not cry but seems lost in thought. Wanting to get closer to the experience, the therapist asks for more vivid detail.] Where were you when these fights were going on?

Mother: I would hide under the stairs and cover my ears. Then when I heard him leave, I would go to see if my mom was alright. I was so worried about her. But even my own room wasn't safe, because he would come find us.

Therapist: You felt scared, all alone, never being sure what would happen next. [Long pause . . . letting the mother be uncomfortable] I can see how terrified you were. I can see it in your face even now.

Mother: I can't even describe it—I was so scared, always watching, and nobody could do anything.

The excerpt above demonstrates a focused, empathic exploration of the mother's early attachment environment. Once this therapeutic moment is created, the therapist lingers in it, holding the parent deep in the ocean of her painful memories. Before coming back up to the surface, the therapist wants to identify the core of the attachment rupture: the lack of protection. So the therapist takes one more breath and dives back into the murky waters of this past.

Therapist: You said that you felt close with your mom. But when you were upset about your father, scared about your father, could you go to your mother for comfort?

Mother: Yes, always.

Therapist: She was able to comfort you?

Mother: Oh, yes. We were very close, even back then.

Therapist: So when the violence occurred in your house and your father was beating your sister or your mother, is that something you could talk with her about afterwards?

Mother: Yeah . . . I could. [Starts to look a bit more uneasy and confused]

Therapist: But did you? Did you go to her to for comfort or help with your father?

Mother: [Stutters, becomes more uncomfortable] Well . . . it was not really talked about.

Therapist: So it just wasn't discussed.

Mother: No. I mean yes . . . I guess not. [Finally, the mother's defenses break down a bit and she is at a loss for a quick answer. This is the first time the mother has accepted how abandoned or alone she felt.]

Therapist: So you were pretty alone . . . with no one to protect or comfort you? So you know what that feels like?

Mother: [Looks down, tries not to cry] I guess so.

At this juncture, some parents may cry or show great discomfort. Some parents have rarely thought about these memories or have worked hard to forget them. Still others continue to be in conflict with their own parents or have chosen partners with which these patterns get replicated. And some have worked through these losses and have developed satisfying adult relationships.

Regardless of how parents have managed these experiences, our goal here is the same. We want parents to connect to and become more reflective about their own attachment history. We want to create a powerful, emotional, reflective moment in which parents confront or examine some of the most profound psychological forces in their lives: childhood attachment ruptures or relational disappointments. As they piece together a more coherent, more complex story of their childhood, they become less avoidant of the painful memories and primary feelings that have often been denied or ignored. You feel this moment in the room. Time stands still. You and the parent or parents are in flow (Csikszentmihalyi, 1997). The authenticity is palpable; the vulnerability and humility is liberating. In this vulnerable state, parents slip beneath their defenses and remember themselves as children, wanting to be loved and comforted. This moment offers a potent change opportunity in which parents see things more clearly, open up to new emotional information, and reexperience their forgotten attachment needs.

Linking the Parent's Own Attachment History to Parenting Practices

We might explore how parents' experiences as children impact their parenting practice. Some parents never wanted to be like their parents and wanted to give their children something better. They often think they are doing the opposite of their parents. They are a bit surprised when they discover they are doing some of the same things their parents did to them. Some parents complain that they had it much worse, so the adolescent should be grateful. Here, the amplifying of empathy and the honoring of each individual person's experience can help parents revaluate some of their parenting strategies. In two-parent families, we often discuss whether the parenting values handed down through the generations are being equally incorporated into the family, or is one family of origin dominating the other? In general, we are exploring whether the ghosts of past parenting are making an important contribution to this family or haunting them.

Whether this brief epiphany has a long-term impact on parents' views of self and other is unknown. We do, however, observe that in this emotional moment, parents have an experience of deepened self-reflection and expanded emotional processing. In this softened, almost sacred space of honest appraisal, parents, at least momentarily, have the opportunity to turn their empathy for themselves toward their own child. Discovering empathy for the child within, parents recover the capacity for viewing their child through this same clear, yet complex interpersonal lens. Therefore, at the bottom of this attachment ocean, we ask them our defining transitional question:

> Ms. Garcia, I can now see how hurt you were, how scared you were. And yet you had no one to talk to, no one to comfort you, no one to protect you. You know, I sometimes wonder if your daughter feels the same way now, that you felt as a child. Alone, isolated, scared, with no one to turn to?

Remembering their own attachment needs and disappointments sensitizes parents to their child's attachment needs. In this enhanced moment of reflective functioning, parents gain a new appreciation of their child's inner strivings, feeling, needs and desires. Some parents resist seeing parallels or protest that their child has it much better than they did. But most parents are stunned, if not pained, by this realization. Some parents cry, saying they never wanted to have happen to their child what happened to them but now realize how history has repeated itself, despite all their efforts.

Regardless of how they respond, as parents' empathy for their child increases, so does their instinctual caregiving urge to protect and comfort their child. Thus, by connecting parents to their own unmet attachment needs, we resuscitate their motivation to provide more secure-based parenting to the adolescent. We build on this epiphany to help parents embrace the treatment plan (the attachment task). In this moment of despair, we offer them hope. We offer them an opportunity to interrupt this cycle of abuse and neglect and spare their daughter or son from living with the unresolved disappointment that has burdened their own life. Rather than have the daughter wait 30 years until she is an adult, in a bad marriage, with a drinking problem, and needing to go to therapy to begin working on childhood attachment injuries, we offer parents an opportunity to help their adolescent work through these relational ruptures now, not only to better understand them but also to repair them so that the safe haven can be resuscitated and sustained.

This moment in the task is really the beginning of the goal phase. If they say, "Yes, I want to work on this," then we have agreement on the goal of therapy. Sometimes this moment becomes a conversation with further explanation or justification of this goal; we return to this later. Just remember, a critical outcome of this session is a *yes* on this treatment goal. If we get a *yes* on goal, we are more like to get a *yes* on task.

To Go Deep or Not to Go Deep, That Is the Question

Before we discuss the goal phase, we need to make one caveat about the bond phase. Trainees frequently express concern that our interventions during the bond phase opens up parents' painful memories, feelings, and struggles, without offering them long-term support. To this concern we have several responses. First, we agree that we cannot offer these parents long-term individual or marital therapy in this process. We have been hired to help parents with their adolescent. However, to pretend that parents' depression, substance use problems, marital conflicts, or negative attachment schemas are not relevant to the therapy underestimates the influence that parents' personal life and history have on their parenting and on the adolescent. Therefore, we have to give some attention to these matters, or they could undermine the therapy. As Johnson (2004) said, "We have to address both their inner world and their outer world if we expect to make profound changes in their life" (p. 27). The question then becomes, How do we find a balance? As we view it, we target their psychological world enough to motivate and free them to try new behaviors in their interpersonal relationships with their adolescent.

Second, depending on the parents' and/or couples' emotional stability, parents react differently to these empathy-building strategies. Many parents are secure and stable and can explore this historical domain without decompensating. Other parents are highly guarded, and we need nothing less than these strategies to break though rigid, defensive structures. With most parents, we do penetrate the defensive armoring and gain access to a softer, more reflective self. But we have to work hard to keep that portal open, as most parents want to return to the surface.

If we are not doing deep and profound life-changing work, then what are we doing? For us, this is the mandate of therapy. Families come to us because they are in pain. If one is not working hard to help them, if one is avoiding the most profound topics because one does not want to disturb or upset them, then one has to think about whether this kind of work is right for oneself. We certainly do not advocate unprofessional and insensitive exploration. But we are psychic surgeons: Our job is to, in an empathic and thoughtful way, get to the core of the emotional cancer that is killing this family and find a way to cut it out. When we do have a more fragile parent, we proceed with more caution.

For instance, with one mother struggling with bipolar disorder, we discussed at the outset of the session our interest in understanding her childhood but respected that she might not want to explore her history of being abused (which we knew about from previous sessions). The mother understood our goal and appreciated our directness. She agreed to have the conversation with us but reserved the right to change the topic or stop the conversation if needed. We then treaded softly as we explored her family history and how it was affecting her parenting. A few times she asked to stop but then wanted to again proceed. She had never thought about how her childhood experiences or years of untreated bipolar disorder had affected her parenting and her son. She found the conversation insightful and tolerable.

Finally, we argue that after the adolescent has stabilized and made necessary progress, family therapy for adolescents often turns into couples therapy or individual therapy for the parents. This happens when the family members feel connected to the therapist and want some continuity to their mental health care. Some more psychodynamic therapists might worry that the adolescent will feel betrayed, abandoned, or replaced by this. But other therapists take a more family practice model of therapy. Just like a family physician might treat the entire family, many family therapists juggle the various alliances and relationships when different subsystems come in and out of therapy at different time points. We find youth and parents are comforted in knowing that the doctor is continuing to help the family.

PHASE 2: GOALS

The bond phase has set the foundation for the goal phase: getting parents to agree to work on the relationship, agree to participate in the attachment task, and agree to learn attachment-promoting parenting skills (e.g., emotional coaching). Sometimes agreement to this goal naturally unfolds from the conversation during the bond phase, just as agreement on the treatment goal (participate in the attachment task) begins to bleed into the task phase. Still, it is worth parsing this apart for pedagogical purposes. So, sometimes the agreement to goal unfolds from the bond phase. Other times, even if we have softened parents and increased their capacity for reflective thinking about themselves and their child, getting agreement to participate in the attachment task can generate resistance. This resistance may occur because in the bond phase, we use empathy and support to focus parents on self-reflection and exploration. In the goal phase, however, therapists begin to ask parents to agree to change their behavior. Still, we rely on the shift in perspective set in motion by the bond phase to help parents embrace these treatment goals.

Offering the Opportunity to Enhance Attachment

There are several ways that the conversation may open a parent to embrace the treatment goals. First, as we said above, in this vulnerable moment of self-reflection, parents gain access to avoided content and emotions. This liberates the psychological energy invested in constraining these memories and feelings, allowing a person to more freely evaluate themselves and others (Main, 1995). J. G. Allen and Fonagy (2006) would consider this an enhancement of *reflective functioning*, that is, the capacity to think about (metacognition) one's own or others thoughts, feelings, and needs. We harness this moment of enhanced reflective capacity to help parents think about their adolescent's thoughts, feelings, and needs. This increases parents' understanding of their adolescent's experience and their sensitivity to the adolescent's primary emotions that hide behind anger or indifference.

Second, at this critical juncture, at the deepest moment of confronting their own attachment ruptures, we offer parents hope and opportunity. This epiphany of perceiving the child's underlying attachment needs activates parents' caregiving instincts. This activation increases desire and optimism about change, thus providing a motivation for trying new behavior (e.g., emotion-focused parenting strategies). Capitalizing on this optimism, we offer them a plan—a pathway to change the future. This is a moment of empowerment, a moment of redemption—the moment when parents know they cannot change the past but, maybe, they can change the future. They can do for their children what they wished someone had done for them. This is a chance to avoid perpetuating the legacy of abuse and neglect and instead offer comfort, support, understanding, and acknowledgement. In doing this, they somehow heal a part of themselves by not falling victim to repeating the past. Perhaps the opportunity to protect and be emotionally present for their child in a manner they did not experience as children also liberates parents from their experience of being passive or defended and affords them a sense of mastery over their past experiences of being victimized.

Therapist: Ms. Garcia, it sounds like you had some difficult experiences as a child and that your parents were not really there for you in the way that you needed. Your father was frightening and your mother was passive. No one was there to comfort or protect you. [Looks for agreement] It is hard to be so alone with that kind of danger.

Mother: [Stares off blankly, not sure whether to cry or scream in rage]

Therapist: I know this is hard to see sometimes, but I wonder if your daughter is feeling some of the same things now, that you felt as a child.

Mother: What do you mean?

Therapist: Well, she has seen some pretty bad things go on between you and your husband: fighting, drinking, police being called. It has not been easy for you, but it has also not been easy for her.

Mother: [Tears up] I promised myself that I would not let my kids go through what I went through. But I guess I have failed. It has all happened to her.

Therapist: I know that is painful and disappointing to think about. [Hands mother a tissue to wipe her tears]

Mother: I guess I have failed her.

Sometimes we allow this sense of despair to linger for a while and explore some of its implications. We help the parents see how these experiences have shaped their child's behavior, influenced the parents' parenting style, and affected the marriage. We are not looking to generate negativity and pessimism but instead self-reflection and understanding.

Assessing Motivation for Change

At a certain point, we want to pull them out of their grieving and begin to offer hope, saying something along the lines of the following:

> I know we cannot change the past. I cannot help you get back the love you needed and deserved as a child. Nor can I take back the years of drinking and violence between you and your husband. But I can help you with your future. I can help you interrupt this legacy of isolation, of abandonment, of children having no one to talk to about frightening experiences. I can help you be there for your daughter in ways your mom wasn't there for you. Would you be interested in that?

Some parents immediately respond positively to this offer. It makes sense to them, and they understand its potential value. With these parents, we acknowledge and admire their courage to try something new. Other parents, however, are more ambivalent, resistant, or even dismissive. For instance, some parents say, "My child's 'suffering' is nothing like mine. She does not know how good she has it!" We respond to this by acknowledging the parent's pain but helping them understand that each person has his or her own experiences in life and feels his or her own pain.

When parents remain resistant, we might try another tactic. Instead of trying to promote emotional comfort, we join with their resistance. We might say,

> You are right. Your adolescent is not as strong as you! You got through your pain and are doing well [even if they are not]. But your child is more immature, more emotionally underdeveloped, and lacks the inner skills to be more resilient. She needs to grow up, to handle conflicts better. Instead of temper tantrums, she needs to express herself directly. We agree with all this. We just have a different strategy to fix it. Where you want to use discipline [and shame], we want to use empathy and understanding. We think she needs to learn to think about and express her feelings more so she can get better at it. Your being more emotionally available to her can really help with this.

Regardless of the strategy or pathway, our goal here is to get to "yes." The outcome marker of this sequence is when the parents say,

> Yes, I see what you are suggesting; yes, I agree that I could be more sensitive to my child's emotional needs; yes, I would be willing to learn some new parenting skills; yes, I will come to the next session [attachment task] and try.

This is our immediate end point. Until we get at least some agreement to this goal, we would be reluctant to schedule a Task IV (attachment task). If the parent cannot understand, agree, and embrace this perspective, then teaching emotional coaching skills will be met with resistance. Without agreement on the goal, parents will be less receptive and motivated for the task.

On the other hand, we always have the "good-enough" principle. Maybe we have moved the parents as far as they can go for now. Maybe we meet with the parents again. Maybe one parent is more on board than the other. Maybe some parents need this to be more concrete and therefore respond better when we start teaching emotion coaching skills. And finally, maybe getting the parents in the room with the adolescent who is prepared to be more direct and honest will help touch the parents' heart, melt their resistance, and bring them willfully into the conversation. All of these pathways are possible and common. Therefore, we do not give up in the face of resistance but remain flexible and creative and look for alternative routes. We do, however, aim to protect all the family members and would not put them in a situation that could be emotionally abusive.

PHASE 3: TASK

Once parents agree to partake in the attachment task with the adolescent, the therapist begins to prepare them, usually in an additional, subsequent session. At this juncture, the therapy moves to a psychoeducational, skill-building format. Four themes typically characterize this phase of the work. First, the therapist assesses how problem- or emotion-focused conversations have gone in the past. Second, we discuss the plan for the attachment task and our expectations of the parents. Third, the therapist teaches specific emotion-coaching skills to use during the conversation. Fourth, the therapist negotiates how he or she can be helpful during the conversation with the adolescent.

Assessing Past Conversations Between the Parents and the Adolescent

We often begin this phase of the conversation by assessing the effectiveness (or lack thereof) of past conversations between the parents and the child. We explore how parents approached discussing sensitive topics with their adolescent, how the adolescent responded, and how the parents reacted. This gives the parents and therapist some insight into the typical negative communication pattern.

Therapist: Randel, you've told me that in the past when you and John try to talk about him failing in school it doesn't go well. Can you tell me more about what happens between the two of you?

Father: Well, first of all, most of the time, when I ask him what is going in school, he lies and says "nothing."

Therapist: What's that like for you when that happens?

Father: It's infuriating! So I push. Eventually he tells me the truth, that he failed a test or, worse, is failing a class.

Therapist: So your pushing gets him to talk and tell the truth. Then what happens?

Father: Then I blow up because I'm so mad and disappointed that he lied at first.

Therapist: When you say you "blow up"—what do you mean?

Father: I yell, I say things I probably shouldn't say.

Therapist: It sounds like John's silence and lying really contributes to these conversations not going well. I can understand why you get angry. I'm wondering how your response, your anger, affects the conversation?

Father: I think I have the right to be mad!

Therapist: I agree. John's lying to you is a huge violation of trust that would make any parent mad. I believe parents should communicate their feelings to their children. How do you see the way you convey your anger to John affect the conversation?

Father: He certainly gets that I'm angry . . . but I guess if I'm really being honest, it doesn't help the situation. John shuts down, so nothing gets talked about. That's pretty much why I let my wife handle these situations now!

Therapist: How do you think John is feeling about failing the class?

Father: He does not seem to care at all.

Therapist: Are you sure? My impression is that he is feeling embarrassed, if not humiliated. And your yelling makes him feel worse. I do not think he trusts that you will be compassionate about this. Remember what you said about never feeling good enough for your father? Is it possible that John feels this way?

Father: I know I certainly did.

Therapist: Yes, exactly. You know how it feels to think you are disappointing your father and wishing for his approval. If you could stop yourself and think about what he might be feeling about this first, it might give you a better starting point in these conversations. I think it is hard for John to know what he is feeling. You could help him with this.

This sequence demonstrates two strategies. First, the therapist helps sensitize the father to his contribution to the negative interactional sequence. Micucci (1998) called this the *symptomatic cycle*, in which negative behaviors elicit negative responses, which in turn perpetuate more negative responses: Father asks about grades, son ignores him, father gets frustrated, son withdraws, father feels disrespected and becomes angry, and son fears talking to his father and avoids him in the future.

Second, the sequence demonstrates how we might offer an emotion-focused strategy to interrupt this cycle. We build on the father's emerging reflective capacity about his own needs as a child and ask him to think first about the child's needs and feelings. We ask him to think about how his son's indifference (secondary emotions) might be masking his hurt and humiliation (primary emotions). This primes the father to become more focused on the adolescent's vulnerable feelings that might drive the adolescent's self-destructive behavior.

Maintaining Adolescent Confidentiality

There is an inherent tension in this conversation between maintaining the adolescent's confidentiality and preparing the parent to address particular topics. We do not tell the parent exactly how the adolescent feels and what the adolescent would like to address during the attachment task. It is not surprising, however, that many parents themselves are aware of the content and affect associated with the attachment ruptures, because there are long-standing issues between them and their adolescent or because some of the content and affect surfaced during Task I. More rarely, parents have no clue about what bothers the adolescent. In those cases, therapists may ask questions about associated topics but do not disclose the specific complaints themselves. For instance, if the adolescent wants to talk about feeling rejected because of his same-sex sexual orientation, the therapist might ask the parents how much they think this is a difficult topic for the son and why. We would never be the person to tell the parent that the adolescent was gay if the parent was unaware of this. In general, we usually find ourselves saying,

> Look, I do not want to speak for your son. He has things he wants to talk to you about. But as you are guessing, his concerns certainly have to do with the kinds of topics you and I have been discussing.

Defining the Structure of the Attachment Task

When the time is right, we explain the structure of the attachment task and our expectations of the parents during the task. The therapist explains that the adolescent will be asked to speak first about what is bothering him or her. The parents' job is to listen, be curious, ask questions, and use the emotion-coaching skills we teach them. We ask parents to restrain themselves from getting defensive or trying to problem solve. We want the adolescent to do the hard work of articulating his or her thoughts, feelings, and grievances. If parents jump in too soon, it will shut the adolescent down. We want the adolescent engaged in a conversation about meaningful and emotionally potent issues.

We also explain that parents will get a chance to speak, but only after the adolescent has expressed himself or herself fully. We explain to parents that, initially, the adolescent needs to be the center of attention and feel fully heard and understood, even if in the parents' opinion it is not the full story or is inaccurate. Only then will the adolescent be more willing to understand and appreciate the parents' point of view. This creates a profound, experiential moment for the adolescent (and the parent).

Preparing for Reactions

The parents may fear feeling blamed and criticized. To help reduce this fear and increase motivation, we sometimes frame this conversation as a skill-building exercise for the adolescent. In addition to solving specific issues, this conversation becomes an opportunity for the adolescent to practice new problem-solving skills. Specifically, we argue that the adolescent needs practice articulating his or her thoughts, regulating his or her feelings, and sustaining engagement in difficult interpersonal relationships. For many parents, this more instrumental strategy helps win them over to the task.

The therapist also explores how parents anticipate feeling and reacting during this conversation. The therapist may ask questions such as, "What do you think will be hard for you during this conversation? What might go wrong? What if you feel criticized, hurt, or angry?" The therapist must anticipate these possible challenges and plan for solutions. For instance, if a parent recognizes that he or she easily becomes offended or angry, the therapist can help the parent plan how to prevent or stop his or her anger once it starts. Parents are encouraged to use internal resources (e.g., deep breathing) or the spouse sitting next to them, or let the therapist coach them into a more listening posture.

In addition to exploring parents' potential emotional reactions, we explore their thoughts and beliefs about what we are asking them to do. Frequently, parents worry that if they acknowledge past errors, their adolescent will lose respect for them. We counter this by talking about the power of honesty, the modeling of more self-reflective thinking, and the emotional liberation that can come from appropriate levels of disclosure and acknowledgment of negative processes and bad events.

More commonly, however, parents worry that validating their adolescent's experience or being compassionate and supportive means losing the authority to discipline their child. We might find this more often in fathers, who stereotypically have a more authoritarian approach to parenting. Some research has also shown that ethnicity and cultural background can influence parenting beliefs. For example, some studies have suggested that African American families tend to use more authoritarian styles of parenting (low warmth, high control; Bhandari & Barnett, 2007; Julian, McHenry, & McKelvey, 1994; Keels, 2009; Kelley, Power, & Wimbush, 1992). However, the data also suggest that this may be more a function of income rather than ethnicity. Low-income families usually live in more chaotic communities with elevated crime rates, poor schooling, and few community resources (e.g., parks, recreation centers). In these communities, authoritarian styles of parenting may also provide a layer of protection from exposure to potentially dangerous situations and interactions with racism (i.e., follow the rules and you won't get hurt; Julian et al., 1994). Additionally, children from these backgrounds may perceive parents with clear rules, tighter restrictions, and higher expectations as more protective and available. Parents who hold strong fundamentalist religious beliefs may also have strong resistance to emotion-focused parenting. Sometimes parents perceive these religious values as conflicting with modern-day developmental theory about child rearing.

Our main strategy for countering this concern is by arguing that setting limits and providing warmth are two different, independent, yet complementary dimensions of parenting. Here we often refer to Baumrind's (1989) parenting model. We say:

> On the one hand [and hold out our left hand], children need structure and expectations. On the other hand [hold out our right hand], children need love and support. Too much of one is not good. Children need a balance of both. And sometimes, certain situations call for more of one than the other. In order to get your adolescent engaged in a more honest, reflective conversation, we mostly need your hand of love and support. Once your adolescent is able to be more reflective and feels heard, they will likely more easily follow your rules. We believe your structure is important, we're just asking you to put it on hold to hear your adolescent's experience first. Ultimately, you are the parent and get to make the rules.

These conversations can be long and challenging, as we are often up against some pretty firm, if not rigid, parenting beliefs. This is why the motivational work in the first part of the task is critical to setting a foundation for this part of the task.

Assessing Comfort With Emotions

When ready, the therapist engages the parents in a conversation about their own comfort with emotions and how to facilitate emotional growth in their adolescent. The length and breadth of this conversation depends on the parents' history and experience of emotions. Some parents might be very familiar with anger but less familiar with vulnerable emotions. For instance, parents may have grown up in a family with a lot of arguing and anger but very little support for expressing more vulnerable emotions (sadness, disappointment, shame). In these families parents may be dismissive of vulnerable emotions or claim they have no parenting model for this. How parents' present will determine where and how we start this conversation. We hope that the discussion of their own attachment relationships as a child will win them over to accept the need for more attention to vulnerable emotions. If we have not won that battle (goal), then trying to teach these skills (task) might be met with strong resistance.

Therefore, we often explore parents' *meta-emotional framework* (Gottman, 2011): their theories, ideas, and feelings about feelings. This conversation begins with exploration and ends with psychoeducation. The therapist typically explores parents' views of emotions by asking questions such as the following:

- Which emotions do you feel most comfortable with and which do you avoid? How comfortable are you with sadness or hurt, with joy and happiness? Are you comfortable sharing strong feelings with others?
- Do you think showing feelings, particularly sad ones, is a sign of weakness?
- How do you respond to others when they show sadness or vulnerable feelings?
- When you are sad, or unhappy, do you want support or do you want to be alone?
- Do you think your beliefs about emotions have served you well?

These kinds of questions begin to reveal parents' implicit beliefs and rules about emotional functioning. In addition to talking about the parents' current comfort with emotions, therapist should explore the place of emotions in their family of origin. Most people learn how to think, feel, and handle emotions from the family they grew up in. Parents may have grown up in families where emotions were not tolerated or not well regulated. For example, in some families it was forbidden or dangerous to be angry. Anger may have meant loss of control or violence. In other families, expressing sadness may be seen as a sign of weakness. Therefore, therapists might ask the following:

- What were emotions like in the family you grew up in?
- Was it OK to express sadness or happiness?
- What emotions were off-limits for girls or women to show in your family?
- What emotions were off-limits for boys or men to show in your family?
- How did you feel about the way your mom or dad showed negative or positive emotion?
- Were they supportive or dismissive when you were sad or upset?

After developing some insight about their emotions and meta-emotion philosophies, the therapist might help parents evaluate the impact of these emotional belief systems on their relationships, marriage, and particularly parenting. Several questions can be asked about the couple:

- Do the two of you have similar views on, rules about, or tolerance for emotions?
- Who is more comfortable with sadness, and who is more comfortable with anger?
- Does one of you get over negative feelings more quickly, and does one of you sustain positive feelings more easily?
- Does one want to express feelings and the other try to avoid them?
- Whose emotional rules have dominated the family?

We are not looking to start a marital therapy moment around these differences. In fact, the psychoeducational tone to the conversation helps to keep these questions from igniting conflict and actually allows parents to reflect about these skills and philosophies in a nondefensive way. No less sensitive is the discussion about how emotional beliefs and practices affect parenting. The therapist's nonjudgmental, almost objective, curiosity helps parents feel less defensive and more willing to be self-appraising. Important questions to ask about parenting might include the following:

- Do you and your spouse have similar or different values about emotions when it comes to parenting?
- Do you think you are teaching your children the same values about emotions that you learned as a child?
- Do you think it worked well then and is working well now?
- Do you think your child is comfortable and competent with his or her emotions?

- Is your child able to talk about sad and difficult feelings or does he or she shut down and avoid them?
- Is his or her approach to emotions serving him or her well?

Teaching Emotion-Coaching Skills

After promoting parents' understanding of their own emotional skills and values, therapists begin to educate parents about the value of emotional coaching as a parenting skill. We highly recommend the resources in the Recommended Additional Readings list to help the therapist deeply understand the value of this parenting style. This will help the therapist convey the importance of emotions when teaching and/or debating about this parenting approach with parents. In a nutshell, we make the following case:

> Depressed adolescents have lost their voice. They have strong feelings but instead of expressing them, they avoid conflict, turn inward, and at worst, hurt themselves. When parents help children accept and express their feelings, it improves children's emotion regulation, which leads to better problem solving and communication. Adolescents who have the ability to express and regulate emotions have better self-esteem, social skills, school performance, and physical health. This also lays the foundation for partner intimacy in adulthood.

Parents can learn communication skills that can promote their children's emotional intelligence. Gottman (2011) referred to this set of skills as *emotional coaching*. He developed this framework while working with young children, but we have adapted his principles for working with adolescents. For some parents, a short review and discussion of these principles and practices is enough. Others may need a longer conversation, role-playing, and/or practice. Overall, emotional coaching is not that complicated, and the skills are straightforward. However, reviewing these skills provides a common language between the therapist and parents that can help during the attachment task. Having a shared set of concepts and vocabulary allows the therapist to more efficiently shape or redirect parents during the attachment task—rather than having to stop the experiential action of the conversation—to teach a concept. Three key areas cover the spirit of emotional coaching: being aware of the adolescent's emotions, listening empathetically and validating the adolescent's feelings, and showing empathy and validation before problem solving.

Being Aware of the Adolescent's Emotions

The first step in emotion coaching is enhancing parents' awareness of their adolescent's feelings. Therapists can ask, "Do you know when your adolescent is sad? Angry? Confused? What are the signs that she [or he] feels this way?" Sometimes adolescents and parents have trouble differentiating between emotions, and often the adolescent feels multiple emotions at once. Parents need to help the adolescents identify, differentiate, accept, and express them all. We also help parents understand the difference between defensive (secondary) emotion and more vulnerable (primary) emotions. Often when an adolescent feels hurt, he or she shows anger. Or when they feel sad, they show indifference. Therefore, we help parents look below the surface of the expressed emotions and think about the sources of the emotion.

Listening Empathetically and Validating the Adolescent's Feelings

A parent's ability to show empathy and validate an adolescent's experience is central to emotional coaching, and it often determines the success of the attachment task. We teach parents active listening skills: to reflect back what they hear. This demonstrates that the parent is listening and makes the adolescent feel understood. Parents should not discount or judge their adolescent's feelings, tell them how they should feel, or try to "fix" their feelings. If they do these things, an adolescent who is depressed will likely become defensive, angry, or withdrawn. When parents had similar childhood experiences as their parents, we tell them to remember how they felt as a child when trying to talk with their parents. This helps parents empathize with their adolescent.

We also encourage parents to ask questions rather than give advice or preach. Again, this challenges adolescents to think for themselves rather than just react to the parent. Parents should, however, not get stuck on "why" questions, which can put an adolescent on the defensive. They should also ask "what" and "how" questions. Thus, in addition to asking, "Why are you so mad?" parents should also ask, "How did that affect you?" "Tell me what that was like for you," or "What about that made you so mad?" We also discourage parents from asking rhetorical questions. Too much of this, and adolescents feel interrogated and manipulated.

Showing Empathy and Validation Before Problem Solving

Often when adolescents share their feelings and problems with their parents, parents are quick to problem solve. Therapists should validate this urge in parents but advise against acting on it. With younger children, helping them with problems is protective. With adolescents, giving them time to express their emotions and think through problems is protective. One way to promote this is by listening, validating, and providing support. This provides emotional scaffolding that helps adolescents build a framework for emotional expression. Many times, listening and validating is all the adolescent wants and needs. Once adolescents understand what is bothering them, they more easily come up with their own solutions. When adolescents are less preoccupied with defending themselves or rejecting parental advice, parents can more easily challenge the adolescent to turn inward and think about what they want and need. As parents give adolescents more responsibility to participate in problem solving, the adolescent will more likely turn to parents for advice and help.

When Not to Use the Skills

Parents often think that emotion-coaching skills means giving up discipline or rules. Nothing could be further from the truth. Emotion coaching does not mean that the parent agrees with the adolescent or approves of what they might be saying. Emotion coaching helps bring the adolescent into the conversation. When faced with serious problems or the need for discipline, other parental skills will be needed. After the conflict, emotion coaching might be used to help sort out what happened, but parents need to know that they will still need to discipline disruptive or disrespectful behavior or set limits around life's day-to-day problems (e.g., curfew, homework, dating). Emotion coaching can bring understanding and compassion to problem solving, which enhances everyone's desire to cooperate and be respectful. In addition, emotion coaching can help sort out the motive behind bad behavior and teach adolescents to be more reflective about their actions. Finally, we encourage parents to practice emotion coaching in the therapy sessions before they start to use it at home. This prevents early failure and discouragement. The upcoming attachment task becomes an opportunity to practice these skills.

Obtaining Permission to Intervene and Coach

One of the most important things we do during preparation for the attachment task is to ask permission to help coach the parents during the task. Even with all this preparation, parents often need help using the emotion-coaching skills to keep them from slipping into defensiveness or problem solving. Therefore, we might say,

> You have done a tremendous amount of work to get ready for this conversation. I want to make sure that it goes well. Would it be OK during the meeting if I jump in from time to time to help you? Just give you a few suggestions or point you in the right direction?

Negotiating this before the family meeting makes parents less defensive when the therapist tries to shape the conversation in real time (e.g., jumping in, making suggestions, blocking anger, encouraging questions). Negotiating this ahead of time also demonstrates the therapist's commitment to supporting the parents.

CONCLUSION

In part, we see alliance building with the adolescent and with the parents as shuttle diplomacy. We work with each side to help them understand their own needs and the needs of others. We teach them some skills that will increase cooperation between them. Important content areas have been identified by the adolescent and parents. Both parents and adolescents have accessed more vulnerable emotional states that will engender a richer, more meaningful, and productive conversation. All parties have agreed to the conversation and have new, more effective communication skills to use during the conversation. All of this sets the foundation for the upcoming attachment task.

6

TASK IV: REPAIRING ATTACHMENT

We have now finished preparing the adolescent and the parents separately. At this point we should be ready to "bring them to the table" for the attachment task. This corrective attachment experience serves as the central change mechanism of the model, where changes in the quality of interaction between adolescent and parents help to revise internal working models of self and other. Ideally, adolescents will feel safe exploring past events, negative processes, and trauma stories in ways that allow new insight, increased coherence, and emotional complexity. No longer psychologically invested in rejecting the parents or preoccupied with engaging them, adolescents have an opportunity to become more reflective thinkers, free to think about and evaluate their own and others' behaviors, thoughts, feelings, and needs. Parents provide the emotional attunement and responsiveness that make adolescents feel safe to explore and share thoughts and feelings. Parents

http://dx.doi.org/10.1037/14296-007
Attachment-Based Family Therapy for Depressed Adolescents, by G. S. Diamond, G. M. Diamond, and S. A. Levy

encourage psychological autonomy, promote reflective thinking, accept difficult emotions, and provide acknowledgment and new information.

During this corrective attachment experience, internal working models of each other are available for revision. Adolescents begin to see their parents as more receptive, supportive, and encouraging. Consequently, adolescents respond with more self-disclosure, honesty, and expression of primary emotions. Likewise, parents begin to see their child as more mature, more vulnerable, and more in need of protection. As a result, they revise their working model (Kobak & Esposito, 2004), a model shaped by the adolescent's depression and negative interactions. Revising their model of the child (e.g., from "he hates me" to "he needs me") activates the caregiving instincts, which generate more willingness and capacity for emotionally sensitive and responsive parenting. Thus, we have engineered a transactional learning experience in which new thoughts and feelings reinforce, and are reinforced by, new interactional processes.

We begin this chapter with some background on enactment, an intervention strategy developed by Minuchin (1976) to create in-session experiential moments of change. Then, we describe the attachment task in depth, including its three phases. We conclude the chapter with a discussion of the process skills that help facilitate this process.

ENACTMENT: A SHIFT IN METHODOLOGY

Facilitating the attachment task requires a different set of therapist skills than the first three tasks. In the reframing and alliance tasks, the therapist adopts a primarily supportive, reflective, and explorative strategy to build a relational frame for the therapy and increase participants' motivation to engage in relationship building. Up until this point, most of the action in the therapy has been between the individual family members and the therapist. During the attachment episode, the therapist's aims shift: We now want to facilitate dialogue and meaningful interactions *between* family members. Minuchin and Fishman's (1981) ideas about enactment form the core intervention strategy. *Enactments* direct people to interact with or talk to each other in the therapy session, thus promoting the new interpersonal skills that create a new interactional experience.

Minuchin first introduced the concept of enactment in 1974. It builds on theories of experiential and behavioral change. Initially, Minuchin used this technique to gain entry into negative interactional patterns. He had parents directly interact with each other in the therapy room so he could observe what they naturally did. In his famous training tape, *Taming Monsters* (Minuchin, 1980), the parents of an 8-year-old boy with attention-deficit/hyperactivity disorder were asked to get the child to sit quietly in his chair. After some embarrassment and resistance, the mother makes ineffective attempts to control the child. The father sits quietly and the boy ignores them both. After a few more of the mother's failed attempts, the father bursts into a rage, screams at the boy, and intimidates the child into submission. The mother feels relief but also humiliation and resentment. Then, a minute later, the child is up again rambling around the room. In this 5-minute sequence, the family acts out, or enacts, their typical dysfunctional interactional style.

The power of enactment goes beyond assessment. Minuchin would then intervene to block some of the negative, unproductive interactions and direct and promote the positive interactions. So, in the training tape just described, Minuchin (1980) later blocks the father's criticism and coaches the mother to be more firm and consistent. Eventually, the boy sits quietly coloring and the mother sits back glowing with surprise and pride. This was one of Minuchin's great gifts to family therapy. Rather than rely only on the development of insight, Minuchin offered an experiential model of change: help people "be" different in the room, and that experience will accelerate the learning and expression of new behavior. Experiential learning is not exclusive to structural family therapy. Cognitive–behavioral therapy and exposure therapy (Foa, Humbree, & Rothbaum, 2007; Kendall, 2011), experiential therapies (Greenberg & Johnson, 1988; Perls, Hefferline, & Goodman, 1951), and behavioral therapies (Wolpe, 1973) all rely on the experience of new behaviors as a central mechanism of change. Also, these models, structural family therapy included, do not ignore the role of insight, cognitive restructuring, and skill building. However, the most potent learning moment occurs in the experiencing of the new behavior.

In attachment-based family therapy (ABFT), we think about enactment slightly differently. First, the old writings about enactment gave very little attention to preparation. Many therapists say, "Turn to your mother and tell her . . . " and the family has no idea of what the therapist wants. Consequently, the interaction often goes badly, and the therapist scrambles to contain the negative escalation to make the interaction more productive. Such a model relies on the charm and charisma of the therapist to help the unprepared family members do something new. It is the vagueness of this strategy that gives enactment a bad reputation (Butler & Gardner, 2003). Even if good things happen, we question the ability to replicate and sustain this experiential change.

Influenced by the thinking of Liddle (2002), ABFT therapists do a lot of preparation. First, although the first three tasks of ABFT represent important therapeutic work in and of themselves, these tasks also prepare the family for the attachment task. In the reframe, we propose a relational focus to the therapy. In the alliance tasks, we generate motivation for participating in attachment sessions, explain to participants the type of behaviors that will be most helpful and explain the rationale, and then identify barriers and facilitators that might make the session go well or fail. By the time we enter the attachment task, family members have agreed on the therapy goals and tasks and feel motivated and safe enough (bond) with the therapist to engage in the process.

Second, unlike Minuchin (e.g., Minuchin & Fishman, 1981), we give much more attention to the content of the conversation. Given the population Minuchin worked with, behaviorally acting out, preadolescent boys, his primary clinical focus was on structure, consistency, and parental teamwork. These goals, however, do not map well onto depressed adolescents, who are withdrawn and isolated. Focusing primarily on parental control will only push them away more. The central aim of ABFT is to promote, at least initially, attachment dialogue, not control and structure. Therefore, to engage depressed adolescents in conversation, the therapy has to focus on salient content, which is personally meaningful to the adolescent (G. M. Diamond, Liddle, Hogue, & Dakof, 1999). Thus, although good process (adolescent remains emotionally regulated, parents remain emotionally attuned) is essential, the content of the conversation is also critical: The content should focus on the negative interpersonal processes or events that have damaged trust.

Finally, discussions of enactment have historically given minimal attention to the important role of emotion in this change process. The family therapy literature has emphasized behavioral change over emotional processing; strategic change over negotiation; and value-free social constructivism over the fundamental, inherent human drive for love and connection. In contrast, our change approach has been greatly influenced by Greenberg and Johnson's (1988) work, and thus we use enactment to invite and guide families into deep and profound emotionally charged conversations about core attachment themes—themes such as betrayal, neglect, abandonment or control. We gain access to these profound content areas by accessing family members' primary adaptive emotions of anger, hurt, love, and longing—emotions that they typically defend against to protect themselves from being hurt. But as we increase safety between family members, more vulnerable emotions begin to surface (Friedlander, Heatherington, Johnson, & Skowron, 1994). As adolescents feel safer to express difficult emotions, parents and adolescents discuss them more freely. In this way, in ABFT we use enactment to facilitate powerful, honest, explorative, safe, and supportive conversations about emotionally charged, extremely important, and often painful attachment ruptures that have damaged trust in the family.

As Figure 6.1 shows, Task IV consists of three phases. In Phase 1, the adolescent discloses his or her thoughts and feelings about the relationship with parents and/or specific traumatic or problematic events that have happened in the family. The parent helps the adolescent explore the memories, feelings, and thoughts about these events. When this phase of conversation

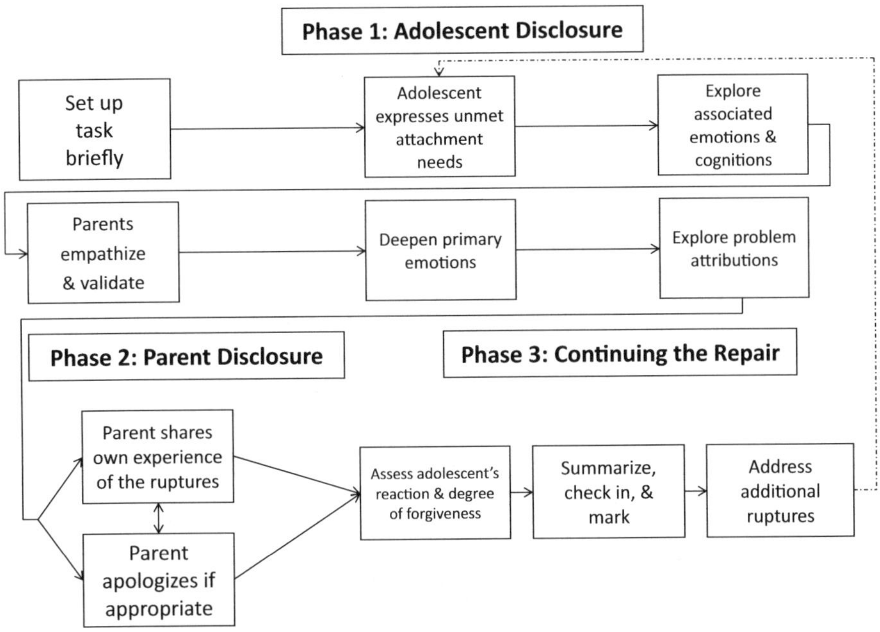

Figure 6.1. Task IV: Repairing attachment. This figure depicts the therapist performance map for facilitating the repairing attachment task.

feels complete, Phase 2 begins. In this phase, the parent may talk briefly about his or her memories, thoughts, and feelings about these events. The therapist encourages the adolescent to ask the parent questions to gather new information about these events or problems. In Phase 3, the therapist sustains this level of honest engagement as the family members continue to discuss the ruptures that have been identified or new areas that need attention. In the end, the therapist tries to consolidate some of the gains of this conversation as they prepare for more attachment-focused conversations or moving to autonomy promoting: Task V. Overall, Task IV focuses as much on process (the quality of the conversation) as it does on content. Generally, this task takes one to three sessions.

PHASE 1: ADOLESCENT DISCLOSURE

Setting Up the Task Briefly

We have laid a strong foundation for this conversation; we do not need further preparation or distractions. Therefore, we quickly check in and then get right to the task. Barring any real crisis (e.g., someone was arrested, someone made a suicide attempt) that may have occurred between sessions, we sidestep any small conflicts or problems of the week and move to the agenda of the day. Here is how the first few minutes might go:

Therapist: So, Mr. and Ms. Smith, I am glad you have made it today. David, welcome back. Look, we have a special conversation planned for today. But, before we start, is there anything critical or urgent I need to know about the week?

Mother: Well, he did get another bad test grade. He might get kicked out of school if this continues . . . and . . .

Therapist: Ms. Smith, let me stop you there. These are serious problems, but no different from what you have struggled with all year. Today I am hoping we can discuss some other issues that might help us find a new direction for this family. OK?

Mother: Sure.

The therapist effectively blocks the parent's pull to focus on the crises of the week. This tendency may be part of the family's general proclivity for negativity, or it may be an attempt to distract the therapist from the planned task. Many parents and/or adolescents come to this session with trepidation and caution. Last week's resolve to engage in this conversation may have dissolved into fears of being hurt, embarrassed, or blamed. In the face of a little nervousness, we usually move forward, lending family members our confidence and courage, trusting that the conversation will take on a life of its own once we get started. If one family member can courageously begin with honesty and vulnerability, the other family members typically feel relief and enter the conversation with the same level of openness and vulnerability. So after the short check-in, the therapist may begin with an opening like the one below.

Therapist: OK, then. So, Mr. and Ms. Smith, you know I have been meeting with your son and have been helping him to identify some things that bother him, that he thinks are pretty important. And David, you know I have been meeting with your parents and helping them learn how to listen to you in new ways. I think they understand what I have been asking of them and have come today to give it a try. [Turns to the father and mother] Right?

Father: Yes, we understand and want this to go well.

Mother: [Nods in agreement]

Therapist: Good. So, David, I'd like you to start. I'd like you to start by telling your parents about some of the things that we have been discussing that get in the way of you going to them.

The above sequence goes well, allowing the therapist to be direct and clear. Sometimes, however, the therapist senses enough nervousness that it should be addressed directly. As Bugental (1992) wrote, "Resistance is not inhibiting the therapy; it is the leading edge of the therapy" (p. 184). So, rather than ignore the tension, the therapist uses the tension as the starting point of the conversation. We might empathically remark, "You seem nervous about today. Can you tell us what you are worried about?" This question directs the family to talk about the nervousness, not the content itself (e.g., the divorce). Often, the process itself (e.g., how something is being discussed rather than what is being discussed) becomes the content (e.g., "Everyone seems nervous. Maybe we should talk about that first"). When the adolescent responds with, "I do not feel comfortable talking with my parents about these events," we empathically ask, "Why?" This directly leads us into a conversation about trust, safety, and honesty—core attachment themes. This is always a decision point. Sometimes the process is inhibiting the conversation (e.g., the parent is being critical). So we either decide to push forward and hope the content moves the process in the right direction (e.g., we get to attachment themes and the mood softens) or we decide to shift and make the process the content (e.g., "David, is your mother being critical of you right now in a way that shuts you down? Can you tell her that?").

Here is a good example of a planned conversation about trust and communication before talking about some specific complaints. The daughter had many topics to discuss with her mother: the parents' divorce, how the mother's anger was keeping the father away, and how the mother did not take her daughter's feelings seriously. In Task II, we planned that the daughter would begin the session by talking about how the mother did not take her daughter's feelings seriously, so she would feel comfortable talking about the other content areas. This discussion filled the hour, became quite emotionally intense, and helped the mother and daughter redefine how they interact with each other. As trust developed, the daughter felt more comfortable discussing her feelings about the parents' divorce and mother's destructive resentment toward her father. This is an example of how attachment task conversations can go back and forth between content (e.g., bad things that have happened) and process (e.g., how we communicate with each other). This has relevance for how the session might start but also for how conversations about process can facilitate an increase in safety and intimacy, allowing for the introduction and working through of difficult content.

The three previous ABFT tasks all had end points: a goal to aim for that denoted successful completion of the task. In contrast, during the attachment task, the process or experience is, in large part, the goal or outcome. We want family members to linger in meaningful dialogue and authentic emotions. From a behavioral perspective, we think about sustained exposure to usually avoided emotional experiences, allowing for new learning and development. From an emotion-focused frame, we think about it as an opportunity to process emotions—where family members access, express, and make meaning of primary emotions, thus improving their ability to use and learn from their emotions. From an attachment perspective, we think about creating a corrective attachment experience during which adolescents seek comfort and parents are responsive and sensitive, thus revising the adolescent expectation of the parents' availability. Regardless of the theoretical perspective, we want to sustain this experience, believing that sustaining engagement in this new learning environment deepens the therapeutic value of the event (Friedlander, Escudero, Heatherington, & Diamond, 2011).

What guides us through this seemingly amorphous process? In one process study, we looked closely at 12 attachment tasks (G. S. Diamond & Stern, 2003). We created an ideal clinical map that captured the complexity and variability of how this conversation might evolve. The clinical map generated provides some understanding of the possible landscape of this pinnacle moment in the treatment process. The map (see Figure 6.1) suggests that the attachment task consists of three phases: adolescent disclosure, parent disclosure, and mutual perspective taking.

Adolescent Expresses Unmet Attachment Needs

After the introductions, the adolescent is invited to share with the parent at least one of the things that has been bothering him or her. In some cases, the adolescent has the courage and self-confidence to take this first risk without any further urging or help. Typically, he or she will look at the parent's face to discern how open and nondefensive the parent seems. In other cases, adolescents have a hard time beginning and we then invite parents to inquire. Either way, for adolescents to share meaningful, vulnerable feelings, they have to feel that the parent is approaching the conversation with empathy, curiosity, acceptance, and a readiness to listen.

Exploration of Associated Emotions and Cognitions

Once the adolescent feels like the parent is ready to hear them, he or she discloses concerns and feelings in a new, more articulate and regulated fashion. Ideally, adolescents disclose stories of pain, disappointment, hurt, or dissatisfaction—typically, themes of feeling unloved, uncared for, or unprotected surface. With the help of the therapist, parents emotionally coach the adolescent to identify and express their primary emotions associated with these experiences in a deeper, fuller manner—feelings such as sadness, hurt, and assertive anger.

Parents Empathize and Validate

The therapist helps the parents restrain their impulse to offer suggestions or solutions, explain things, or otherwise defend themselves. We want the adolescent's experience to be the center of attention. We do not want the adolescent feeling the need to monitor and/or respond to the parent's reaction. Instead, we want the parent to witness and encourage the adolescent's self-exploration. This challenges the adolescent to examine and articulate his or her thoughts, feelings, and wishes, promoting psychological autonomy and self-reflection. When parents are sensitive and responsive, adolescents disclose and explore more thoughts and feelings. In like fashion, as adolescents become more reflective and forthcoming about attachment needs and vulnerable emotions, parental support, empathy, and validation increase. The adolescent's vulnerability pulls for parental caregiving instincts. In this iterative fashion, sustained engagement around themes such as loss, longing, and unmet attachment needs deepens the adolescent–parent bond.

The therapist helps the family sustain this conversation for as long as possible. We want the adolescent to have a prolonged experience of being in contact with his or her attachment needs while feeling supported and understood by his or her parents. We want him or her to openly and freely experience these needs and the frustrations associated with not getting these needs met, while experiencing his or her parents as open, empathic, and loving. Sustaining these efforts allows parents' and adolescents' anxiety to diminish and increases their experience of success. This provides experiential evidence that a more satisfying and rewarding relationship can be possible. From an attachment point of view, this interaction helps revise the adolescent's expectation that the parent can be sensitive and available, thus helping him or her develop a more secure attachment style. The therapist should be cognizant that, in many instances, such episodes provide a once-in-a-lifetime opportunity to work through current or past relationship problems. After the therapy, the family is not likely to return to these particularly loaded, traumatic events/processes on their own initiative. This may be the only opportunity to rationally discuss and explore what these experiences or processes have meant to the family members. With this in mind, the therapist helps the family remain in this reflective, explorative state for as long as possible and makes sure all corners of this conversation are explored.

Deepening Primary Emotions

Expressing Anger in a Regulated Way

Typically, the adolescent begins by disclosing anger, often expressing for the first time feelings and memories that have been neglected or avoided for years. Sometimes the adolescent will begin with secondary anger, complaining about the usual concerns ("My sister gets treated better than me"). We might tolerate this momentarily, but then we begin to look for more vulnerable, primary feelings. For some adolescents, anger might be the avoided primary feeling. Anger about abandonment, anger about abuse, and anger about overly critical parents might all represent avoided, denied, or ignored—yet justified—feelings.

It is important to note, however, that we are not encouraging expressing anger for the purpose of catharsis or fostering the expression of unbridled anger. During Task II, the therapist helps adolescents learn to express their anger in a more regulated fashion. Consequently, we have increased the adolescent's skills in articulating his or her anger directly, coherently, and with less blaming and attack. As a result, parents feel less threatened, defensive, and more curious and empathic about their adolescent's experience. When adolescents are given permission to express primary anger, it frees them up to also feel more vulnerable primary feelings as well.

Mother: Sally, I wanted to ask what you were thinking and feeling when you saw your dad come home and he was in one of those moods.

Adolescent: I don't know.

Mother: [Persists] Well, what were you feeling?

Adolescent: Angry.

Mother: [After a long pause] Oh, OK. Can you say what you were angry about?

Adolescent: Him of course. He was a jerk. I wanted to . . . [Pauses]

Mother: Go ahead, you can say it.

Adolescent: I wanted to kill him . . . to get him out of our house and never see him again. I hated him.

Mother: [A bit taken aback by her rage] Oh . . . ah . . . I don't think you should kill him, but you did have reason to hate him. . . . He was not very good to us.

Adolescent: [Looks down; looks angry]

Therapist: [To the mother] You are doing great. Keep it up!

Mother: OK. Ah . . . well . . . Sally, what were you angry about?

Adolescent: About how he treated you!

Mother: Do you mean yelling at me?

Adolescent: Yes, and hitting you! [Expresses frustration with mother]

Mother: [Surprised] Oh, ah, I didn't know you saw that.

Adolescent: What do you think I am . . . stupid? Of course I saw it . . . we all saw it.

Mother: What was going on in your mind when you saw that?

Adolescent: I was angry. I wanted to kill him.

Mother: You would not really do that, would you?

Therapist: Ms. Wilson, I think for now, it is OK to say the ugliest, strongest feelings. Give her permission to let this out.

Mother: Yes, I know. I just did not know you felt that way. I knew you were upset at times, but not that mad. [Becomes tearful but remains focused on her daughter] OK, what else? Were you scared?

Adolescent: Yeah I was scared! I thought he was going to kill you!

Mother: [Tearful, pauses]

Adolescent: I was also angry at myself.

Mother: [Surprised] Why were you angry at yourself?

Adolescent: I was angry that I couldn't do anything. I wished I was bigger so that I could come downstairs and do the same thing to him that he was doing to you [e.g., hit him].

Mother: Oh, Sally! That was not your job. I should have protected you, not made you feel like you had to protect me. . . . Were you . . . ah . . . were you ever angry at me?

Adolescent: [Looks uncomfortable; looks down]

Mother: It is OK . . . you can say it.

Adolescent: [Long pause] Yes . . . you were stupid for staying with him.

Mother: What do you think I should have done?

Adolescent: [Moans in frustration] Mom! You are the mother. Why are you asking me? Of course you should have left him. Picked us all up and left!

Mother: So you are angry at me, disappointed in me?

Adolescent: Arggg . . . Mom . . .

Mother: It's OK. You have a right to be mad. I did not handle it well. I did not protect you.

The mother does a great job of tolerating the daughter's rage, even though she feels uncomfortable. The daughter has never expressed this level of emotion before, nor has she told these stories and memories before. Usually, she just shrugs her shoulders with indifference when asked about her feelings. But the mother knows this anger has been eating away at her daughter for years, so she accepts direction from the therapist to let the daughter express her anger more fully.

Accessing Softer Emotions

Anger is sometimes necessary, but parents will tolerate anger for only so long, especially when directed at them. Even as a primary emotion, this mood will eventually wear down even the most patient, empathic parents. So we monitor this process and look for the openings to move to softer emotions. We encourage parents to help the adolescent, or we help the adolescent, to access softer, more vulnerable emotions:

> Sally, I know you are mad and you have a right to be, but I also know you feel hurt. You feel like your mother let you down. We have talked about this. I wonder if you can share some of these feelings with your mother.

Ideally, this will lead to an exploration of sadness, disappointment, sorrow, and/or grief.

Bringing these vulnerable, primary emotions into the conversation helps the adolescent have a richer and more complex understanding of his or her own experiences. In general, we do not value sadness over anger. It is client specific. Typically, however, vulnerable emotions are more frequently denied or avoided, thus blocking adolescents from feeling the full range of their emotions. In addition, for many of our adolescents and parents, this is a learning moment. They come to better understand that sad or hurt feelings often fuel anger and behavioral acting out. To emphasize this, we might clarify what we think is going on emotionally. We do not stop to do a psychoeducational intervention; that would interrupt the experiential action of the conversation. Rather, we just weave it in and coach the parent.

Therapist: Ms. Wilson, your daughter is clearly very angry. And she should be. But I wonder if she has other emotions as well. You know this is a pretty complex situation.

Mother: Yes . . . ah, so Sally, what do you think? Did you have other feelings?

Adolescent: Like what?

Mother: Well . . . ah . . . I wonder if you felt disappointed . . . like Dad let you down . . . like I let you down. I was not there to protect you.

Adolescent: [Starts to cry]

Mother: [Moves over and puts her hand on her daughter's knee as she hands her a tissue]

In this heightened aroused state, the daughter's usual defenses are penetrable. Mother softly asks about sadness, and the daughter cannot hold back those emotions. As she starts to cry, it opens the door for the mother to move closer, to offer comfort and solace. These hidden or disavowed emotions of loss and longing are now available for sharing and conversation. The daughter has silently carried both rage and sadness for many years, protecting both herself and her mother from these feelings. But this emotional restriction and relational ambivalence exacerbates, if not causes, her depression, withdrawal, and isolation, closing the door on her mother's attempts to love and protect her. Yet here the door opens. The daughter allows her mother to comfort her, and the mother provides the support and protection that she was not able to provide during the years of abuse. As trust emerges, the parent can guide the adolescent to explore thoughts and feelings such as helplessness, guilt, and shame.

The sequence above represents what we would consider a meaningful moment. Within this one interaction, Sally tells her mother, most likely for the first time, that she felt unprotected and sad. Perhaps she thought her mother did not care. Perhaps she thought her mother was unavailable. Regardless, Sally was, in her experience, left alone. Just as important in this sequence, the mother responds in a completely nondefensive, empathic, genuine, caring, remorseful manner. This is far from trivial. For many parents, hearing their child express feeling unprotected, scared, and angry might feel like a stake in the heart—the pang of feeling like one has failed their child. The mother contains and regulates her own sadness, self-criticism, and other difficult emotions and instead focuses on her daughter's experience, thus promoting the reparative attachment process. It is impossible to overstate the courage and selflessness that the mother shows in this sequence, setting aside her reactions to focus on her daughter. It is exactly this act of responsiveness and availability that helps the adolescent begin to revise her expectations of her mother.

Exploring Problem Attributions

Once adolescents have expressed their own needs and feelings, we often help them think about why these kinds of events have occurred: What attributions do they give to these problems? Who do they blame? Can they consider other people's motives and choices? The divorce, the father's alcoholism, an overcontrolling parent, an adoption, the death of a parent; how do they understand these things? This direction of exploration helps uncover negative attribution schemas of self-blame and low self-worth: "If I were a better child, maybe daddy would not have left us." This phase of the conversation also begins the process of promoting perspective taking: Can the adolescent begin to consider or guess the motives and needs of others?

The emergence of perspective taking has long been a hallmark developmental task of adolescence (Steinberg, 1990). As adolescents acquire new cognitive abilities for abstract thought, they begin to realize they are not the center of the world and that other's needs and feelings might be worth considering. Thus, this exploration of attributions about why bad events or processes have happened enacts at least a momentary emergence from one's self-focused perspective and engenders an appreciation of other people's needs and experiences. Perspective taking is also at the heart of mentalizing—Fonagy, Gyorgy, Jurist, and Target's (2005) proposed mechanism for understanding secure attachment. When children have had their own inner world acknowledged and responded to by parents, they internalize the ability to do that as well, to acknowledge their own inner thoughts and feelings and those of others. The capacity to appreciate other's needs, feelings, and motives forms the critical foundation for successfully negotiating one's needs in interpersonal relationships.

Thus, the repairing attachment task builds on this development task. If the conversation has gone well, adolescents feel understood and acknowledged. This frees them from the need to avoid or repress their hurt feelings and from battling to be heard and taken seriously. When adolescents feel parents understand and acknowledge their point of view, they become less consumed with the battle to be heard. As they begin to find their own voice, they more willingly examine their own negative contributions to problems and how their attributions and behaviors might have affected others.

Most therapists end the disclosure phase too soon; they do not carry out a sufficiently full exploration of emotions and cognitions. Most families may never again discuss these core attachment ruptures with this much focused attention, so we want it to be as complete as possible. The therapist should help the parent sustain the adolescent's reflection and expression for as long as possible. Again, the Angus, Levitt, and Hardtke (1999) model of emotion-focused narrative processing is helpful here. The therapist helps the parent immerse the adolescent in the details of the memories and assists parents in excavating the primary emotions that underlie these experiences. The therapist helps the parent explore what meaning these events had for the adolescent in the past, has for them in the present, and holds for them in the future.

Sometimes this conversation feels sacred, a timeless, protected space of honesty and integrity. Usually, family members will feel tremendous relief, both from finally talking about avoided issues and from learning that the conversation was not as frightening or difficult as anticipated. Eventually, however, this disclosure phase does come to a natural end. The parent (and therapist) has pushed the adolescent as far as he or she can go, or needs to go at this time. At this point, a calm stillness and profound mutual respect often fills the room. The parents often admire the adolescent's honesty and maturity, and the adolescent feels relief and pride.

PHASE 2: PARENT DISCLOSURE

Parents Share Their Own Experience of the Ruptures

After the adolescent disclosure feels complete, it can be time for the parents to say a few things about the subject. This is a delicate moment. We want the parents to talk about their own experiences, but we do not want them to be defensive, invalidating, or dismissive. Nor do we want them to intellectualize about what the adolescent just said. We certainly do not want the parents' needs and feelings to suddenly dominate the conversation such that the adolescent feels ignored or responsible for taking care of their parents' needs. Many of our adolescents already feel *parentified*: that is, they take care of parents' emotional needs. In this task, we attempt to engineer the opposite experience, whereby parents parent the adolescent, not the inverse.

So, what is the goal here? We want the parent to give the adolescent some new information about the context of his or her own life, information that might help the adolescent put the attachment ruptures into context. We want the adolescent to have more pieces of the story so that he or she can construct a more complex and coherent understanding of the ruptures. We want the adolescent to gain new information but not become flooded with it or overwhelmed. A parent might talk about his or her own experience with the alcoholic spouse or why he or she stayed in an abusive marriage so long. A parent might talk about his or her depression and how it has made parenting difficult. A parent might talk about his or her own childhood and how those experiences shaped their relational capacity. A couple might talk about their marital conflicts and how it has negatively affected their parenting. The parents might talk about their pending divorce and how they will both remain committed to the child.

The parent disclosure phase should be brief. Sometimes the child will ask questions. The parent may respond, but we remind them that they should not feel compelled to tell everything. In cases where we anticipate that parents will share some of their own story, we plan for it during the parent alliance task. Kids do not need all of the details. They need to know enough to understand the context better. In some cases, this is the first time the adolescent has heard their parent's story, so maybe we linger here longer or plan to revisit this in another session. Sometimes the adolescent has an awareness of these stories but has never fully understood them or had the chance to ask questions.

This moment of parental disclosure helps adolescents see their parent as a person, perfectly imperfect like everyone: He or she is not just the adolescent's father or mother but is also a person with life struggles. Sometimes it helps the adolescent reinterpret the parent's behavior as more positively motivated, "So you stayed with dad because you wanted me to have a father, even though he was abusing you?" For some adolescents, especially older teens, this can be a remarkable developmental moment, a shift in perceiving parents in a childish, naive, idealized manner to seeing parents simply as people, with strengths and weaknesses. In one case, an adolescent had been struggling for two years with a rape experience, often screaming at her mother, "You will never understand what I went through . . ." In the attachment task, this very guarded and emotionally restricted mother, to everyone's surprise, stated, "I do know very well what you went through, more than you know," implying that she too had been raped as a child. Without providing any more detail than that, the daughter suddenly saw her mother differently and, finally, felt her mother did understand her. Parents' appropriate disclosure helps the adolescent better understand parents' motivations behind their behaviors. In doing this, the adolescent begins to appreciate the parents' feelings and needs.

Some parents worry that these disclosures will reduce their child's respect for them. In our clinical experience, we typically find that the opposite is true. This phase of the conversation, if done well, generates empathy and promotes perspective taking and understanding on the part of the adolescent. Now that the adolescent feels heard and understood, they are psychologically freed up to consider other people's points of view, psychological needs, and motives. We are enhancing the adolescent's capacity for mentalization (J. G. Allen & Fonagy, 2006). As adolescents appreciate their parents' needs more fully, warmth and positive regard increase between them. Parents feel more respected and appreciated by their adolescent, and adolescents feel more patient and understanding of their parents. In this moment of mutual trust and care, the adolescent's attachment desires can more safely emerge and parents are more likely to respond. We find many adolescents become more protective of parents after these parental disclosures.

Therapist: [To adolescent] You know, Sally, I imagined that you sometimes wondered why your mom stayed with your dad.

Adolescent: I did, but I never came up with a good answer. It couldn't have been because she wanted us to have a father, because he never acted like a father in the first place.

Mother: Well, Sally, I struggled with that question every day. I didn't want you all to grow up without a father. I know he wasn't always the best father. I also loved him as much as I hated him. I struggled with trying to help him as well.

Adolescent: I guess I could see that.

Therapist: [To adolescent] I wonder if you thought mom was a pushover. That she believed all of his promises to change his ways, to make things better.

Adolescent: [To mother] I don't know why you let him hit you like that. Why didn't you fight back?

Mother: [To adolescent] Oh, I did hit him back. I hit him back real good, many times.

Adolescent: [To mother] I don't know why you didn't kick him out of the house. I can tell you, no man is ever going to hit me like that. I would never put up with that. How come you didn't ever kick him out?

Mother: [To adolescent] Sally, you are a much stronger person than I am. There was not a day that went by that I don't think that I should have been stronger. There were times when I kicked him out of the house. You remember that time I told you that Dad would be out of the house for a couple of weeks because he got a job working out of town? Well, in reality, I had made him go to a drug rehabilitation center during that time. I told him that if he didn't go, he wouldn't be able to live at home.

Therapist: Did you know that, Sally, that sometimes mom was strong even though sometimes she was not?

Adolescent: [Shakes her head "no"]

In this sequence, the daughter was free to ask questions she had never dared to ask before. Before this conversation, Sally perceived her mother as naive, weak, and misguided. Now, she better understood her mother's motives, thoughts, and struggles and had new information about her mother's actions and behaviors. She also better understood that her mother had tried to protect her (e.g., the father's 2-week absence was an act of the mother protecting Sally). This new information helps change the daughter's perceptions of who her mother is, how much she cares, and that she will fight for her. These kinds of conversations begin to change the daughter's internal working models of the mother.

This parent disclosure phase requires some close monitoring. Three elements guide us here (G. S. Diamond & Stern, 2003). First, is the timing of the disclosure appropriate? If it is too early, it might cut off the adolescent talking about herself or himself and seem inauthentic. Second, does the content represent new information for the adolescent? If not, the adolescent will feel bored or even lectured. Finally, we have to make sure the emotion is appropriate. Is the parent angry or vulnerable? Does the mood invite adolescent understanding and empathy, or is it defensive and dismissive? Is the adolescent experiencing the parent's disclosure as an attempt to excuse his or her behavior? These elements help us decide when the parent should talk, what they should talk about, and if it is promoting growth.

Parent Apologizes if Appropriate

In some cases, there has been a severe violation of love and trust, where the adolescent may have experienced abuse, neglect, rejection, or abandonment. The parent participating in the attachment task may have been the perpetrator of this abuse, or the parent may not have done a sufficiently good job protecting the child from these experiences. We are not speaking here about a parent who sexually abused a child. That is a more complicated circumstance that requires thoughtful consideration, extensive preparation, and lots of planning, if it is appropriate at all. Instead, we are referring to situations such as the parent who is now a recovered alcoholic, the parent with previously undiagnosed bipolar disorder, or the parent who did not protect the child while the other parent or another family member was neglectful or abusive. In these circumstances, the parent disclosure phase often concludes with the parent making a spontaneous, authentic, heartfelt apology.

This complicated moment needs to be monitored closely. A parent's apology can be an incredibly validating and moving act that solidifies acknowledgement for the adolescent. It punctuates the fact that the parent has heard and understood the adolescent's pain. It is a tremendous act of humility and strength on the part of parents when they accept responsibility for their contribution to these problems and apologize.

PHASE 3: CONTINUING THE REPAIR

Assessing the Adolescent's Reaction and Degree of Forgiveness

When an apology is made, parents often expect, or at least hope for, forgiveness. This, again, is a complicated, delicate moment. Some adolescents feel touched by the parent's honest repentance and feel moved to spontaneously forgive their parent. This can be a powerful psychological moment, in which the adolescent lets go of his or her resentment and demands for restitution (McCullough, Pargament, & Thoresen, 2000). Other adolescents, although happy to receive the apology, are not so ready to forgive, or maybe they forgive but do not exonerate. These adolescents remain cautious or suspicious, waiting to see if things will change. We have to be sensitive to these possible variations and nuances in the adolescent's experience and responses during the conversation. We do not want the adolescent to feel compelled to forgive out of guilt or obedience. We want to slow the adolescent (and parents) down and offer them a chance to think through what they are thinking and feeling.

Mother: Sally, I want you to know that whatever I did, I had no intention of hurting you . . . and Sally . . . I was doing the best I could at the time. You know, I was pretty depressed then too. [Pauses] But I am so sorry for everything I did that caused you pain.

Adolescent: [Looks down in thought for a long time]

Therapist: [Long silent pause to adolescent] I was curious what you thought of mom's apology. Did it feel sincere? Did you believe her?

Adolescent: Yeah, I guess I believe her.

Therapist: [To adolescent] I guess I wasn't quite sure what was going through your mind just now. Was it too little too late? I just felt like you didn't really accept that apology, which is OK.

Adolescent: No, I accept it. I believe her. I just don't know what it means yet.

Here the therapist gives permission to the adolescent to not automatically reciprocate or feel compelled to forgive just because her mother made a heartfelt apology. This is a complicated yet profound moment, and the therapist wants it to have integrity. The therapist also uses this moment to sensitize the adolescent to the complexity and subtle variations involved in emotional processing and grants permission to feel many different and sometimes conflicting emotions/impulses. For example, maybe the adolescent does not believe the apology, maybe the adolescent forgives but does not forget, or maybe he or she still feels vengeful and wants restitution. There is no right or wrong response, other than trying to help the adolescent understand and be honest about what he or she is feeling.

Summarizing, Checking in, and Marking

The type of enactment described above can be both emotionally painful and uplifting. The topics discussed may have involved particular incidences, but they also touched on more general relational themes. As the session draws to a close, we try to make sense of what occurred, check in with how everyone feels, and use the material/event to mark the future course/tasks/goals of the treatment.

Therapist: Well, we aren't going to get to everything today. You guys have done a tremendous amount of work. How are you doing right now?

Mother: I think it was good. Sally shared with me a lot of things I hadn't been aware of. I mean, some of them I kind of thought in the back of my head, but I am glad she spoke about them.

Therapist: Sally, did it feel like mom listened and really heard you?

Adolescent: Yeah, she did.

Therapist: Good. You all did a great job. I think we will do a bit more of this over the next few weeks. Ms. Wilson, you were worried that Sally might lose respect for you the more she learned about how and why you made the decisions you did. Do you feel like that happened?

Mother: I don't know. [Turns toward her daughter] Sally, did anything I say make you feel even more like I was weak or made the wrong decisions?

Adolescent: No. The opposite!

Mother: Really?

Adolescent: Yeah. You did the best you could.

Mother: [Gives a smile of appreciation to the therapist]

Therapist: OK, you guys were great, really great. I know that there are some immediate, practical issues we need to address soon, but today was special. Today you crossed a bridge. I am hoping that going forward hard conversations will feel less threatening.

One final decision is whether and how much to process what has just occurred. On the one hand, we like to let the mood of intimacy, warmth, and success linger. We want the pride, closeness, and hopefulness to set in as a means of counteracting the past negative expectations and poor interactions. On the other hand, we know from research on emotion-focused, experiential therapies that meaning making is associated with better outcome (Greenberg, Auszura, & Herrmann, 2007; Greenberg & Watson, 1998). Also, research on exposure therapy suggests that some review and assessment after experiential learning helps to solidify the learning experience (Foa, Huppert, & Cahill, 2006). For that reason, we often ask the family to reflect a bit on what just happened.

> How did this conversation feel? What did your mother do to make it different? Mom, what did you see your daughter do that helped you have this kind of communication? What helped make this so successful? What do you think each of you personally did differently?

These kinds of questions, and the discussions they engender, help anchor for the family the kinds of skills and processes that make for positive communication.

Addressing Additional Ruptures

After the adolescent's disclosure of his or her anger, pain, and unmet needs, and the parents' acknowledgement, empathy, disclosure, and in some cases, apology, there is typically a sense of relief, intimacy, and even love in the room. The secret, or unspoken truth, finally comes out. Family members have said what they most feared saying and have survived. Even in this short conversation, the tension has dissipated and the level of trust, at least momentarily, increases. The adolescent and the parent, at least momentarily, see each other differently. The adolescent is more competent; the parent is more responsive and available. At this point, the therapist has at least two options. Sometimes the conversation has been long and exhaustive, and ending the session seems the most appropriate thing to do. In other cases, however, there is still time left in the session. The therapist may try to capitalize on the special mood of comfort and safety created. The therapist may pursue some of the themes or issues raised during the session or address content that did not necessarily come up in the planning stage nor was on the initial agenda for the attachment session.

The content in this third phase can cover a variety of issues. At times, we continue talking about the core relational issues. The adolescent may have more questions, or the parents may have more stories. Alternatively, we might move onto other relational topics if the initial topic has run its course. The therapist has to make the decision as to what other topics might be appropriate or if it is too much and the family needs something lighter to discuss. In fact, we may engineer a more positive conversation that springboards off the goodwill elicited by the reparative moment. How do family members want things different going forward? How can we keep up a feeling of goodwill and love? What we are careful to block, however, is the conversation turning to behavioral management problems. We do not want to talk about school attendance, curfew, or helping out around the house. We want to linger in the warmth of this interpersonal bonding moment. Behavioral problems typically pull the family back into negativity and confrontation. Moreover, they distract from the emotional closeness created in the moment.

Phase 3 involves a shift in process. Whereas in Phase 1, the adolescent was center stage and parents were "attentive witnesses" and in Phase 2 parents did the talking and adolescents asked questions, in Phase 3 the interaction is more balanced. Family members have learned to be curious and to respectfully listen to one another. Tension has been diffused. So we often find this third phase has more interaction. Each person is asking questions, responding appropriately, and reflecting and exploring. As long as the conversation is working well, we allow the process to unfold naturally. We may not need to monitor the process so tightly. However, we are mindful of when and how to end this session. We want to maintain the positive emotion and goodwill that has emerged. If Phase 3 does not occur at the end of this first attachment task session, this phase will occur in future attachment sessions.

PROCESS SKILLS THAT FACILITATE THE ENACTMENT

Thus far, we have been describing the general structure or pathway of the attachment task. As we said, however, the session is as much about process as it is about content or goals. In fact, in many ways the process is the outcome. So, unlike the other tasks, the structure and phases of the attachment task are less distinct and can blur into each other. We do try to dedicate time for Phase 2 (parent disclosures), but generally the rest of the session is about sustained, authentic respectful dialogue as long as it meets our general goals (adolescent center of attention, parent as witness). To assist with the productive flow and course of the session, we describe a few therapist process skills that we use to keep this enactment of the attachment task on track.

Content, Affect, and Process

The most important therapeutic skill required for conducting attachment sessions is the ability to evaluate and monitor the value of the content, the quality of affect, and the moment-by-moment process of the conversation. By *content*, we mean what the family is actually talking about. Are they complaining about the adolescent not doing his homework or talking about the pain and disruption caused by the parents' divorce? Are they talking about curfew or trust? For the attachment task, the content should not be about behavioral management or rules. Instead, the focus should be on attachment injuries. This can include specific events, such as abuse, neglect, or abandonment, or negative interpersonal processes, such as criticism and/or overcontrol. These themes should have been well developed during the alliance sessions, so at this point the therapist should not be searching for the right content during the attachment task. Finding paradigmatic content is an essential element of the alliance sessions, and that is what we bring to the attachment task. New content may come up and, when it does, the therapist has to decide if it supports and promotes the goals of this task or distracts from it.

For example, at the start of one attachment task, the therapist turned to the daughter and asked her to begin. The daughter began by complaining that her sister is a pest and she wants mom to punish her. The therapist listened for a minute to see how the conversation evolved, but then the mother became defensive and started criticizing the daughter for being too hard on her sister. At that point, the therapist stepped in and redirected the girl to different content—content reflective of underlying attachment themes, such as trust, commitment, and abandonment: "Alexis, maybe you should talk a bit more about what we discussed last week . . . about how upset you are that your mother sends you to grandmother's every time you and your sister fight." The issue of abandonment serves as a foundational organizing theme for how this girl understands her life, her relationships with her parents, and her self-worth. Helping her speak about this, and identify more primary adaptive emotions (hurt), rather than her more reactive anger, made this a much more profound and meaningful conversation (Greenberg, 2011).

By *affect*, we mean what emotions the adolescent or parents are expressing at any given moment during the session and whether such emotions are facilitating or undermining our treatment goal: rupture resolution. This is a complex judgment call and always depends on the story of the family. Thinking about primary and secondary emotions helps us decide what to amplify and what to block. Sometimes the adolescent's anger is a defense against hurt, and sometimes withdrawal is a defense against anger. Which emotions are defenses, and which emotions are avoided but important to access? Helping the adolescent acknowledge his or her primary adaptive emotions, bringing those emotions into awareness, naming them, and integrating them into the story of the attachment rupture helps the adolescent better understand past and present negative life events or processes. Helping parents tolerate the adolescent's primary, vulnerable emotions helps soften even the most defensive parents. In this regard, getting the right (e.g., accurate and helpful) affect determines whether this conversation is going to be transformative or just familiar. Evaluating how productive parents' emotional stance is, is a bit easier because we primarily want them to be empathic and supportive. If parents become irritated, judgmental, blaming, or belittling, then we know we need to help them access a softer, more receptive emotional state.

When accessing vulnerable emotions, how you ask a question becomes very important. First, if you ask about thoughts, you are likely to get a cognitive response. If you ask about anger, you are likely to hear about anger. If you ask about sadness, you are more likely to hear about sadness. You get what you ask for. When you are not able to access primary emotions, you need to block distracting, nonproductive secondary emotions and ask again. Second, therapists can ask family members to think about feelings or feel feelings: "I wonder if this makes you feel sad sometimes?" versus "You seem very sad right now . . . I can see it in your eyes. . . . Can you tell your mom what you are feeling?" Both questions are valuable, but therapists need to consciously select the right one for the right moment. We *recommend* therapists ask the latter question more often. Third, parsing out the feelings sometimes helps adolescents feel less defensive. For example, framing the questions as "Part of you feels one way and part of you feels another" increases the likelihood the adolescent will explore some of these more avoided, emerging, "dangerous" feelings. This frame makes them feel safer and helps them build scaffolding for acknowledging competing emotions. Fourth, requests for softer emotions must be packaged with empathy and admiration. Accessing these emotions is hard for many people, especially adolescents, and especially depressed adolescents. The therapist has to be the perfect parent at these moments, offering comfort, protection, and admiration, while still having expectations, as in the example below.

> Luisa, I know this is hard for you to talk about. I am so impressed with you. You have so much strength and insight about yourself. I know we can get through some of this. But right now you look so sad, and I want your mother to understand that part of you better.

By *process*, we mean how the family members interact with each other. During most of the attachment task, we want the adolescent talking and the parent listening. We want the adolescent telling previously untold stories and expressing previously avoided emotions. We want the parents asking questions, evidencing curiosity and empathy, and giving acknowledgement and new information. If, instead, we find the adolescent becoming belligerent or withdrawn, or the parent starting to lecture or problem solve, we know that the process of the conversation is not good and may inhibit the family's reaching their goal.

The therapist has to monitor the content, affect, and process all of the time. Ideally, all three are synchronized and supporting the goal of this task. Sometimes we might have two of these domains working well but not the third. For instance, suppose the content is wrong (e.g., not the core attachment rupture we had planned for). Instead of talking about the divorce, the daughter talks about her frustration at school. The affect, however, may be good because she expresses her worries and the parents offer empathy and support. The process is good in that we have our corrective attachment moment: The girl is asking for help and the parents are offering protection through their thoughtful listening and willingness to help. So the content is not about relational ruptures, but the affect and process are good. Under these circumstances, we might let this conversation progress, thinking we are building goodwill and trust that will later serve to support more difficult conversations to come.

In another example, suppose the son is talking about the father's harsh, punitive parenting style. The father might actually be listening pretty well, but the son gets progressively angrier as the conversation continues. Although the adolescent's anger may be justified, too much anger, expressed inappropriately, will shut down the father. To keep the session on track and productive, the therapist might help the adolescent modulate his affect, or express other, additional emotions related to these circumstances: disappointment that he cannot get closer to his father. In general, it is the monitoring of content, affect, and process that helps the therapist judge the relative value of the conversation at any given moment in the session.

Engineering the Enactment and Deciding Whether the Conversation Needs Shaping

A core assumption of an enactment is that the family must have the experience of talking to each other in new ways. As much as possible, family members should be encouraged to talk with each other. If the therapist remains the center of attention, or too tightly maintains control over the process, then the family does not have the experience of engaging in and navigating the conversation directly with one another. We find that many therapists have difficulty not being the center of the action.

In general, after setting the stage and determining the content, the therapist tries to stay out of the way as much as possible during the enactment. This is a process that occurs between family members and not through the therapist. Enacting productive conversations about attachment ruptures is typically a powerful, moving experience, with family members highly attuned to one another's responses—verbal and nonverbal. Therefore, the therapist must restrain herself or himself from interfering too quickly, speaking for family members, or explaining what family members meant by what they said. Sometimes this means letting the family struggle a bit.

Mother: Chantel, I wanted to ask what you were thinking and feeling when you saw your dad come home and he was in one of those moods.

Adolescent: I don't know.

Mother: Well, what were you feeling?

Adolescent: Angry.

Mother: [Long pause] OK, anything else?

Adolescent: Nope.

At this point in the conversation, the mother turned to the therapist to ask for help. However, instead of taking over, the therapist encouraged the mother to proceed. The therapist said, "You are doing great. Keep it up!" The therapist serves as a witness to the unfolding of this important dialogue. As long as the topic reflects core relational themes, the material is new, and family members are sincere and open, the therapist allows them to find their own path. But what happens when the family needs some help or the conversation is not going well? How much does the therapist need to get involved to keep the conversation on track? How much are we in the conversation and how much are we out? And when we are in, what should we do to get the conversation on track? We think about this at four levels.

First, although we attempt to not be central, we do coach parents, offer and shape the content, ask questions and lend language to deepen the affect, and urge family members to persist and delve deeper to sustain the conversation. As much as possible, this is done through the parent. The therapist might suggest that the parent ask the adolescent a question or tell him or her to slow down and let the adolescent talk more. Sometimes we model for the parents what to ask and direct the adolescent to tell their parents the answer. The therapist is the conductor guiding the musicians on when to come in, when to get softer or louder, when to emphasize a point, and when to begin the next movement. Hence, the therapist is very active in shaping the conversation, but as much as possible, the family members talk to each other, and not to each other through the therapist.

Second, when the therapist sees things getting off track (e.g., the content is wrong, the affect is alienating people rather than bringing them together, and/or the process is reinforcing familiar counterproductive interactional patterns rather than supporting new ones), he or she may need to do more than slightly redirect. In such instances, the therapist relies on the preparation work from previous sessions, as well as the strong alliance he or she has built with each family member. The therapist might briefly stop the action of the conversation, draw the family member's attention to himself or herself and remind him or her of conversations from previous sessions: "Dad, remember what we talked about when we met alone. We discussed the importance of you being an emotional coach? Your son needs that from you now. Can you turn to him and offer that now?" This type of intervention briefly interrupts the experiential action of the enactment to remind a parent of skills previously discussed. A brief reminder is often enough to remind the parent of what he or she learned in the session the previous week. The parent says to himself or herself, "Ah, yes, I remember what she taught me. Yes . . . yes . . . I can do that." The therapist then invites the parent (or adolescent) to try again, restarting the experiential conversation in the here and now.

Third, when a brief redirection or reminding does not get family members back on track, the therapist may have to be even more directive. This is necessary, for example, when a conversation has gone very poorly and the conversation rapidly dissolves into an unhelpful, if not destructive, repetition of what usually happens at home. Faced with this challenge, the therapist must be more directive quickly. The therapist might stop the action completely and begin to reestablish the goal of the task and commitment to it. More didactic instruction and positive reinforcement will be needed; for example, "Let's hold on here for a minute. We need to revisit some of the themes we discussed last week." This may lead to more therapist–parent or therapist–adolescent conversation, both to diffuse the tension and to try and recapture the intent of the session. The therapist must use his or her interpersonal strengths and clear theoretical perspective to wrestle this process from complete regression back to negative interactions.

Fourth, and in the most extreme circumstance, the therapist must be prepared to stop the conversation completely and regroup. Maybe the severity of the adolescent's depression inhibits the adolescent from engaging in this process. Maybe the parents' marital conflict or psychiatric distress remains a barrier. Maybe there was a disagreement that day that the family members just cannot get past. There can be any number of reasons this process can become compromised. But when the therapist cannot salvage the process, even after several valiant attempts, we might ask the more cooperative family member or members to step out of the room while we challenge the more resistant person. In one case, the daughter had clammed up and refused to talk about the issues that had been prepared and agreed upon. The therapist asked the mother to step out of the room while she gave the adolescent a pep talk:

> Listen, you cannot back out on us. We have worked so hard for this moment. You can do this. You can get through this. Next week you leave for vacation, and we do not want this to linger. Now is the moment. This is your time to work this out.

In another case, the therapist asked the son to step into the waiting room while the therapist addressed the parents about letting their marital conflicts enter the room:

> Look, you two . . . it happened again. Did you see how crushed your son was, how disappointed he was that you two could not listen to him for even 5 minutes without starting to fight with each other? I know you both love him, but I have to say you abandon and ignore him when you two fight. Can we try one more time, for his sake? [Gets agreement] OK, Dad, can you go out to the lobby and get him? When he comes in, I think you owe him an apology.

CONCLUSION

The attachment task can be not only a transformative moment for the family but also one of the most rewarding moments for a therapist. When it goes well, we come out of the session remembering why we went into this profession. These conversations can be profound, intimate, and life changing.

These conversations resuscitate trust, reactivate attachment needs, refurbish caregiving instincts, and set a foundation for a new relationship ahead. Of course, these conversations may also be frustrating and exhausting, and may need to be repeated over and over. We take small steps that we try to build on each time, but the therapist has to work hard to sculpt this conversation. It is the fourth quarter, the therapist is the quarterback, and he or she must take charge of the team and try to get a win. If this task is successful, or even partially successful, the therapist can shift to Task V (promoting autonomy) or begin to integrate Task V conversations into these Task IV episodes. Moving to Task V too quickly can water down Task IV, but sometimes moving to Task V can help identify new content for, or shore up, Task IV. This back and forth between these tasks is explored in the next chapter.

7

TASK V: PROMOTING AUTONOMY

In the autonomy task (Task V), we begin to help family members use their newly established or improved secure base to develop a better goal-corrected partnership. The task involves helping adolescents and parents begin to negotiate the normative developmental challenges of adolescence. This does not mean that the therapy suddenly becomes focused on behavior management. Instead, we aim to bring forward family members' reflective functioning, emotion awareness, improved emotion regulation, and enhanced communication skills honed in the previous tasks into the conversation that can focus on adolescent autonomy and competence. From our perspective, developmental challenges are not only specific problems to solve but also opportunities to (a) strengthen secure base interactions between the adolescent and parents and thus revise their internal working models of self and other and (b) practice new interpersonal skills.

http://dx.doi.org/10.1037/14296-008
Attachment-Based Family Therapy for Depressed Adolescents, by G. S. Diamond, G. M. Diamond, and S. A. Levy

If we have reached the autonomy task, then we are assuming that enough relational conflict has subsided that we can return to work on some day-to-day family challenges or help parents help their adolescents work through some of the other issues contributing to his or her depression. Or we think making progress on some daily conflicts will help build goodwill in the relationship. With either strategy, it is helpful to keep in mind some of the normative developmental issues that serve as the backdrop for these conversations. Having a template to predict, understand, and/or normalize these conflicts helps the therapist bring structure and focus to these common areas of conflict. Thus, after a brief overview of the structure of Task V, we begin this chapter with a discussion of these developmental issues. Next, we describe autonomy-promoting therapeutic processes, with an emphasis on how they differ from attachment-promoting therapeutic processes. We identify three levels of autonomy promotion for the family and therapist to address. Finally, we discuss the steps of Task V.

The autonomy task (Task V) does not have the same kind of systematic structure as the previous tasks. In the first four tasks, we prescribe the treatment content, placing the attachment narrative at the center of the therapeutic dialogue and preparing both parent and adolescent for specific, difficult conversations. In the autonomy task, the family members are increasingly more in control over the content and focus of the conversation. As shown in Figure 7.1, the autonomy task is not clearly broken into different phases.

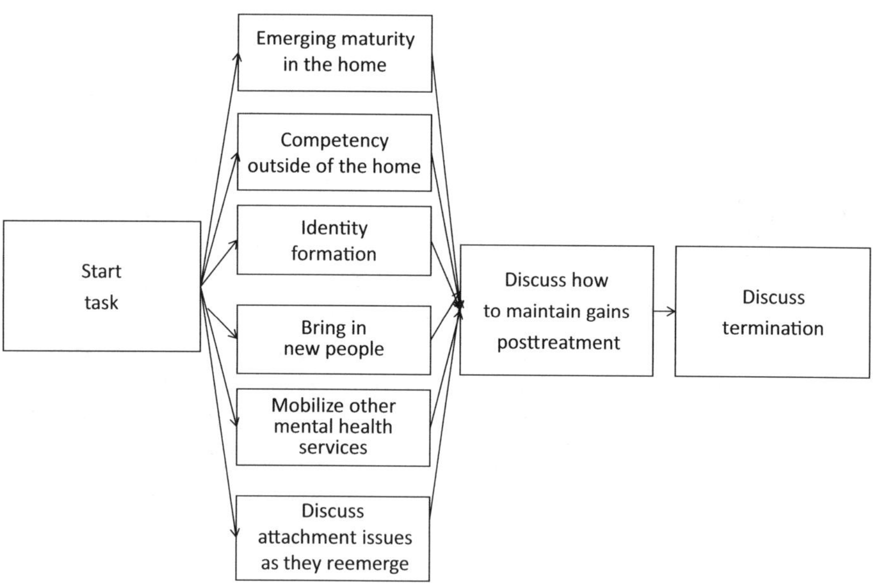

Figure 7.1. Task V: Promoting autonomy. This figure depicts the therapist performance map for facilitating the promoting autonomy task.

Multiple steps occur with the general goal of promoting autonomy. We help family members identify and prioritize challenges. We help them strategize (both alone and together) about how to approach and discuss these problems and then help them follow through with those plans or modify them if needed. We help them think about the interpersonal skills they have learned and how to bring them into conversations about concrete, specific problems rather than long-standing, interpersonal disputes.

The autonomy task usually involves the entire second half of treatment. In the context of a 16-week treatment course, Tasks I, II, III, and IV typically take about 8 or 9 weeks to complete (not a rule, just an estimate). Then, Weeks 9 through 16 focus on Task V, the autonomy-promoting task. Outside of a 16-week treatment course, the autonomy task could last from a few weeks to months, depending on the issues the family is facing.

WHAT CAN WE LEARN FROM THE ADOLESCENT DEVELOPMENT LITERATURE?

Adolescence is a time of rapid change in a child's biological development, social context, and role in the family. The onset of puberty and sexual maturation ushers in a host of biochemical and physical changes (e.g., weight, height, secondary sexual characteristics). These changes alter one's self-image and relationships. These changes can intensify parents' worries and lead to more behavioral control and conflict. Interestingly, most research does not support the common assumption that adolescent moodiness results from rapid hormonal change but rather attributes it to the dramatic increase in social interaction and other situational factors.

Adolescents also experience significant cognitive developments that allow them to think more abstractly and conceptually. They more easily question social convention and moral standards and increase their expectation to be included in decision making. This reinforces an emerging sense of autonomy. The ability to reject parents' values, the development of independent views on life, and the expectation of more equality in decision making with parents necessitate that parents adjust their view of authority and control—a transition that can be fraught with tension and conflict.

The adolescent years signal the beginning of the quest to develop a firmer sense of self and identity in the social world. Emerging independence leads to increased affiliation with peers, which can compete with family time and values. Increasing psychological and behavioral autonomy can be quite challenging for parents who want to maintain children's dependence, expect obedience, and demand continuity of family norms. The inability of an adolescent to respectfully negotiate his or her emerging autonomy, and of parents to tolerate and modulate such autonomy development, can be a great source of conflict during adolescence.

In addition to developmental changes, adolescents are experiencing changes in their social context. At least in Westernized societies, adolescents experience a loosening of restrictions and an increase in independence. These manifest as extending unsupervised time; expectation for self-directed responsibility, especially in school; and wider and more frequent exposure to mass media. Adolescents increasingly determine how to spend their time as parenting shifts from supervision to monitoring, and parents have to increasingly rely on the adolescent for information about activities and school performance.

In addition to adolescence ushering in major changes for children, parents also enter a major transition phase (Steinberg, 1990). Although this may vary by culture or social class, parents are commonly in their 40s when their first child enters adolescence. Unsatisfying marriages often reach a low point during these years, and rates of divorce increase. As adolescents enter a period of peak growth and opportunity, parents begin to face the limits of their success, dreams that did not come true, decline of physical fitness, aging and dying parents, and thus a deeper realization of their own mortality.

Whether or not parents and adolescents are aware of these developmental perturbations, these themes often play a role in normative family development. Within a moderate range of intensity, these conflicts can spur growth. Adolescents push the limits of their freedom, learn how to voice an opinion, begin to define themselves separately from their parents, and practice interpersonal problem solving. At the same time, these minor conflicts push parents to recalibrate their perspective on their adolescent, themselves, and their parenting as the adolescent moves into a more autonomous stage of life. Family flexibility during these transition phases is critical for successfully renegotiating new rules and expectations (Walsh, 2006). Keeping this developmental context in mind provides a template and baseline from which to accommodate the emerging goals and challenges faced by the adolescent.

DISTINGUISHING ATTACHMENT-PROMOTING AND AUTONOMY-PROMOTING THERAPEUTIC PROCESSES

The boundary between the attachment-promoting and autonomy-promoting tasks should be distinct but also permeable and fluid. In general, the focus on promoting autonomy increases as attachment security becomes more strongly established. Therapists must make clinical judgments about this balance at all times. Some families have made profound progress during the first few treatment tasks and have established a new foundation of trust and security. Others continue to have conflict and tension. Thus, conversations may go back and forth, as needed, between strengthening attachment and promoting autonomy. Sometimes there is strategic value in moving away from attachment-related themes to reduce the intensity in the moment. Turning to autonomy related themes can provide new opportunities for positive experiences of each other without directly focusing on attachment themes per se. As always in the attachment-based family therapy (ABFT) framework, there are no rules, only principles to guide decision making.

We find it helpful to distinguish between attachment-promoting and autonomy-promoting therapeutic processes. In general, we define *attachment-focused themes* as conversations about trust, care, safety, acceptance, and love in the adolescent–parent relationship. Attachment themes also include conversations about past traumatic events or ongoing negative process (e.g., persistent criticism) that undermine trust, safety, and the adolescent's sense of being loved and appreciated. These are not discussions about organizational or behavioral conflicts such as chores, curfew, or homework. At a metalevel, attachment-focused conversations aim to help family members understand and renegotiate the very expectations, needs, and ground rules of the relationship itself. During these attachment-focused conversations, adolescents express their views, feelings, memories, and concerns and parents facilitate this conversation through empathy, curiosity, and receptivity. These conversations often make hidden or unacknowledged themes (e.g., resentment, distrust) more overt and up for discussion rather than ignored or denied. Fonagy, Gyorgy, Jurist, and Target (2005) might refer to these conversations as promoting *mentalization*, where each family member reflects on his or her own inner experience and tries to understand the inner experience of others.

In contrast, *autonomy-promoting conversations* focus on dilemmas or challenges that the adolescent faces in the process of becoming more autonomous. For teaching purposes, we think about three different domains of autonomy promotion: emerging maturity in the home, functioning competently outside the home, and identity formation. We discuss these three levels of autonomy promotion more in depth next.

LEVELS OF AUTONOMY PROMOTION

Emerging Maturity in the Home

Emerging maturity in the home refers to the normative negotiation of autonomy within the family: rules (e.g., curfew), chores, responsibilities, and contributions to family life. When the attachment fabric was fraught with distrust and fear, negotiation of normative adolescent developmental challenges were often used to indirectly express angry feelings about attachment injuries (e.g., "You were never there for me as a child, why should I listen to you now?"). In contrast, when adolescents perceive their parents as available and responsive, they become more willing to negotiate (rather than demand or sabotage) their independence. When adolescents feel respected, listened to, loved, and supported, they are more invested in maintaining the relationship, even if it means making sacrifices (e.g., staying home for Sunday dinner). In fact, we find that if the attachment task resolves some of the relational ruptures of the past, or changes some of the insidious family interactions in the present, adolescents more willingly accept parents' limit setting (if they are developmentally appropriate). Thus, as a result of the attachment task, parents can use a more authoritative parenting style (e.g., balancing warmth and control), and adolescents will become more mature and collaborative participants in the process of negotiating autonomy—a goal-corrected partnership (Bowlby, 1988). However, some adolescents continue to violate their parents' rules. When this occurs, the therapist helps parents talk with adolescents about their expectations and set appropriate boundaries and consequences. When parents are overcontrolling, therapists will usually meet alone with them first to help define age-appropriate rules. This conversation might include psychoeducation about balancing autonomy and attachment and setting limits that support that goal. We remind parents that, ultimately, their word goes, but it is important to let their adolescent have a voice in the conversation.

Therapist: I know today that José wanted to talk with you about some of the rules in the house. How does that sound?

Mother: Fine by me.

Adolescent: Me too.

Therapist: Great! Then I'm going to turn the conversation over to the two of you. José, remember, you need to be honest, stay calm, and talk about your concerns and how you are feeling. Ms. González, remember—hear José out first, use your emotional coaching skills to talk about this. OK—go ahead, José.

Adolescent: I'd like to have a later curfew on the weekends since I'm 16 now.

Mother: Your curfew is the time that it is for a reason—you know that.

Adolescent: See, I knew you wouldn't listen.

Therapist: José, I know this is hard, but try to be patient. Both of you guys are new at this. Ms. González, I know you have reasons for why curfew is 9 p.m., but remember, you want to try to hear José out before deciding on the final rule. Why don't you find out from José why this is so important to him?

Mother: José, why is it so important to you to have a later curfew?

Adolescent: I'd like to be able to hang out with my friends more now that I'm feeling a little better. I think that would be good for me.

Mother: I agree that seeing your friends would be good for you, but it depends which ones.

Adolescent: Mom, you know I stopped hanging out with the ones you don't like! I haven't been in trouble for 2 months. I've been hanging out with Ryan and Lucas [family friends].

Mother: That is true; you've managed to keep out of trouble at school and in the neighborhood. Why do you need your curfew raised though? What can't you do before 9 that you can do after 9?

Therapist: That's a great question, Ms. González.

Adolescent: Well, my friends like to go to 8 o'clock movies, and they've been getting into the local music scene at coffee shops around town. Usually the acts don't start until 8:30 p.m.

Mother: I see, so what time do you think is reasonable?

Adolescent: Midnight.

Mother: No way!

Therapist: Ms. González—why don't you tell José some of your concerns. As you and I discussed, agewise, 9 p.m. on the weekends is a bit early, but I know you've had very good reasons for making José's curfew 9 p.m.

Mother: OK. What I'm worried about is you getting into trouble again and breaking curfew. I know you've been good for the past 2 months, but I worry about you falling back into the group you were getting into trouble with. You need to remember, your curfew used to be later, but you didn't abide by it. And when your curfew was later, that's when you hung out with those kids who you got in trouble with.

Adolescent: I know I broke my curfew before, but I haven't broken the 9 p.m. curfew in the past 2 months. And I already told you: I'm not hanging out with those other guys anymore. Jeez, when are you going to start trusting me again?

Therapist: José, you're doing great—Remember, if you get angry here, this conversation will go nowhere. You brought up a great question, when is your mom going to start trusting you again?

Mother: I have started trusting you again, but it takes time to rebuild all the trust.

Therapist: Ms. González, you are right. I wonder if we can use this situation as an opportunity for José to continue earning back your trust. Maybe there is a compromise that can be made here. Maybe you guys could decide together on a time and then try it out for a trial period?

Mother: Hmmm. I'd be willing to try it, but José if you mess up your curfew is back to 9 p.m.!

Adolescent: I get it, Mom. What time are you willing to go to?

Mother: Let's try 10 p.m. for the next 2 weeks. If you can do that, I'm willing to talk about 11 p.m. But if you're late, the curfew goes back to 9 p.m.

Adolescent: I can live with that.

This excerpt shows how parents and adolescents can use their new skills to negotiate autonomy and emerging maturity. Adolescents need to feel heard. They need to feel as though parents are taking their requests seriously. Parents need to be able to listen to their adolescent and understand his or her perspective. In the end, parents ultimately make the rules, but if they can engage the adolescent in the process and compromise enough, resolutions can be made that are satisfying to both parties.

Competency Outside of the Home

Asserting competency outside the home pertains to dilemmas or challenges the adolescent faces in his or her life with school, work, siblings, or peers. This can include present and future school performance, social involvement (peer conflicts, romantic relationships, bullying), reengaging in activities (e.g., hobbies, finding a job), risk-taking behavior, or functional life goals. Challenges in this domain can contribute to, if not cause, depression. As we have argued throughout this book, family conflict and relational ruptures can cause depression, contribute to depression, or arise as a result of depression. Regardless, depressed adolescents always present with a host of family, school, and social challenges. In ABFT, we aim to repair the fabric of attachment security to remove or reduce these conflicts, as well as increase the parents' capacity to provide a secure base from which the adolescent can solve these problems. That is, we do not resolve family conflicts and then move to individual therapy to address other challenges. Instead, we use the family (as much as possible and appropriate) as the context for problem solving.

Some adolescents struggle with bullying, school failure, body image, negative peer involvement, sexual identity, prejudice/racism, substance use, and risky sexual behavior. Throughout the beginning tasks of therapy, the therapist is listening to the family and noting which topics seem relevant for the adolescent. Challenges that can cause depression from outside the family usually get identified in Tasks I and II when the therapist is gathering information about the adolescent's depression. The case below illustrates our general approach to shifting to the autonomy task. It also exemplifies some of the typical challenges we encounter when selecting the content focus and discussing autonomy development.

Therapist: So we have now been working together for about 10 weeks. I am very impressed with how hard you have all worked to resolve or at least acknowledge some difficult problems from the past. I am not saying that we are done with those topics, but I think you are in a better spot now in regard to these things. Do you agree?

Adolescent: [Shrugs shoulders offering restrained, passive agreement]

Mother: Well, it has not been easy, but I think we have a chance to start some things over and be a better team.

Father: I agree.

Therapist: So we have about 6 weeks left, and I would like to try and sort through some of the other things that are contributing to Sara's depression. OK? [Family members nod in agreement.] Sara, you have said over these many weeks that there were a few things that contributed to you feeling depressed. You mentioned that you worry about school, your weight, being home without your mom, and your relationship with your brother. Which of these topics would you like to start with and talk about today?

Father: I think we should talk about school. . . . You know, she is starting to get behind and that worries me.

Therapist: Can you tell that directly to your daughter?

Mother: Sara, we are both worried about that.

Adolescent: [Rolls eyes]

Therapist: Hmmm. This is hard. School is an important topic. But Sara, what do you think? This is our first time addressing some of these problems. Tell your parents, are you worried about school?

Adolescent: No! [Looking at both parents] You don't know what you're talking about. I am going every day. I got an A on my last test.

Father: So you think that means that school is going well?

Adolescent: It is better than last year.

Therapist: Let's give Sara the benefit of the doubt. [To parents] You are going to an open house this week. Right? So let's say you meet with her teachers and gather a bit more information. And then we can take this on next week. Sara, is that OK?

Adolescent: Sure.

Therapist: You know, this is 11th grade. I know you are still thinking about college. Even going away to college, right?

Adolescent: Yes.

Therapist: So, school has to be your challenge this year, not your parent's problem.

Adolescent: Yes, I really want to get out of the house.

Therapist: I know you do. And your parents want to see you launched. But you are going to need their help.

Mother: Anything we can do, we will. I know we were hard on you and not helpful enough last year. We need to. . . . [Turns to therapist] What did you say last week? We need Sara to teach us how to be helpful to her.

Therapist: Exactly!

Adolescent: [Smiles for the first time in the session] OK . . . ah, well. There is a meeting with my guidance counselor next Tuesday. They said parents could come. [Looks down, a bit embarrassed] It is during school, so you probably cannot come . . .

Mother: Of course I could come [restraining her enthusiasm].

Adolescent: But who will watch the baby?

Mother: Oh, ah, well.

Father: What day did you say it was? Tuesday? I, well, ah, I could go in a bit late that day to the office. I will watch the baby. You go with Sara to that meeting.

Therapist: Very nice!

The therapist is able to block the parents' panic about school, a panic that, the previous year, spiraled into anger, conflict, and disengagement. The therapist also points out that it is also the girl who is worried, not just her parents, making this a problem she is as motivated to solve as her parents. As the parents back up and give the daughter space, the daughter comes forward seeking help.

Therapist: What do you want to talk about today, Sara?

Adolescent: My weight has really been bothering me a lot, maybe that one?

Therapist: Great, Mom, why don't you talk with Sara about her concerns about her weight?

Mother: [Shocked that Sara would invite her to talk about this problem] Ah . . . well . . . ah . . . Sara, what worries you about your weight?

Adolescent: I don't like being overweight. I'm bigger than all the other girls in my class and my clothes are tight. I know I'm supposed to love my body, and all that crap . . . but I don't!

Mother: Sara, you're beautiful!

Therapist: Mom—Remember what we talked about? I know you want to make your daughter feel better—but find out more about her experience.

Mother: Oh . . . ah, yes . . . ah, well, what's that like for you to be around the other girls that you think are smaller?

Adolescent: It makes me really self-conscious.

Mother: Do you want to do something about that?

Therapist: Mom—remember you want to continue to find out about her experience before problem solving.

Mother: Oh right, OK, um, Sara, what does that do to you when you become self-conscious?

Adolescent: It makes me cry.

Mother: So it makes you sad and upset?

Adolescent: Yeah, because I start to worry I'm not good enough and then I start thinking boys aren't going to like me.

Mother: I can see how upsetting this is for you. I know what it is like to struggle with weight.

This excerpt demonstrates many things. First, the therapist must track the process closely. We want the adolescent to begin to take the lead in solving the problems in her life. We want the adolescent to want to solve the problems and ask his or her parents for help. We often joke that the adolescent is now hiring the parent as a consultant and advisor. This puts her in the position of having some control over the parents' type and level of involvement. The parents remain in charge, but the adolescent begins to feel a bit more self-efficacy. Second, the parents must use their new emotion-coaching skills. Even in this problem-solving conversation, parents must be empathic, emotionally attuned, and respectful and use the conversation as a learning experience. In therapy, helping adolescents think about the challenges in their life is as important as solving these challenges.

Sometimes it is the parents who are generating the topics for discussion related to concerns they have about their adolescent. Parents often have many topics of concern that they wish to address with their adolescent—challenges that impact their adolescent's functioning. Areas of concern can vary from being worried about whom the adolescent spends time with and school achievement to substance abuse and risky sexual behavior. If necessary, the therapist will meet individually with the parents to prepare them for this conversation. When parents have expectations that are not developmentally appropriate or are not in line with the adolescent's temperament or abilities, the therapist will provide psychoeducation. The goal is for parents to engage their adolescent in a conversation about their concerns, listen to the adolescent, validate her or his adolescent's experience, and then discuss how to move forward. There may not be resolution to some of these topics, but the ability to have open and productive dialogue better ensures a good outcome in the future.

Therapist: Last week, we discussed Talia's concerns about school. Mr. Brown, I know you said you have concerns that some of her friends really impact her school performance, should we pick up there today?

Adolescent: I guess.

Therapist: OK, Mr. Brown, why don't you tell Talia what your concerns are.

Father: Well, it really has to do mostly with your one friend, Riley. You spend a lot of time at her house and you don't seem to get your work done. Riley's mom doesn't really seem to care about her schoolwork. I don't agree with that. Plus, I don't like the fact that you guys are there alone a lot of the time.

Adolescent: Are you telling me I can't be friends with Riley now? This is just great! She's the one person I feel like I can really talk to, and you're trying to take that away from me.

Father: I'm the parent here, Talia . . .

Therapist: Mr. Brown, you are the parent and ultimately you make the rules, but remember what your goal is here—you want

Talia to be able to concentrate on her work. Try to remember the emotion-coaching skills you used last week with Talia. Maybe you can find out why Riley is so important to Talia.

Father: Uh, OK. . . . Why do you like Riley?

Adolescent: She's the one person that gets me, Dad. When I was going through everything last year, she was the only one that cared and stuck by me for the whole thing! She gets what I'm going through. She's a huge part of why I'm able to walk through the school doors every day; you can't take her away from me!

Father: She's really important to you, I can get that. I don't want to hurt you. I need you to understand though that I need to make sure you're OK and part of that is making sure you are passing school. I don't dislike Riley—I'm just really uncomfortable with you at her house so much.

Adolescent: But, Dad, we don't do anything wrong!

Father: Well, you don't get your work done either though.

Therapist: Talia, can you get what your dad is saying, that he's trying to support you in school and protect you?

Adolescent: I guess, but he won't be protecting me if he takes my friend away.

Father: Listen, I get that Riley is important. But I think we both agree that you want to get the best grades you can so you can get into the environmental science college you have been talking about.

Adolescent: [Nods]

Father: So I would be more comfortable if you guys were at our house after school more often.

Adolescent: Ugh, so you can watch us the whole time?

Father: No, I'll give you guys your space, but I will expect you guys to do your work. If you can get your work done, then great—you guys can see each other every day after school. If you can't, then you'll be limited to the weekends with her.

Therapist: Talia, that seems like a pretty fair offer from your dad. You give him a bit of what he wants (which you want also) and he will give you want you want. Are you willing to give it a shot?

Adolescent: I guess we can try it.

As seen here, sometimes parents and adolescents move toward temporary solutions or preliminary plans that allay the parent's concerns. This leaves the door open for future conversations and adjustment of plans. More important, however, parents and adolescents get practice at productively negotiating the adolescent's autonomy. If parents can show that they are willing to listen to the adolescent's concerns and take them into consideration, they are less likely to encounter strong resistance from their adolescent when they set boundaries and limitations. In this sequence, the father negotiates with the daughter but maintains his expectation that she will succeed (e.g., maturity domain; Baumrind, 1989) and the daughter's own stated long-term goals. This makes the negotiation ultimately about the daughter's autonomy rather than a power struggle over control.

Along with discussing parents' concerns, it is important for parents to help their adolescents become behaviorally activated. From the perspective of behavioral activation (Lewinsohn, Clarke, Rohde, Hops, & Seeley, 1996), we know that experiences of competency and positive experiences can help reduce and buffer against depression. Adolescents who are depressed have difficulty sustaining positive feelings, quickly returning to a more negative mood state (Yap, Allen, & Sheeber, 2007). Therefore, increasing the duration and frequency of positive emotions can help counteract the depressive tendency. Sometimes parents are needed to help the adolescent identify and acquire opportunities for competency. Parents have to know when to be more assertive about these life challenges. We have had parents say, "I want him to get a job, but he is old enough, he should do it on his own." To this we say,

> In an ideal world with a happier child, this might be the right approach. But we want him to be challenged by having a job, not trying to get one. So help him get the position and then we can turn over more responsibility to him about keeping it.

Parents want to include the adolescent in the decision-making process but also want to make sure problems get solved and opportunities get developed.

Behavioral activation is to help adolescents reengage in their social world and activities that had been lost due to depression. Reengaging in the social world can help adolescents increase their self-esteem and sense of competency, which has been shown to buffer against hopelessness, depression, and even suicidal ideation (Cole, Martin, & Powers, 1997). Additionally, reengaging in pleasant or meaningful activities, or engaging in such activities for the first time, has been known to be an effective intervention for those with depression. The therapist should have knowledge about these activities from conversations earlier in the treatment. The therapist will help parents and the adolescent discuss these topics. The therapist may also assist the parent in advocating for their adolescent when necessary.

Therapist: One thing I've been thinking about is how Kim told me she really likes dancing but has not done it in a long time. Maybe it is time to think about this again.

Adolescent: Yeah, I used to dance, but I don't anymore.

Mother: Do you want to dance again?

Adolescent: I don't know.

Mother: Oh, well, OK.

Therapist: Mom, maybe you can find out what she liked about dance.

Mother: Why did you like dance so much?

Adolescent: Well, it was fun and it was actually something I felt I was good at.

Mother: You were great at it!

Adolescent: Thanks. I guess when I dance I don't think about my problems. But it just takes so much energy to do it.

Mother: Hmm. You're right, it does.

Therapist: Mom—maybe you can tell your daughter what you think dance did for her.

Mother: I loved to watch you dance! You look so at peace with yourself. Plus, it's healthy for you and it gets you out with other people.

Adolescent: I guess.

Mother: I think you should do it again.

Adolescent: I missed the window to sign up; it's too late.

Mother: Oh?

Therapist: Mom, I wonder if there is a way you can help her either get into the class or find another class.

Mother: I guess I could, normally she doesn't want my help.

Therapist: Why don't you ask her?

Mother: Would you let me help you?

Adolescent: I guess so. I mean, I don't want my mommy doing everything for me, but I guess it would be good to dance again.

As the excerpt shows, the therapist helps guide this conversation. It's a deeper conversation than merely whether the adolescent wants to do the activity again. It is a conversation about the meaning of the activity as well. Additionally, we see that the adolescent is more open to allowing her mother help her than she has seemingly been in the past.

Identity Formation

At a third level, we think about autonomy-promoting conversations as opportunities to facilitate identity development. Adolescence is a critical time for forming ideas about one's self in relationship to family, peers, community, and culture. These conversations aim for a higher level of reflective thinking, and the adolescents need to have a pretty high level of trust in the parents. Sometimes these issues have to do with normative adolescent challenges: dating, sex, and drugs. Parents may not need to know the specific details of these domains, but they should be able to ask adolescents about their values, worries, and questions. Parents have to tread gently here if they want to keep the lines of communication open. They do not have to pretend they do not have an opinion, but they do have to remain open to hearing the adolescent explore his or her thoughts about these complicated topics. Parents might say,

> Look, I think you know how I feel about drugs and alcohol. I have not kept it a secret. But I am wondering how you feel about it. You do not have to give any details about what is going on, but I do wonder how you think about all this.

When parents take this more open approach, adolescents are more forthcoming about details, thoughts, and worries.

Ethnic, racial, religious, and cultural identity can also be important topics of conversation with many families. Identity formation in adolescence has been shown to influence adolescent well-being and resilience (Arnett, 2000; Martinez & Dukes, 1997). These issues can impact adolescents' sense of belonging and self-efficacy, both in the family and in broader social contexts. Feelings of thwarted belongingness can contribute significantly to feelings of isolation, confusion, depression, and suicidal ideation (Gomez, Miranda, & Polanco, 2011; Joiner & Coyne, 1999; Polanco-Roman & Miranda, 2013). Discussions about racism, sexism, homophobia, and other forms of discrimination can be extremely difficult and emotional even for highly functioning adults. When adolescents are able to use their parents and families as a secure context in which to discuss these issues, they learn that even topics they thought were taboo and very difficult can be safe and gratifying areas to explore with their parents. These conversations help adolescents think about, articulate, and try out different points of views about critical, yet often ignored, challenges to their self-identity.

Therapist: Lita, you have said a few times that sometimes you feel that people stereotype you. Mom, can you find out more from her about what she means by this?

Mother: Sure. I think I might know. But, what did you mean by that, Lita?

Adolescent: I guess we're always hearing about all these statistics, you know? About Latinos and Hispanics and stuff, like about getting pregnant and not finishing school, and sometimes I feel like that's what people will think about me, so I feel, like, motivated to not end up like that. But it also feels unfair that people might think that.

Mother: I think both of those things are right. It is unfair but it's definitely a reality. Do you feel like you have to act a certain way or be a certain way?

Adolescent: Yeah! Like you've always said that we have to leave the "street" in the neighborhood. Like, we watch you act completely different at times. Like, when you get on a work call, your voice totally changes, you sound like you're trying to be like the people at your work.

Mother: Oh, you've said that to me before. That I'm putting on my "White voice." [They both chuckle]

Adolescent: Yeah, but, I really hate it sometimes.

Mother: Why do you hate it?

Adolescent: It feels fake. I mean, I get that it's important and there are boundaries and stuff, but sometimes it just bothers me.

Mother: I understand that. It seems like I'm not completely being myself maybe?

Adolescent: [Nods]

Mother: It has been important for me to learn how to adapt, though. When I started working as a real estate agent and I was working in different neighborhoods, sometimes I felt funny at first. Sometimes I felt like people did not take me seriously. It made me mad sometimes. I felt like I had to fit in with the people I was working with, in order to move up and make it in my business. But even when I talk differently for a work call or something like that, I am still the same at heart. And, I want that for you too. I want you to be proud of who we are and where you come from.

Adolescent: I am, Mom. I mean, it's hard, but I think it's good. I think being Latina makes you stronger. You know you have to work hard for everything, and like, I've heard all the stories from you and Nana and Pop-Pop and how far everybody has come, and I'm proud of our family. But I know there will just be some things that are still not fair.

In this example, mother and daughter broach several topics of importance to ethnic identity development. No firm conclusions or resolutions are made. The mother remains curious about her daughter's thoughts and experiences while providing perspective based on some of her own experiences. Most important, both mother and daughter reported that they have never talked about this before and the daughter found relief in knowing that her mother struggled with some of the same issues.

In other cases, parents and teens have discussed religion and how it will or will not fit into the adolescent's life. In yet another case, parents helped a teen who was homosexual think about what it means to be gay in light of his strong religious beliefs and how to reconcile these two parts of his identity. Task V conversations about identity development help to set the stage for continued healthy and open discussions about sometimes difficult and sensitive topics related to family and individual identity. Adolescents are thinking about and grappling with these issues. Task V conversations open the door for them to use their parents in their explorations of these areas and what they mean to their emerging autonomy and sense of self.

CONDUCTING TASK V

Starting the Task

To start Task V, the therapist may signal an explicit, distinct shift in focus (e.g., "OK, it is Session 10 and we need to begin thinking about school"). In other cases, the transition is gradual, where Task V–like topics begin to seep into attachment-focused conversations. The majority of sessions in this task include both the parent (or parents). During these sessions, family members discuss topics directly with one another, with the therapist becoming increasingly less involved in coaching both parties. Although parents and adolescents are learning to master their new communication skills and negotiate, the therapist encourages, monitors, and supports this process. Therefore, there may be times that the therapist meets alone with individual family members. In general, the autonomy-promoting task focuses more on problem solving. We are returning to the normative family function of negotiating autonomy while maintaining attachment. But we do not lose sight of promoting secure-based relationships. In fact, we are using the process of solving day-to-day problems in order to practice or solidify the families' new interpersonal skills.

Involving the Adolescent in the Conversation

Adolescents should be active participants in the discussion. This needs to be a conversation, not a lecture. If adolescents are not participating, the therapist must help the family figure out why not. This process becomes the content of the discussion: Is the topic not interesting? Does the process feel off-putting (e.g., parents are being a bit demeaning)? Is the adolescent still resistant to working with the parents? If the underlying problem goes back to a more fundamental interpersonal distrust, then the conversation shifts back to a focus on trust and safety. Moving forward to problem solving is very difficult when unspoken feelings and thoughts undermine the family members' level of trust and motivation to cooperate. However, sometimes we overfocus on the process when just moving forward with the content, even in the face of minimal resistance, might create a positive experience of change.

Determining Who Owns the Problems

Is the parent more worried about this issue than the adolescent? If so, why and how can we change that balance? We want adolescents, especially depressed adolescents, to feel some responsibility for and investment in working out these problems. We are trying to challenge the adolescent's tendency for passivity and feeling like a victim. We are challenging the adolescent's conflict avoidance. We have changed (we hope) the environmental pressure that was reinforcing an internal working model of the parents as controlling or indifferent, unresponsive or unavailable. The adolescent has to perceive and trust in this change, and begin to turn inward and challenge themselves rather than (a) continuing to blame the parent or (b) relying on the parent to solve everything. The adolescent's battle to be heard is over. They should no longer be preoccupied with feeling dismissed or misunderstood or undervalued. These barriers should be gone by this point in the therapy. The degree to which these complaints/fears are being used to avoid engaging in the conversation should be challenged, as follows:

> Look, Billy, I am not sure what your hesitation is. Your father is here really trying to be different. I know it will take time to trust him on this, but we have to give him credit for trying so hard. It is time for you to step

up and take some leadership in your life. Get out of the back seat and at least into the front seat, if not the driver's seat. Your parents are not in your way anymore. You can start to make some decisions for yourself and begin to find out who you want to be. They are standing close by if you fall, but they are ready for you to take the lead here! What do you want? What time do you think you should have to come home now that you are 16, and how will you earn their trust on this? Take a chance. Put an offer on the table.

Helping Parents Use Emotion-Coaching Skills

We must help parents find the balance of support and control. Parents must carry forward the emotion-coaching parenting skills they learned in the first few tasks and apply them in more concrete day-to-day problem-solving discussions and discussions about the adolescent's challenges and identity development. During the preparation for attachment tasks, many parents resist emotion-focused parent training. They accuse us of advocating too liberal a parenting approach, where everything is about the adolescent's feelings and with no consequence. Nothing could be further from the truth. We educate parents on how they can both emotion coach and set limits at the same time. Unlike in Task IV, now the focus is not just on having the adolescent learn to express his or herself but also, in many cases, on negotiating and solving some serious problems in the adolescent's life. Therefore, the parent has to find a new balance of support and control. On the one hand, adolescents should increasingly participate, if not take the lead, in these kinds of challenges. Maybe it is time for the adolescent to assume responsibility for his or her homework without the oversight of the parents. Maybe the adolescent should come to the school meeting to discuss reenrolling or scaling back classes to a more reasonable schedule. Maybe the adolescent should complete some job applications without his or her parents' help. Parents may still have to contribute, but adolescents should increasingly assume leadership for life decision and activities. In the normal course of events, adolescents increasingly assume responsibility for making decisions in the various domains of their life. It is unfortunate that there is no clear formula for this balance and it must be tailored to the individual needs of the adolescent, parents, and cultural context of the family.

In determining the balance of support and control, lending assistance and promoting independence, therapists must help parents consider the adolescent's personality traits, temperament, and intellectual and emotional resources and vulnerabilities. For example, gauging the adolescent's intellectual skills and proclivities, parents may need to lower or increase expectations about academic success. Many depressed adolescents find themselves far off the normative high school track and may need to think creatively about how to rebuild this part of their life. Solutions might include repeating a grade, getting a GED, enrolling in community colleges or trade schools, or just working for a year. We do not want to aim low for these youth, but we want realistic goals that will maximize the chance for success.

Parents also need help appreciating the adolescent's temperamental traits. Many depressed adolescents are shy and do not have the confidence to manage some things on their own. For example, one adolescent loved animals and imagined working with them as a career. Her parents recommended that she get a job at the local pet store to gain some experience and some confidence and to have some time out of the house—all good things. But the daughter was too shy to go and put in the application and follow up. The parents, unfortunately, thought that it was an important lesson for her to get the job herself. In the therapy, we helped the daughter articulate how uncomfortable she felt selling herself, given that she had so little belief in her own skills. With their new listening skills, the parents became more empathic about the daughter's challenge rather than dismissive of these feelings. Working out a plan together, the parents became more involved in the job application process; getting the applications, helping her fill it out, doing the follow-up phone call, and taking her to the interview. The daughter got the job and worked in the store for 2 years while she finished high school. So, in this case, the parents had to adjust their expectation of the daughter's independence and provide more initial support than they originally thought would be helpful. However, once in the job, this became a great experience of responsibility and competency for the daughter.

Parents must also consider the adolescent's depression itself. It is unfortunate that depression complicates this progression toward autonomy. Low self-esteem, hopelessness, and social isolation lead to dependency on parents. Depressed adolescents are home more and have less self-directed activities. For many adolescents who are depressed, the collision between their depression-generated dependency on parents and their desire for autonomy and independence from parents can become a source of frustration and anger. For parents, this becomes a no-win, push–pull process. If parents help too much, adolescents complain they are controlling; if they help too little, adolescents feel abandoned. Often, depressed adolescents are confused and unclear about what they want. They may withdraw and refuse help or may become passive and expect parents to take care of everything.

Therapists must help parents be patient with this dilemma. Rather than be frustrated by the adolescent's ambivalence, parents need to understand that negotiating through this is an essential developmental task that is, it is unfortunate, complicated by the depression. Rather than unilaterally solving problems or leaving the child on his or her own to work it out, parents need to help the adolescent understand the dilemma he or she finds himself in.

Parents need to invite the adolescent into these conversations and expect that he or she will take as active a role as possible in sorting out these challenges. These challenges are opportunities for the adolescent to exercise new emerging skills in self-reflection and problem solving. Take, for example, a child enrolling back into school after a month in the psychiatric hospital. Parents can help adolescents think about whether they are capable of going back to school, need to scale back their schedule, need a different school, need home school, or should decide to get a GED. Parents need to help the adolescent think through these options so they feel more like an active partner in planning his or her life. The thinking-through process is therapeutic and developmentally appropriate, even if at the end of this conversation the parent has to make the final decision.

The balancing of support and control also must be considered in the context of the culture and environment of the adolescent. With inner-city families, parents often need to increase their monitoring, exert more control, and expect more from their children. These neighborhoods are often unsafe and have many negative distractions. Given these concerns, what may be considered safe, developmentally appropriate levels of freedom offered to adolescents in the suburbs may expose a child to danger in the city. For instance, with our inner-city families, parents may need to make more clear rules about when to be home, where to go and not to go, and who they can be with. To promote autonomy, these rules need to be formulated and negotiated with the adolescent. We want the adolescent to understand the rationale behind the rules and understand that such rules emerge out of love and protection rather than out of the parents' need for control and obedience. In more dangerous environments, parents may need to make special efforts to help the adolescent find and participate in more-structured activities, like community centers, sports, or after-school activities. The pull of peers and social life is natural and strong in any community and cannot be completely restricted. But respectful negotiation and discussion can make these battles more manageable and good learning opportunities.

THE PROCESS OF TASK V

Models for effective problem solving have been well developed and are included in many parent education manuals (Barkley, 1997; Forehand & Long, 1996; Kazdin, 2000; Patterson, 1975; Robin & Foster, 2002). These models usually consist of several steps: identify problems, generate solutions, pick one solution, make a plan, and evaluate the outcomes. We recommend therapists review these models if they are unfamiliar with them. Here, we outline our approach for conducting a problem-solving or autonomy-promoting conversation.

The Arc of the Conversation

Essentially, we think about a conversation like an arc: a sort of rolling, moving, bending dialogue that has a beginning, a few points along the way, and maybe some tangents. We use these conversations as learning opportunities. We initially want to promote self-reflection and emotional awareness. We therefore begin with exploring feelings, thoughts, meanings, memories, and fears before moving to solutions and behavioral plans. Many of the problems faced by depressed adolescents are multilayered, involving many psychological, interpersonal, and environmental factors. We aim to increase the adolescent's capacity to talk about, explore, and understand these dilemmas through dialogue with his or her parents. We want adolescents to view their parents as safe havens where they come to understand themselves better through parents' guidance, safety, and acceptance. No longer preoccupied with anger or distrust, the adolescent is freer to turn inward and begin to develop more self-awareness. We do not, by any means, want to give the impression that we avoid behavioral change—nothing could be further from the truth. We find, however, that if the adolescent does not feel ownership of the problem, understand at least a bit of the complex landscape that drives the problem, and feel motivated to change it, those behavioral change strategies suggested by the parents slam up against a brick wall of resistance.

So, in our change model, we want the conversation to be as much as possible between the adolescent and the parents. We help as much as we are needed. Sometimes we see that the process is good (parents asking questions, adolescent sharing thoughts and ideas) even though the content is not that important. We let this go, trusting that family members are building some goodwill. We come into the conversation to clarify a point, help keep the conversation on track, and offer some new information. But we keep our eyes on the process and do not get consumed by the content.

In a recent session, the older sister of an adolescent came to support the adolescent in talking about past and current problems. The older sister had always been supportive and protected the younger girl from their mother's chaotic style. Things were much better now, but during the session, the older sister quickly began talking for the adolescent, explaining to the mother how the latter felt about things. The therapist had to politely stop the older sister, appreciate her attempts to protect her younger sister, but then ask the adolescent if she wanted this much help. Initially the adolescent said yes. But after some conversation, we all agreed that the adolescent had to find her own voice and needed to speak up for herself. The older sister continued to be helpful, but by supporting and challenging the adolescent to express her thoughts and feelings to her mother more directly. The content was the same, but the process better supported our goals of adolescent autonomy development.

When the process is good, we can focus on the content and arc of the conversation. We often begin with problem definition. Therapist and parent help the adolescent define specific issues or challenges that he or she would like to resolve (e.g., lose weight, make friends, get back in school, have more privileges at home). With agreement on content, therapists then coach the parents to encourage the adolescent to explore this dilemma. We block parents from jumping in to solve the problem and, instead, help them remain positive, open minded, and curious. Parents should encourage their adolescent's independent thought, honesty, reflective thinking, and acceptance of difficult and contradictory emotions; validate their adolescent's experience; and offer support. Parents need to make the adolescent the center of the conversation, empowering him or her to have a voice, a sense of self, and a sense of agency. Meanwhile, adolescents are expected to be honest, self-reflective, open-minded, and regulate their emotions.

After adolescents have taken the lead, have had their say, have felt understood, and have a better understanding of themselves, they will become more open to listening to their parents' perspectives and thoughts. This cannot suddenly turn into a lecture, criticisms, or offerings of a resolution. All of these pitfalls close down conversation. We encourage parents to be honest about their perspective but to remain open-minded:

> Look, it is no secret that I do not like the boy you are dating. But I cannot make these choices for you any longer. But can I just share a few of my concerns? Not to criticize or control you. But I am just curious how you see these things . . .

These are not easy moments in a conversation. Parents might be angry, scared, or hurt, but it is this kind of respectful exchange of ideas that keeps the adolescent engaged. We often, for example, say to a parent:

> Look, your daughter is no longer 6. She is not going to be cooperative just because you say so. It is more give and take now. This is how you would talk to a friend or a coworker. You cannot just tell them what to do without some kind of negotiation or explanation. If you cannot begin to see your adolescent as a young adult, to honor her emerging sense of self, she will not listen to you. You are still the parent and still in charge, but the process of negotiation has to be different.

The arc keeps bending, and the conversation moves to resolution. Once we feel we have some investment from the adolescent in solving the issue and some understanding of the meaning, fears, and hopes from the adolescent, then we can begin to negotiate some solutions, some behavioral expectation, some plan. Even here, the parent should begin by asking the adolescent what he or she would like to be different, what changes he or she is willing to make. With the foundation of respect in place, the parent can then make a counteroffer or express his or her concerns about the adolescent's plan, and recommend some modifications:

> Look, I know you would rather do home schooling, but I just feel that is not the best option for you. I worry you will feel isolated and even more disconnected from your friends. Maybe we could meet with the school counselor and see what options are possible.

At this point in the conversation, the parent is able to have a say. If done with respect and empathy, the parent can even take a stand that will not anger the adolescent.

> Look, I can see how much you like this boy, and how important he is to you. But he is 19 [adolescent is 14], and I just cannot accept that kind of relationship for you. I know you will be mad at me, but I would not be a good mother if I let this go on.

Here, the arc of the conversation ends with a specified outcome that will lead to a plan for behavioral change. But this plan stands on the foundation of respect and understanding.

The arc does not always end in behavioral change. In fact, in many conversations the parent needs to help the adolescent explore and understand options but leave the ultimate resolution up to the adolescent. Sometimes the adolescent will want the parents to make the decision; sometimes the parents will decide; sometimes they will let the adolescent struggle with taking responsibility for themselves; and sometimes the conversation is not about something that requires a decision or a conclusion but that just involves the sharing of thoughts and feelings in a manner that helps the adolescent learn more about himself or herself. The path to follow is indicated by the content of the conversation.

OTHER CONTENT AREAS

Bringing New People Into the Therapy Process

During this task, we may also consider and begin to focus on other family relationships that may be impacted by, or contribute to, the adolescent's depression. These could include nonparticipating parents, siblings, romantic partners, other family members, or other supportive people in the adolescent's life: for example, a sibling with whom the adolescent has a long-standing conflict or who has struggled with the parents in similar ways, a grandparent who is willing to be more of a resource but has been in conflict with the parents, or a friend who helps the adolescent through difficult times but has no relationships with the parents. We look into the ecology of the adolescent's life and think with him or her and the parents together about who may be impacting the adolescent's depression and/or who could be a resource in these dark and troubled times: Can they come to the treatment? Should they come to the treatment? Are they willing to come to the treatment? These are questions to reflect on with the family, and not everyone will agree on these choices. For example, a parent may want a sibling to attend, against the wishes of the adolescent, or the therapist may want the disengaged father to come, against the wishes of the mother. These complicated decisions are not a barrier to the treatment–they *are* the treatment. Uncovering and understanding these barriers can be illuminating and productive.

As a general framework and recognizing that each case may present with its own unique circumstances, we approach this treatment task in the following way. Once we decide who should attend and what to work on, we think about preparing for these meetings much like we prepared for the attachment task. Our first move is to think about who should invite the person to the treatment: the parent, the therapist, or the adolescent. Then, we often set up a meeting alone with that person or with the parents if that seems appropriate (e.g., mother and older sibling). In the initial meeting with the new participant, we find ourselves combining elements of Task I (relational reframing) and Task II (alliance building). Therefore, we initially spend time joining with the new person and getting to understand the context of his or her life. Then we try to assess his or her understanding of the adolescent and the depression. We then turn to his or her contribution to the depression and other problems. This obviously can become complicated, especially if the visitor feels blamed. So, we go slowly, increase our empathy and admiration that they came to the meeting, and highlight the visitor's good intentions even if they are not working so well. Sometimes we might even do some intergenerational work, to help the visitor get in touch with his or her own attachment longings so he or she can be more empathic toward the adolescent. Who the visitor is and why he or she was invited can lead us down multiple pathways in this conversation, far too complex for us to fully explore in this chapter. But we aim to generate the visitor's empathy for the adolescent and desire for reconnecting with the adolescent or helping the adolescent work through some of his or her challenges. If we get some approximation of this goal, we begin to talk about setting up a meeting. As in Task II, we assure the visitor that we will protect him or her if the session becomes uncomfortable. We assure the visitor that we are not interested in him or her being yelled at or criticized but that we want an opportunity to open up an honest, direct conversation about issues that get in the way of the visitor being a better resource to the adolescent.

In one case, the mother pushed to have an older sibling (Jesse, 17) attend the treatment to help resolve some differences with her sister. This was a particularly complicated case in which the depressed adolescent (Dana, 14) had been sexually molested by the older sister's friend (2 years before coming to our clinic). The depressed adolescent and mother reported the assault, and the boy arrested in the case was in and out of trial during our work with the family. The depressed adolescent felt that the sister was more protective of the boyfriend than of her, and in fact thought the sister still did not believe the assault had really taken place.

In Week 12 of the treatment, we met alone with the mother to plan the next few sessions. We wanted her to take the lead on this process, hoping that this would further internalize her new parenting skills. We helped the mother understand that she would have to make everyone feel safe, understood, and supported. She would need to monitor the conversation to make sure everyone felt heard and that the most difficult issues got on the table. To some extent, the mother was becoming the therapist who would facilitate an attachment task between the two sisters. We certainly would be there to help, but as much as possible, we wanted the mother to take the lead. We then had the mother and older sister in for a session. The older sister was worried about the adolescent but did think she was being a bit dramatic and histrionic over the whole thing: "The assault was not that bad." Both the mother and therapist were surprised at this cavalier attitude. The therapist encouraged the mother to explore the sister's attitude. The mother used her emotion coaching skills to discover that the girl's comment was really a defensive strategy. The sister herself had a lot of anger toward the adolescent over the sexual assault because she lost all of her own friends after the arrest. The more the mother offered validation and empathy, the more the sister was able to express sorrow for her younger sister. She acknowledged she did feel bad for what happened but that it was hard to get past her own anger about the fallout that resulted between her and her friends. With this new understanding of the sister's perspective and the softening of the sister's affect, the therapist felt comfortable bringing her into the session with the adolescent.

Therapist: Jesse, thank you for joining us today. We know that you and your sister have not been getting along for a while now and it is upsetting to both of you. It is also no secret that these problems got worse after Dana reported that she was raped by one of your friends. So we all agreed that getting together to talk about these things might be good for everyone. I think mom wants to lead this discussion, so I will turn this over to her now.

Mother: OK, I'll do my best here. Dana, can you tell your sister what has been making you so upset?

Adolescent: Um, I guess it seems like you didn't believe me when I told Mom about the rape, and I feel like you're blaming me for everything that happened afterwards with your friends and everything.

Sibling: How many times do I have to tell you, I did believe you, but you don't understand how it has been for me?

Mother: Jesse, you'll get your chance to say your part. Can you try to listen to your sister first?

Sibling: I guess, but I don't know what you want me to do here, Mom. We've been through this a million times.

Mother: Ask Dana what it was like for her when she felt you didn't believe her.

Sibling: [Sarcastically] Dana, what was it like for you?

Adolescent: It made me feel really alone! I mean, I know I've messed up before, but to think my own sister didn't believe me, that you chose your boyfriend's friend over me, you don't know . . . it crushed me.

Sibling: But I DID believe you!

Adolescent: You sure have a funny way of showing it!

Therapist: Mom, maybe you can have Jesse ask Dana why Dana thinks she didn't believe her?

Mother: Thanks, yes! Jesse—ask Dana why she doesn't think you didn't believe her.

Sibling: So, Dana, why?

Adolescent: Well, you kept asking me so many questions again and again. It seemed like you were trying to trip me up. You were grilling me, it seemed like you were accusing me of lying or doing something wrong.

Sibling: [Starts crying]

Mother: What's going on, Jesse?

Sibling: I can't believe that's what you thought! I was asking so many questions because I was in shock! I couldn't believe that you could be hurt with me in the house. I feel so guilty that I didn't know, that I didn't know more. That's why I asked so many questions.

Adolescent: I had no idea. [Begins crying]

This case demonstrates the value of bringing in other family members to address big or little issues that may be fueling the depression and thwarting the recovery. In this case, the mother assumed some leadership in setting this up and facilitating the conversation. Her success increased her sense of competency and authority in the family. Were this a divorced father we were bringing into the session, the mother could not assume this role and would likely not attend the session at all (again, depending on the relationships, issues, and logistics). Once again, as throughout this entire therapy model, clinical judgment is needed in determining how one implements the principles.

Mobilizing Other Mental Health Services

At some point during therapy, during either Task I or II or Task V, it may become clear that for some adolescents, other services are needed as well. For instance, some adolescents may have severe anxiety, substance dependency, or posttraumatic stress that requires more systematic intervention than the parents can offer. Some adolescents may benefit from additional therapy such as cognitive–behavioral therapy, exposure therapy, rehabilitation, or dialectical behavioral therapy. We see the family treatment as laying the foundation for the individual therapy. It both removes the family tension from the recovery equation and increases the parents' potential to be a resource to the adolescent. In addition, this is often the time when individual or couples therapy for the parents may also be discussed.

Discussing Attachment Issues as They Reemerge

Given that the attachment issues that inhibited parents from being a secure base for their adolescent are usually long-standing, it is typical during Task V to see a reemergence of some of the attachment issues discussed in Task IV. If attachment issues reemerge, therapists should focus on them explicitly or as they pertain to the autonomy issues. Unresolved attachment issues will inhibit movement toward autonomy. The therapist has to be sensitive and flexible about how he or she moves back and forth between attachment and autonomy themes.

Discussing How the Family Will Maintain Gains Posttreatment

When termination of therapy is approaching, the therapist may direct the family to discuss the gains they have made. What has each person changed about themselves to contribute to the interpersonal changes? What do they think others have done to support these changes? This type of self-reflection helps solidify the treatment gains. The therapist might also invite the family to discuss how they would like their relationship to be moving forward. This helps family members create a shared vision of the future. The therapist helps the family discuss their fears related to reverting to old behaviors and their hopes for the future. When all fears have been discussed, the therapist encourages proactive problem solving regarding what to do if someone begins reverting to old behaviors. He or she makes the family stick with problem solving until all family members acknowledge their comfort with the plan.

Discussing Termination

Once the family has a plan for how they will move forward, the therapist intentionally engages them in a conversation regarding termination. This includes a discussion about how the family feels about ending this therapy. The therapist thoroughly explores all family members' feelings and thoughts. We find this conversation to be especially important when conducting this work, as ABFT is a deeply experiential, emotion-focused therapy leading to strong bonds with the therapist. The therapist also provides the family with feedback about their progress over the course of treatment and has them reflect on the comments made by the therapist. Often, as they start feeling better, family members forget about the amount of progress they have made. This is another opportunity to help the family reflect on the positive changes that they have made.

CONCLUSION

In Task V, families shift attention to address the adolescent's developmental challenges, which can involve promoting maturity in the home, competency outside of the home, and identity formation issues. By involving both the adolescent and the parents in these conversations and helping the parents use emotion-coaching skills, ABFT therapists help strengthen secure-base interactions between the adolescent and parents. This develops or reinforces the family members' new, more positive internal working models of self and other. Task V also provides an opportunity for family members to practice new interpersonal skills. At this point, the therapist may also introduce new people into the therapy process or mobilize other mental health services. Toward the end of treatment, the therapist addresses termination issues. Chapter 8 applies the principles of the preceding chapters to show the entire arc of treatment for one ABFT family.

8

CASE STUDY

In this chapter, we present a case study.[1] Josh, a 17-year-old boy in the 11th grade, was referred because he had been depressed for several years and was recently kicked out of his academically competitive magnet school because of poor performance and disruptive behavior. (Guy S. Diamond was the therapist.)

TASK I: RELATIONAL REFRAME

At the intake, Josh came with his mother and father. Josh's 10-year-old sister did not attend the session. The family was friendly, but the tension between the parents was obvious. I spent some time learning about each person, getting the general context of their lives, and looking for strengths.

[1]All identifying information has been changed to protect the family's identity.

http://dx.doi.org/10.1037/14296-009
Attachment-Based Family Therapy for Depressed Adolescents, by G. S. Diamond, G. M. Diamond, and S. A. Levy

I learned that Josh had few friends and fewer hobbies, which was unfortunate. He was, however, clearly very smart and had a remarkably good understanding of current electoral politics. I saw a glimpse of pride in his father's face as his son gave me an analysis of the current presidential race. The mother grew up in Philadelphia, Pennsylvania, and the father grew up in Washington, DC. The maternal grandparents were still alive and lived in downtown Philadelphia. They provided some financial help at times but did not offer the parents any emotional support, nor were they emotionally invested in the grandchildren. The paternal grandmother had passed away when the father was an adolescent, and the paternal grandfather was quite old now and living in a retirement home. Neither parent was very religious. The mother had a large circle of friends that frequently kept her busy after work. The father, to the mother's obvious disdain, was less social and spent his free time watching TV. He had often wanted to get involved in local politics but reported that he felt obligated to be at home with the children (a jab at his wife, who was rarely home for dinner). The tension between the parents was so thick it was hard to remain focused on strengths, so I moved quickly to problem definition.

Josh had a typical early childhood, with a slightly irritable temperament. Once he started school, his high degree of intelligence became apparent, and he excelled in math and reading. By the third grade, attention and organizational problems began to emerge. In the seventh grade, Josh had a severe depressive episode. This lasted for several months, causing him to miss a lot of school and lose touch with his small peer group. Meanwhile, he got further behind in school and consequently began to lose interest in academics. Eventually, poor performance and lack of motivation led to his being expelled from his academically competitive magnet school, and he now attended regular public school. Outside of school, Josh spent most of his time at home playing computer games, staying up very late, overeating, and isolating himself from friends. He presented in treatment as very reserved, withdrawn, and angry.

Both parents were in their mid-40s, educated, and engaging but overweight and underachievers. The father graduated from the University of Maryland with a degree in computer science and worked as an assistant supervisor of technology at an advertising firm for 20 years. He reported having his own history of mild depression that plagued him off and on through adolescence and young adulthood. He was laid off a year ago and eventually took a similar position at a publishing house, but with less pay and leadership responsibilities. This midlife setback brought on a more severe depression, and he spent the first 6 months of unemployment watching TV.

The mother was a self-employed event coordinator. She was proud of her work, but it was part-time and unreliable. She went to Pennsylvania State University, where she spent more time socializing than studying. The couple met after college, married within a year, and gave birth to Josh a year later. At that point, the mother decided to not work for a few years. The parents reported that the marriage had been a struggle from the beginning. Around the same time that Josh started having difficulty in the third grade, his parents separated but then got back together when the mother found out she was pregnant with their daughter. Since the father's recent depression and unemployment, the mother had become unhappier and again had begun talking about divorce. Josh knew about these circumstances but did not know whether his parents were going to follow through with the divorce.

Josh had been in therapy in the fourth grade and then again in the seventh grade. The therapy was mostly supportive but included social skills training for Josh and limited parent involvement. He had been put on attention-deficit/hyperactivity disorder medicine in fourth grade, but it did not seem to help. He had not been on any medicine since. A year ago, they saw a psychiatrist for a medication consultation, but the mother did not like the psychiatrist, so the family never went back. The father had some successful therapy in his 20s but had not been in therapy or on medication for 20 years. He had educated himself about medication and clinical trials and interpreted the literature to say that the benefits were minimal, if not mere placebo. On the basis of the mother's own negative experience with therapy, she was suspicious of most mental health services. She had had a complicated childhood and still struggled with issues with her own parents. She also was skeptical about medication and refused to take it herself, even though her mood was labile and her depression was severe at times.

The history of this family was very complicated and painful. I decided I would need to explore it further in the individual sessions with the parents. In the meantime, I turned to the reframing process: I began to explore whether Josh could use his parents as a resource in sorting out his depression and school problems. The parents immediately disagreed about who was the better and more helpful parent. The father accused the mother of being emotionally erratic and unavailable, and the mother blamed the father for being depressed and unmotivated, and thus a bad role model for his son. As they argued, Josh faded into the background and became more withdrawn from the conversation. I had to interrupt the parents and reach into Josh's growing darkness.

Therapist: Josh, you seem to be drifting away. Does their arguing upset you?

Adolescent: [Surprised] What? No . . . I don't even pay attention. . . . They can fight all they want.

Therapist: So you are just indifferent about it?

Adolescent: Sure, you have to be. They should just get divorced. That would make them both happy.

Mother and Father: [Listening, with a bit of shame and sadness]

Therapist: Do they know how you feel about all this arguing?

Adolescent: Sure. They know I hate it.

Therapist: [Blocks parents' attempts to defend themselves] They know because you tell them or because they just see how you react?

Adolescent: [Shrugs as he briefly checks out his parents' reaction to this conversation] I just ignore them.

Therapist: I wish you could, but I worry that it is impossible. You live there. You hear it. You see it.

Adolescent: Yeah. I suppose. But it has always been that way. So what is the difference?

Therapist: [Turns to the parents] How do you think he feels about your arguing?

Father: [Seems a bit defensive] Sure . . . I see it in his face. I know he does not like when his mother and I fight. But he has to understand it is not about him. We love him.

Mother: I don't know. He never says anything about it.

Therapist: Really? So he keeps his feelings to himself.

Mother: All the time. Just stays in his room.

Therapist: So, this is my concern. [Turns to Josh] I think you have been pretty unhappy lately, in fact, for a long time. You have been depressed, having problems with school, feeling a bit isolated. Right?

Adolescent [Suspicious] I suppose. OK, yes.

Therapist: What worries me is that you have no one to turn to for help, especially that you cannot turn to your parents for help.

Adolescent: What do I need them for? They can't help me.

Therapist: That's exactly my point. You feel they cannot help you. Why is that?

Adolescent: [Looks uncomfortable] It would not help. And besides, Mom is never around and Dad is too . . . ah . . . busy.

Therapist: Oh, so you feel like they are not available even if you wanted them.

Adolescent: I did not say that. You said that.

Therapist: Mr. and Mrs. Stern, what do you think about that? Did you know that Josh feels you are not there for him?

Mother: I don't know how he could say that.

Adolescent: [Pointing at therapist] I did not say that, he did.

Mother: I mean, we always ask him how he feels and what he needs.

Father: Yes. I am home every night . . . he can come to me.

Therapist: But he doesn't. He does not come to you. Why not? [Silence in the room] Can you ask him?

Mother: Josh, why don't you come to us for help?

Adolescent: [Looking angry] I told you. I do not want your help. And even if I did, you are never home and Dad is always in his room.

Mother: That is not true. That is just what your father keeps saying.

Father: It is true and we all know it. Even the last few nights . . .

Therapist: Look. Look. Mr. and Mrs. Stern. If you want to understand Josh's experience, you have to be more curious about how he is thinking and feeling. Even if you do not agree, we all like to be heard, right? We like to have our perspective understood, right? [Parents agree and calm down.] Why don't you ask Josh what is it is like to think that no one is available.

Mother: Um, Josh, what is it like?

Adolescent: What do you think it is like? It sucks.

Mother: I don't understand why you haven't told us that before.

Father: How could he, you're never home!

Mother: That's not true!

Therapist: Josh, I wonder if what is happening now is part of the problem. That you might start to talk and then they start to argue?

Adolescent: Sure. It happens all the time.

Therapist: So that might also make it hard to go to them for help?

Adolescent: Sure, I guess. [Turns away to hide his tears and rage]

Therapist: You know, there is no doubt a lot more to understand about all of this, but maybe we can do that later. What

I wonder [turns to the parents], is if the two of you wish Josh would come to you for advice and comfort?

Mother: Well, of course. He knows he can come to me.

Therapist: But he does not. So what I am asking you is if you would like him to.

Mother: Sure!

Father: Yes, of course!

Adolescent: [Remains silent; does not react]

Therapist: [Turns to the parents again] I wonder if Josh knows how much you miss him. He is now 17, getting ready to leave home in a year, has been pretty depressed and withdrawn. It seems that you are all not as close as you used to be. [The mother gets teary; the father, silent; Josh, annoyed.]

Mother: Of course I am going to miss you.

Therapist: I know that. But do you miss him now? Do you wish that you were closer now?

Mother: [To therapist] Josh knows I love him and would do anything for him.

Therapist: Mrs. Stern, can you turn to Josh and tell him that?

Mother: [Turns to Josh, who looks up in anticipation] Josh, you know how much I love you. And that I will miss you deeply when you leave.

Therapist: [Coaches mother] . . . and that you miss him now.

Mother: Yes, yes, I do miss you now. Neither Daddy nor I like to see you so lonely.

Father: [Hands mother a tissue]

Therapist: What about you, Mr. Stern. Do you miss Josh?

Father: [Uncomfortably joking] Sure . . . sure I miss beating him on the basketball court. Now he is so big . . .

Mother: John . . . can you ever be serious?

Therapist: Mrs. Stern, please.

Father: No, all kidding aside, I will miss you when you graduate. [Reaches out and puts hand on Josh's leg] Really, I am so proud of you. We both are.

Therapist: [Turns to Josh] What do you think of what they are saying, Josh?

Adolescent: [Shrugs his shoulders]

Therapist: If it were possible, do you think you would like to feel closer to your parents again, before you leave home?

Adolescent: [Looks down, looks uncomfortable, mumbles] Sure, I guess.

Therapist: [Lets the tender silence linger for a few moments] Good. Look, this is what I want to do. I want to help Josh feel connected to the two of you again. I know there are some difficult things we might have to sort through, but I think there is enough love and strength to accomplish this. We find that when adolescents, even those as old as Josh, feel connected to their parents, that the depression is easier to manage and overcome. So can we make this the first goal of our therapy: finding out what is getting in the way of love in this family and helping to revive it? [Everyone gives some kind of agreement.]

TASK II: ADOLESCENT ALLIANCE

The following week, I met with Josh alone for Session 2 with the goals of building a bond, getting agreement on the goal of therapy, and then building some skills that would prepare him for a conversation with his parents, if he would agree to have it. I began the session by checking in on his thoughts about the first session. He was a bit indifferent about it and still not sure if he wanted a better relationship with his parents. I did not push the issue right then but did acknowledge his ambivalence, and we agreed to talk about it more later in the session. The conversation then turned to hearing more about his interests, areas of competency, peer group relations, hopes, and dreams.

For all his intelligence, Josh had not really become curious about the world around him. He did not like sports, had no real hobbies, and had few friends. He did fancy himself becoming a journalist, given that he was interested in politics. Even he could laugh at the irony that he was so isolated but interested in the workings of the world. It was the first self-reflective moment I saw in him where he had some perspective and humor about himself and his problems. I lingered a bit in his dreams about journalism. He used to assume he would go to college and then hoped to move to Washington, DC, to look for a newspaper job. His ambitious vision of himself was a contrast to the sullen, angry, and withdrawn adolescent I had met in the first session. I asked if his parents knew about these plans, and again, he just shrugged his shoulders. Josh said he talked with his dad about this long ago but was not sure if his dad remembered.

We also talked about his first girlfriend and how drinking beer at parties helped him be more outgoing. I acknowledged how depressed and/or anxious youth often use alcohol to feel less inhibited, but I did not make this a focus of our conversation. At this moment in the therapy, I wanted Josh to feel free to talk about anything and not feel judged by me. After about 20 minutes of this conversation, I thanked him for talking about himself and praised him for his insights and sensitivity.

I then focused the conversation on his depression and family conflicts. We talked about his depression and how it had taken over his life. He admitted that it had been more frustrating than he revealed in the first session. He saw his friends succeed easily in things like school or sports, things that now seem so hard for him. He clearly was unhappy about being depressed and felt helpless to change it. We then began to discuss his parents and how his relationship with them influenced his depression. At first, he was guarded and dismissive, claiming they were not important to him and that he did not even think about them. I observed his mood change and watched him disengage. To circumvent his resistance, I asked for more facts and details, trying to stay away from feelings. He began to talk about his parents' arguments. As he offered more details and got more into the stories, more emotions emerged. When he was young, he remembered feeling scared. He did not know if the fights would end, someone would get hurt, or his parents would divorce. As he got older, he became more angry and resentful. He felt closer to his mother but hated how she belittled and berated his father. He felt protective of his father but angry at his emotional distance and sarcasm. He often found himself in the middle, trying to defend someone or distract them from fighting. Eventually he just gave up and withdrew, feeling the situation was hopeless. In the past few years, he often wished they would get it over with and divorce.

As we talked further, I was able to identify and amplify his feelings of disappointment and sadness that accompanied the anger. For Josh, it seemed that both anger and sadness were primary, legitimate feelings that he attempted to avoid and ignore. He had angry outbursts, but usually over behavioral disagreements. His anger at his parents, and certainly his sadness, had hardly been acknowledged by him and certainly never expressed or acknowledged by his parents. He was not sure he agreed that these problems made him depressed, but he agreed that his anger at his parents was causing him a lot of stress that maybe was affecting him at school.

The conversation then turned to the therapy goal: talking to his parents about these issues. At first he was vehemently opposed to the idea. He did not think it would help, arguing that he was almost out of the house anyway. I explored whether he worried that his honesty would make things worse or upset his parents. He eventually said he worried that if he made trouble, his parents might divorce. I took a deep breath and empathized with his dilemma:

"That is a big burden to carry; no wonder you feel depressed." Josh brushed it off, but I challenged his problem-solving strategy and began to talk about the consequences of not speaking up, of not getting these things off his chest. I reminded him of how unhappy he was and how worried he was that his dreams for his future were slipping away. I also expressed my worry that some of these family problems were in fact contributing to his depression. I said, "You are clearly very angry at them, but you hold it all in, and I worry that it is eating you up." He tentatively agreed that this might be true. As we developed that thought, I added that maybe he did not have to carry that burden, that holding on to all this anger actually made him more embroiled (preoccupied) with his parent's problems. Maybe if he could get some of these things off his chest, he might be more freed up to focus on his own life. This theme seemed to resonate with him better than the theme of getting closer to his parents. He agreed that things needed to change but felt he did not know what to do. I praised him for his maturity and insight about the situation. I then asked him if he thought his parents loved him. He was surprised by the question but assured me that they did and would show it more if he let them. I agreed and said I thought they would do anything to help him feel better. Josh agreed but still felt confused. I then said that I thought he was using all his life energy to hold back his anger and his parents knew it. I went on to say that I thought it was essential to get these feelings off his chest and that I believed his parents would be willing to listen to him, if they thought it would help him. He responded with ambivalence but had a hard time disagreeing. He had agreed with all the premises of the argument and now could not ignore the conclusion. Still, Josh resisted and said he would think about it. I empathized with his hesitation and agreed that he should think about it a bit and that we would meet again to talk about it.

TASK III: PARENT ALLIANCE

Given the conflict between the parents, I decided to meet with each parent alone and then see them together. This would give me a chance to understand each of them without being constantly drawn in by the conflicts between them. It also seemed that neither would allow themselves to be very vulnerable in the presence of the other. The father was busy that next week, so I started with the mother.

Session 3 was with the mother. The marital stress was so pervasive and such a dominant theme that it was hard not to start with that topic. The mother quickly launched into a diatribe telling me about her years of unhappiness in the marriage. She complained that her husband was depressed, withdrawn, critical, and lifeless. She told me how she had wanted to leave him years ago but then got pregnant with their daughter. Although she loved her daughter, she felt trapped into staying in the marriage. As the story unfolded, she also talked about a few episodes of infidelity but swore it was always short lived and that her husband never knew. She also discussed her drinking, which she said was not a problem but was at times excessive. I listened, empathized, and tried to see whether she could recognize ways in which she contributed to the unsatisfying marriage. She could respond with a few comments, but the topic was so charged for her that it was hard for her to step back and have any perspective on the situation. She felt like a victim and a prisoner.

I easily could have let her rant for the entire hour; no doubt she would need a lot of that before she could develop a more complex understanding of her marriage. But I decided to move the conversation forward and see whether there were other doorways that might give me access to a softer, more reflective self. I punctuated her pain, anger, and frustration and then asked if I could ask her about some other issues. Not looking to make a huge leap in topic, I asked her if she had any sense of how the marriage affected her parenting and the children.

She nearly burst into tears, expressing deep remorse and guilt. She described feeling like a failure as a mother and lacking the skills to parent. She said that she was never loved as a child and, consequently, felt she did not know how to love her own children. I empathically noted that comment and promised to get back to it, but I wanted to finish these thoughts about how the marriage has affected the kids. The mother was remarkably honest with herself about this and admitted there was little warmth between the parents.

She said she wanted to be a good mother but feeling trapped and angry about the marriage made it difficult. I reflected to her that Josh did feel like he was close to her and that she was someone he could come talk to at times. Mother smiled and agreed but felt that that kind of connection had faded long ago. She was a bit naive about how upset Josh was about the marital problems. She knew he was upset but figured he was not that aware of the fighting most of the time. She said that she knew she could be a bit prickly at times but that she has a soft side and could share that with the kids. She also said that the kids had a much better childhood than she did so she was happy about that. This reference to her childhood seemed a good time to move in that direction.

The mother's childhood was horrific. Her mother was depressed and passive. Her father worked three jobs to support the family but when home was an abusive alcoholic who used extreme physical punishment with the children. Josh's mother was the good child, did very well in school, and learned to be independent early on in life. This included expecting very little emotional support from her parents. She said she learned to cope from her father: work so hard you have no time for anything else and be emotionally cold and harsh so no one can hurt you. As we tried to detail her memories of these attachment failures, the mother had difficulty remembering ever expecting any love from her parents, making it hard to access her grief or sadness about not getting it. I asked her to remember when she was 8, before she became more defended and independent. She silently shook her head, and then started to cry. When I asked what she was feeling, she said, "I cannot remember wanting her love. I was already dead inside." I nearly cried myself, feeling how lonely and abandoned this mother must have felt, then and now. I punctuated her pain, her sorrow, and the tragic lack of love in her life. On her own, the mother made the link between this deprived emotional upbringing and picking a husband who was depressed and withdrawn. But this brought back her anger and frustration. Wanting to block the anger, I asked her again about her childhood. She told me she worked hard at school and tried to help around the house, but it never made a difference. Mother fought back her tears. I empathized deeply with her attempts to win love and how unfair it was for her to feel she had to earn it. At this point, I felt the mother has sufficiently accessed her own grief and loneliness to empathize with her son's grief and loneliness. I always feel the tension of wanting to stay "down there" longer, but I also want to use these painful memories to help a parent begin to better understand their child.

The timing felt right, so I took the next step, which was beginning to link her experience to her son's experience. "You know, each person has their own experience in life, but I wonder if your son struggles with some of the same things that you did?" She was caught off guard and was a bit tentative, but this mother was obviously psychologically minded, when not consumed by her intense anger. After a moment, she again began to tear up, claiming that she had always said to herself that she would "make things different for her children." At this moment, she realized she had not:

> I am so angry at myself; I have become cold and harsh just like my mother. My husband hates me, and sometimes I cannot blame him. I am so critical of him. I can see why Josh has pulled away from me and protects his father. It is just what I did with my parents.

The conversation continued by exploring the parallels between her deprived childhood and how Josh felt isolated and alone at times. We certainly agreed that the mother's childhood had been more frightening and unstable, but that despite the differences, she also could see how Josh felt alone and felt angry about the marital problems. For these few minutes, the mother was honest and self-reflective. She was able to appreciate Josh's predicament without feeling defensive or dismissive. She could rise above her own emotional reactivity and take Josh's perspective, if only momentarily.

As the conversation evolved, I tried to evoke some sense of urgency and competence and hopefulness in the mother. I talked about how, even though she had not been well loved as a child, she could break this intergenerational legacy and be there for Josh in a way that her mother had not been there for her. The mother protested that it was too late, that Josh did not need, nor want, that kind of love from her. He was a young man. I countered this by saying that he may not need her to mother him like he did when he was 6 but that he still longed to be understood and nurtured in different ways now. I talked about how Josh might feel as angry and lonely as she had and, like her, did not feel entitled or safe enough to express any of those feelings: "And it is eating him up just like it did to you." My goal at that moment was not to win her over or get her to sign on to trying anything new, just to have her think about what I was saying. I told her that I believed in her and her love for her son and that she could do for him what her parents failed to do for her. The mother brushed off my compliment but welcomed my belief in her. I was not asking her to change the past but to try to acknowledge what Josh was going through in the present: "Imagine if your parents had even once sat down with you and asked how you were feeling about all this. You might not have had to carry around such deep resentment all your life." The mother remained silent but began to understand what I was asking of her. We talked this through a bit more, and as I ended the session I asked her to just think about this and we would return to this in our next meeting.

TASK II: ADOLESCENT ALLIANCE (CONTINUED)

In Session 4, I met with Josh alone again. We initially talked about some problems he was having at school and with friends. His few friends were starting to use more drugs and he was feeling the need to pull away from them, but this left him more isolated. We did some problem solving and then explored whether his parents could be helpful in working this out. He scoffed at my suggestion, but it brought us back to the conversation from the previous week. I had to recap the last conversation to get us back to where we had ended. He was actually more in agreement with me and had even found himself being slightly more overtly angry with his parents. This allowed me to help him understand the difference between anger over daily routines and anger over more profound relational issues. He was a smart kid, so he quickly got the distinction. This was a perfect opening to try to identify the things that hurt him the most regarding his parents. It was not new content, but he was now more open and reflective about it. The topics mainly revolved around his father's depression, his mother's emotional ups and downs, and her staying out so much. Most of all, he complained about the fighting and threats of divorce.

While discussing each of these topics, we tried to better understand his complex and sometimes mixed emotional responses. He was at times sad, sometimes worried, and always angry. With this content and his emotions more clear, we began thinking about how his parents might respond if he talked to them more directly about these things. He was worried that they would either be hurt, angry, or start fighting over who was more to blame. We discussed each response and how he might react to it. Most of all, I tried to help him feel entitled to express himself, regardless of how they responded—that he was not responsible for taking care of them.

We then reviewed a few self-regulation skills to help him manage his emotions and keep him from exploding or shutting down during the conversation with his parents. We also discussed whether he would let me help him if he got stuck or was not being clear. He was fine with this and jokingly welcomed my assistance. I assured him that I would help him stay on track. I also reminded him that I would be meeting with his parents to get them prepared to listen to what he had to say. The conversation then turned to him joking about a girl that he liked at school and that maybe he would ask her out if the meetings with his parents went well. I joined in with his humor and said that if it motivated him, then I was all for it. Then I added that he might want to ask her out no matter how the conversation went with his parents. He smiled as he left the session.

TASK III: PARENT ALLIANCE (CONTINUED)

In Session 5, I met with the father alone. The session was not quite as satisfying as the one with the mother but seemed good enough to accomplish the goal of this task. The father was moderately depressed and hopeless, feeling undermined by the mother and unable to have an impact on the family. He talked about the marriage as if it were "not that bad" and said his wife should just accept that people are not perfect. His tolerance of her rejection, sexual refusal, and absence from family life was startling. His depression reinforced his low self-esteem, lack of healthy entitlement, and his passivity. He did not express as much anger at the mother as in the relational reframe session, but rather more remorse and regret about the marriage. Again, the problems in the marriage felt so entrenched that staying on this topic seemed unproductive.

The father let me easily transition to his childhood experience of attachment. The early years of his childhood were fairly normal. The family lived in Washington, DC, and his father worked for a nonprofit, liberal social policy think tank. He often went to work with his father and, thus, was exposed to pretty high-level national politics. As a teenager, he dreamed of running for political office and spending his life as a public servant fighting the good fight. At the age of 15, his mother died quickly of a rare disease and in the blink of an eye, his life crashed. His father became depressed and unavailable. His grades dropped and his college career was in jeopardy. He described how, as a result of his mother's passing, he had lost faith that he had any control over his life. After empathizing about his tragic loss, I focused on his feelings of abandonment, trying to get him in touch with his needs for love and support at that critical juncture.

After exploring his memories and feelings about those critical years, I asked whether it was possible that Josh had some similar feelings of abandonment. The father initially became defensive, but then began to understand the different, yet parallel, experience that Josh might be having. The father embraced the idea that maybe he had not been there for Josh when Josh needed him. We explored the father's rationale and regrets about this for a bit, but then I tried to resuscitate some feelings of responsibility and compassion. "You know, Josh really needs you now, just like you needed your father at 15 and 16." The father wanted to sink into his passivity and hopelessness, but I tried to keep possibility afloat. As I had with the mother, I tried to inject the possibility of him mustering the desire and motivation to help his son. The father protested that he always tried to help, but it never worked. I suggested that at this point in time, maybe he was trying the wrong thing. Josh did not need discipline and tutoring; he needed his father to help him better understand some of the feelings that were eating him up. Josh was feeling anger and disappointment, just like the father felt when he was 15. The father protested that Josh did not want to share his feelings, and I countered that I was not sure Josh thought anyone really wanted to hear about them. The father was hesitant but curious. I talked some more about how hard it was for Josh to express himself, how his emotional muscles were very weak. He needed some emotional exercise and to get a few things off his chest. The father certainly agreed with that and began to be more receptive to my ideas. I asked if he would like to learn how to listen to his son in a way that might help Josh talk more; this resonated with the father. I complimented the father on how sensitive he was and on his ability to understand Josh's struggles. I assured him that he could be a great resource to his son if he would let me help him. He agreed.

TASK II: ADOLESCENT ALLIANCE (CONTINUED)

In Session 6, I met alone with Josh again. I was not ready to do the attachment task but did not want to wait another week before I saw him. After an assessment of his current depression and general emotional state, we turned to the topic of school. After hearing some details about a few of his school failure stories, we began examining the accuracy of his beliefs about his school performance. It turned out that he had a tendency to focus on a few negative events and then make stable, global attributions about himself ("I am just stupid and will never go to college"). We were able to identify evidence that countered this view of himself and he began to envision attending college, even if he did not attend Georgetown.

About midway through the session, I turned back to the attachment task. He said he had thought about it, and he sort of agreed that it might help. I praised him for his courage, and we began preparing for the task. We reviewed the goals, what he wanted to say, and how he could better manage his emotions during the conversation. We talked about how his parents might react and his fears of hurting their feelings. He responded well to my challenge that his distancing himself is actually hurting his parents more than his saying what was on his mind. He agreed. We then talked about how I could help him during the session. I wanted to both challenge him and support him. He agreed that I could jump in if I felt that he needed it.

TASK III: PARENT ALLIANCE (CONTINUED)

Session 7 included both parents together. I began by thanking both of them for meeting alone with me and telling them how impressed I was with their sensitivity and insight about themselves and their son. I also said that I was not there to do marital therapy, although we might have to touch on a few issues. Instead, my goal was to help them to help Josh: to help him get launched so he could begin to prepare for his approaching adulthood. Both parents expressed confidence that I could help them and said that they were willing to work on whatever I thought would help their son.

I began by explaining my impressions of them as individuals and as a family. First, I expressed deep empathy for both of them, acknowledging that they both, in their own ways, had very hard childhoods. I said, "When we grow up like this, we sometimes have a hard time feeling safe in relationships. We want to love and be loved, but sometimes we feel self-protective and get hurt by small mistakes from our partner." I told them that I saw in them great hurt and yet great resilience. They had not done that much couples therapy and certainly not recently, so I encouraged them to give it one more try before seriously thinking about divorce. Even if it meant using the therapy to make the breakup more civil and bearable for themselves and the kids, it would be worth it. The father was open to the idea, but the mother was more hesitant. She agreed, however, that it might help even if they decided to separate. I also turned to the father and talked to him about medication for his depression. I was sympathetic to his ambivalence but challenged him to explore it with a good psychiatrist. He had nothing to lose and a lot to gain if it reduced his depression, even a little. I remarked that no matter how things moved forward in this family, having some relief from the depression could give him more energy to help Josh and deal with whatever lay ahead. He agreed to think more seriously about it. The mother was so antimedication and anti–personal psychotherapy that I decided not to bring this up for her, even though she knew I was thinking about it.

I then started to talk about Josh. My approach was not to blame his problems on the marital conflicts. Instead, I emphasized that the marital problems were creating an environment that made it hard for them to help Josh fight his way out of the depression. I began by expressing admiration and concern for him. I saw a very smart, kind, insightful, and ambitious young man who seemed trapped by his depression. I reiterated that he needed his parents' help in two specific ways. First, he needed to find a voice. He was a boy filled with feelings and little ability to express them. I reminded the parents that they both knew what it was like being a lonely adolescent with a lot of confused feelings and no one to turn to, no place to get them out. They both acknowledged this. I then offered them the opportunity to help Josh have a different experience—to have parents who could listen to his sadness and maybe even his anger and who could help him learn how to better manage his emotions. Both parents also understood this. They wanted to see him gain some maturity and express himself better, rather than retreat from conflict and people. I prepared them by saying, "Some of what he has to say might be hard to hear. I am sure some of his feelings are about the two of you." Rather than be defensive, the parents readily agreed and assumed that he was angry at them for many things. I quickly added that I was not saying that their conflicts caused his depression or that it was the only thing on his mind. But I did worry that these feelings might be the ones getting in the way of him turning to them for help about other problems. I was being a bit cautious and protective of the parents, but they both had enough insight to understand that Josh was angry about their arguing. We spent a bit of time discussing this, and I vigilantly monitored the parents to prevent them from blaming each other. Staying focused on Josh, I asked them to think about how they would feel if Josh said some honest but harsh things about them. They both understood the need for this, but I still reinforced the need for them to listen, be curious, and not get defensive.

With some goodwill emerging, I was able to address the bigger problem. I gently, but directly, said that my biggest concern was their tendency to argue and blame each other. I shared with them that when we met in the first session, I observed that Josh faded into the background each time they began to fight. Their constant fighting left little emotional space in the family for him. At that moment, the mother became critical of the father and he became defensive; I stepped in forcefully to stop the escalation and pointed out that this was exactly what I meant, that they were like a tinderbox that ignited in an instant. I empathized with their anger at each other and assured them that I did not assume that this could be resolved easily. However, I reminded them about how they felt as children when things were frightening and they had no one turn to. I asked whether they could find it in themselves, motivated by their love for Josh, to put aside their anger long enough to give Josh a chance to speak. I explained that Josh would give up and sink back into his isolation if they could not do this for him. At that point I was only asking them to at least do this in the session, as I did not want to convey unrealistic expectations for change. The parents seemed to understand my challenge and advice.

With agreement on the goal and task in place, our conversation turned to skill building. The tone became a bit more psychoeducational and focused on teaching some basic listening skills. We talked about the need to have Josh be the center of attention and that the goal was to have them listen to him, ask him questions, be curious about his thoughts, and permit whatever feelings might arise. We talked about why this was important and how it would help Josh learn to put feelings into words and gain trust that he could address problems without feeling rejected or punished. It might also help him get some things off his chest that he was holding against them or just extremely worried about (e.g., their getting a divorce). The parents were compliant and agreeable to these directions.

I then turned to the harder material. I expressed my concern that not only would they both be likely to be defensive but also that they would start fighting about things in a way that would divert the attention from Josh. The parents felt a bit chastised by me, but I had to persist and make this point clear. I acknowledged their discomfort with what I was saying and emphasized how important it was to acknowledge. In a gentle and nonaccusatory way, I was direct about how the arguing, regardless of who started it or who was right or wrong, took up all the emotional space in the conversation. Josh just gave up and retreated when this happened. We discussed this some and the parents became more accepting of this analysis of the dynamic. We also did some problem solving together about how I could be helpful in getting them to stop fighting if it occurred during the session. We then reviewed a few other listening skills and how the parents needed to support each other in this session. We ended with a pretty good feeling, the parents feeling hopeful that they might actually begin to hear what their son was thinking about and feeling.

TASK IV: REPAIRING ATTACHMENT

All three family members came to Session 8. After a brief check-in, I turned to the goals of the session.

Therapist: So, thanks everyone for coming today. As you know, I have been meeting with each of you to try and prepare for this conversation. I think everyone knows what we want to accomplish and has agreed to work on this. So, Josh, is there somewhere you would like to start or do you want me to suggest an opening?

Adolescent: You start.

Therapist: Well, you and I had talked a bit about feeling lonely at home. Why don't you start there?

Mother: How could you feel lonely? I am there all the time. . . . Why don't you come talk to me? If you are lonely, why don't you talk to me?

Therapist: Mrs. Stern, that is what we want to understand, but let's remember to slow down a bit and try to understand what Josh is feeling, OK?

Mother: Yes. Yes, OK. So Josh, what do you mean you feel lonely? I really want to know. Say whatever you want . . .

Father: Yes, Josh. Say whatever you need to say.

Therapist: Do you believe them, Josh . . . that they really want to hear what you have to say?

Adolescent: No!

Therapist: Why not?

Adolescent: 'Cause they never have listened before. They either just yell at me or at each other.

Father: What do you mean?

Therapist: Mr. Stern . . . please, please just try to listen. You do not need to defend. You want to hear what he has to say, right or wrong.

Father: Yes . . . OK . . . I guess. . . . So what do you want to say?

Adolescent: [Starts to shut down]

Therapist: Wow, wow, Josh, this is what we talked about . . . you standing up for yourself. Don't retreat now. Don't go back. You can do this.

Adolescent: You see how they are.

Therapist: I see two parents who are doing their best to try and listen. This is not easy for them, and they are not so good at it, but they are here. This is your time to get some things off your chest, don't lose this moment.

Adolescent: [Cautiously looks around the room] I can't stand it anymore . . . your fighting. I hate it . . . I hate it . . . it makes me want to kill myself.

Mother: Josh. You . . .

Therapist: [Interrupts] Mrs. Stern. Let him talk. Give him the space. Keep going, Josh.

Adolescent: For years, you have hated each other, and we've had to watch it. [To the father] You yell at her, she leaves the house, you get depressed. Then I have to try to take care of you. Then mom calls me to see if everyone is OK . . . and I . . . I have to take care of her. I hate it. Just leave me out of this!

The parents were speechless—They had never heard Josh talk like this and never knew how much they had dragged him into their problems. I restrained the parents from interrupting and from comforting him. This was not the time for that.

Therapist: So you feel you have to take care of them?

Adolescent: Shit yes. They are idiots.

Therapist: [Worries this will insult the father] Josh . . . what . . . what do you want to say? Don't insult them, just tell them what this has been like for you.

Josh then went on for 15 minutes talking about how life had been at home over the past 10 years: the arguing, the chaos, the instability, the unpredictability, the mother's mood swings, the father's passivity. He also talked about all the times he felt he needed their help and they were either not there for him or too busy fighting with each other. The parents restrained themselves, mostly listening, but also asking a few questions and encouraging Josh to tell his story. At one point the mother said to Josh, "So you think we should get a divorce?" Before Josh could respond, I blocked her question and reflected how her asking that question invited Josh to comment on things in which he should not be involved. The father began to jump on her for asking such a stupid question, but I blocked him, remarking that this is how the focus on Josh quickly gets lost. I attempted to pull for some of Josh's disappointment, feelings of loneliness, and sadness. He softened a bit and shared some of that, but mostly he felt angry that day. Those were legitimate, usually unacknowledged feelings, so I did not push him too hard on softer feelings. The fact that he was talking and the parents were listening was a major breakthrough for them—a major shift in the emotional rules of this family. I monitored the conversation to make sure it was not too much for the parents. Although they were uncomfortable, they were moved by Josh's honesty and pain.

After a while, Josh seemed worn out, like he had just crossed a hot desert with no water. The disclosure had a natural end, and the interaction felt complete for a first conversation. At that point, I turned to the parents to see whether they wanted to say anything, reminding them to keep it simple and about Josh. To everyone's surprise, it was the father who sat forward, a bit closer to Josh and apologized. He admitted he had dragged Josh into his problems and that he had given into his depression when, at times, Josh really needed him. The mother started to jump in, but I blocked her, wanting the father and son to have this intimate moment. Josh kept his head down but was clearly listening. The father said that his depression had really made it hard for him, but he knew that was no excuse and he wanted to try and do better. Josh remained silent. I asked Josh if he believed his father. Josh shrugged his shoulders and said, "Sort of . . . but will things really change?" The father said he would try. Trying to build on this successful moment, I commented that this conversation already felt different to me. Josh then looked to his mother.

Adolescent: [In a vulnerable, curious tone] So what are you going to do . . . leave Dad?

Mother: [Looks at the therapist, knowing what to say]

Therapist: I think it is a legitimate question and topic for Josh to ask about. This has a big impact on his life. Let's just think about what he needs to know or be involved in and what should be between the parents.

Mother: I do not know, Josh. Dad and I have to figure this out.

Adolescent: But you two seem to hate each other so much.

Mother: We do not hate each other.

Adolescent: Seems like it. You are always fighting.

Therapist: You know, Mrs. Stern, I wonder if Josh worries that you might leave him as well?

Mother: [Starts to cry] Josh . . . I will never leave you . . . no matter what Dad and I do . . . you are my son, and I will always love you and be there for you.

Adolescent: [Tears up]

Mother: [Moves over on the couch to hug Josh; he does not let her but does let her put her hand on his shoulder.] Josh, I love you. We both love you. I am sorry if we . . . I . . . have made things hard for you.

We lingered in the silence of that moment for a few minutes. The family was exhausted and relieved. After a few moments, I complimented them all on how well they did and empathized with how hard this was. I also injected hopefulness by saying this was a new beginning, a new chance to have a different kind of family. I acknowledged that there were many difficult things ahead to talk about and sort out but that if they could be this honest and supportive of each other, that Josh would emerge from this a stronger person. The parents were grateful for the meeting, and the family planned to return next week.

Over the next few weeks (Sessions 9–10), we had a few more conversations like this; although the conversations were not quite as intense, we covered some important memories impacting Josh's relationship with his parents that Josh felt the need to talk about. The parents told me they were doing their best to fight less, and the mother was home for dinner more. The father made an appointment with a psychiatrist to explore whether medication could help reduce his depression. The marriage was still bad, but the fighting had diminished. I offered to meet with the parents in a few weeks, after we had a few more things settled with Josh.

TASK V: PROMOTING AUTONOMY

Things were not perfect at home by any means, but some of the tension had been reduced. Sessions 11 through 13 began to center less on the relationship between Josh and his parents and more on how Josh was going to put his life back together. The father had begun to see a psychiatrist and suggested that maybe Josh should be evaluated. Josh had mixed feelings about this but was willing to go for an appointment. Josh was more concerned about school. His parents were also very concerned about Josh's academics. He still wanted to go to college but feared that he had ruined his chances because his grades had slipped. Both he and his father had always talked about Josh going to Georgetown University on scholarship so Josh could be in DC. But this seemed beyond reach, given Josh's grades. I suggested that Josh meet with his school counselor and try to get an assessment of what his options were, given his grades. The remarkable moment occurred when he turned to his father and asked him to come to the meeting with him to help him sort this out. The father was surprised, and the mother was a bit hurt. The moment could have gone any number of ways, but the father, without seeking his wife's approval or trying to take care of her hurt feelings, just looked at his son and said, "Yes. I would be happy to come to that meeting." Josh looked at his mother, expecting a hailstorm of mixed emotions and undermining of the father. Mother looked at me and felt my support for her. Then she said, "Oh, that would be great."

I asked Josh if it was hard asking his father for help. He said, "Mom is usually the one to help me. Dad sort of stays out of these kinds of things." The father wanted to blame his wife for that, and the mother wanted to complain about father's passivity. I blocked both impulses and asked the parents to see whether Josh needed help with anything else. Josh was a bit embarrassed but then said under his breath that he wanted to go to the 11th grade prom. The parents were somewhat surprised. They never would have suspected that. They asked how they could help. He said he was not sure, but he thought it might be too late to buy a ticket. The mother said she would call the school and find out, then caught herself and suggested he go to the student office tomorrow and see what he could learn. Then they could talk.

In a few weeks, I met alone with the parents (Session 14). Things were not perfect with Josh, but he was working harder at school. They had taken him to a psychiatrist, and she had recommended an antidepressant. The three of us discussed it in a session and the family decided to give it a try. The important shift was the parents' ability to better cooperate about plans and needs for Josh. The marriage was less hostile but no more functional. The mother had moved out of the bedroom and was sleeping in the guest room. They told the kids it was because of dad's snoring, but everyone knew the truth. They had not yet sought marriage counseling, but the father's medication was helping him feel better and giving him more energy at work and home. Without blaming each other, the parents talked about separating. The father was more invested in making the marriage work, but the mother was anxious to get out. Their question to me was whether separating now in the beginning of Josh's last year of school was helpful or detrimental to him. We talked about the need for stability but also the need for civility. I again encouraged them to seek out a marital therapist where they could get some help with this transition, regardless of what they decided.

In the last few weeks of the therapy (Sessions 15–17), we had a few crises and setbacks. Josh had stayed out all night at a friend's house without calling home. The parents were furious and overly punitive. Josh flew into rage, arguing that he finally was having a life and they were being too controlling. This normal developmental transition of increasing independence was uncharted territory for this family. Josh did not know how to negotiate with his parents, and the parents did not know how to incrementally give him more freedom and appropriate consequences. This was complicated by the fact that Josh was 17 years old and nearly an adult. In the session, I initially helped recalibrate the hostility by normalizing the problem as a common developmental challenge that this family had avoided for years because of Josh's depression. The parents apologized for overreacting, and Josh apologized for not calling. With emotions under control, I helped the parents express their support for Josh's independence but also validated their need for more cooperation. Josh agreed but claimed that he was nearly an adult and he wanted more freedom. The session focused on trying to understand each other's perspectives and expectations, and finding a balance of attachment and autonomy, of responsibility and independence. In subsequent sessions, the family practiced finding this balance in the context of other developmentally appropriate challenges, such as Josh being concerned about how to handle his friends' drinking.

In our last session, the family reflected on the changes that everyone had made during the course of treatment, as well as the challenges that lay ahead for the family. Everyone commented on how Josh's depression had decreased significantly. According to the clinic's assessments, he was experiencing minimal depressive symptoms. Additionally, Josh was reaching out more to his parents when things bothered him. Josh continued to improve in his academics and was becoming increasingly social. Josh and his parents continued to disagree about rules, but they were improving their ability to negotiate these challenges and appropriate consequences when Josh defied the rules. The parents continued to be more civil to one another. Josh's father tried to do more caretaking of Josh and appropriately managed his own depression without putting a burden on Josh. The mother increased her quality time with Josh and, with effort, was able to start giving Josh more responsibility in taking charge of his own life. Everyone in the family was concerned that they might slip back into old habits. They discussed how they could tell each other when they noticed this happening. They came up with code words they could say to one another to signal that someone had "fallen off the wagon." Finally, the family talked about how they would like their relationships to be in the future, once Josh went off to college, regardless of whether the parents remained together or not.

A year later, I got a holiday card from the mother. Josh was in DC in a small private college and doing well. He was a political science major and succeeding in school. His depression had decreased, and against the parents' wishes, he had decided to discontinue the medication. In the meantime, he seemed to be alright without it. He did meet a few times with a therapist near the school, so he had some support if he needed it. He came home about once a month and called weekly, usually to talk with his father about politics. The mother felt left out but found other ways to be involved in Josh's life. The parents were still together, raising their now 15-year-old daughter. However, after a year of couples therapy, they decided to separate in the coming fall. The mother asked whether she and her husband could come to see me again with their daughter to help with this transition. The mother thanked me for saving her son's life and helping everyone in the family "grow up" a bit.

CONCLUSION

This case was not easy but was not as hard as some. We have treated a range of cases in our clinical trials and our outpatient psychiatry clinic at Children's Hospital of Philadelphia, the original home of the Philadelphia Child Guidance Clinic. The performance models we have outlined in this book are just that, an ideal sequence that provides a path to follow. The model fits some cases like a glove; other cases have different challenges or processes, which requires us to modify and adjust our approach. But regardless of the cases we see, the principles still guide us: Are the family relationships providing the support needed to help a child overcome the adversity of depression? Will the family agree to relationship building as at least part of the treatment plan? Meeting alone with each family member helps us better understand their unique perspective and prepares them for future conversations. Bringing them back together, we try to create honest, reflective, supportive conversations about ruptures in the very fabric of the conversation itself and then move on to problem solving daily issues, with an eye toward creating more appropriate competency and autonomy for the adolescent. As we said in the Introduction, our primary aim is to help the reader be more of a thinking therapist. If we have done that, then we have accomplished our goal.

RECOMMENDED ADDITIONAL READINGS

FOR THERAPISTS

This appendix presents a list of must-read books and articles for the person serious about attachment-based family therapy (ABFT). These materials will deepen your understanding and sensitivity to the subtle but profound nature of this work. Some of the writings directly address core elements of the model (e.g., Kobak & Duemmler, 1994), whereas others address common family variations that present unique challenges (e.g., Beardslee, 2003). But as a whole, these works provide the theoretical and clinical backdrops for ABFT. This list closely parallels the syllabi we use at Drexel University when teaching ABFT.

Depression- and Suicide Related

Beardslee, W. R. (2003). *When a parent is depressed: How to protect your children from the effects of depression in the family.* Boston, MA: Little, Brown.

This book discusses how depression can affect both parents and their children. Despite the link between parental depression and subsequent symptoms in children, the author discusses how these problems can be prevented and how families can help combat this illness together. He combines empirical evidence and clinical examples to create a comprehensive work aimed at addressing this serious mental illness.

Brent, D. A., Poling, K. D., & Goldstein, T. R. (2011) *Treating adolescent depression and suicide: A clinician's guide*. New York, NY: Guilford Press.

This comprehensive clinician's guide to depression and suicide addresses the assessment and treatment of adolescents with these symptoms. It touches on a wide range of psychosocial and pharmacological interventions so that clinicians can help develop highly individualized treatment plans geared toward specific clients. It also includes a wide variety of examples to illustrate how these ideas are implemented in practice.

Goodman, S. H., & Gotlib, I. H. (2002). *Children of depressed parents: Mechanisms of risk and implications for treatment*. Washington, DC: American Psychological Association.

Goodman and Gotlib consider how parental depression can impact children, including their likelihood of developing depression. In addition to shared genetic risk, exposure to a parent's symptoms can increase the risk of a child developing the same symptoms. Given this knowledge, this work also considers protective factors that can reduce a child's risk, regardless of parental symptomatology.

Joiner, T. E., & Coyne, J. C. (1999). *The interactional nature of depression: Advances in interpersonal approaches*. Washington, DC: American Psychological Association.

This book examines the ways in which relationships can (a) on the one hand, contribute to and perpetuate depression and (b) on the other hand, protect against depression. Even though the illness lies within the individual, depression is a fundamentally interpersonal illness and cannot be treated without taking these factors into account.

Attachment Related

Allen, J. P., & Land, D. (1999). Attachment in adolescence. In J. Cassidy & P. R. Shaver (Eds.), *Handbook of attachment theory and research and clinical applications* (pp. 319–335). New York, NY: Guilford Press.

These authors explore adolescents' attachment to their parents, even as they attempt to establish autonomy. This chapter explores both the developmental challenges faced by all adolescents and differences in development as a function of attachment.

Bosmans, G., Braet, C., & Vlierberghe, L.V. (2010). Attachment and symptoms of psychopathology: Early maladaptive schemas as a cognitive link? *Clinical Psychology and Psychotherapy, 17*, 374–385.

Bosmans et al. discuss a study that investigated whether early maladaptive schemas can explain the relation between attachment anxiety and avoidance dimensions and symptoms of psychopathology.

Cassidy, J. (1994). Emotion regulation: Influences of attachment relationships. *Monographs of the Society for Research in Child Development, 59*(2–3, Serial No. 204), 228–249.

This monograph explores how children's attachment experiences in early childhood shape their ability to regulate emotions later on. Specifically, it links secure attachments with more flexible, adaptive emotion regulation abilities later on, and insecure attachment styles with tendencies to either heighten or minimize negative affect.

Greenberg, L. S. (1999). Attachment and psychopathology in childhood. In J. Cassidy & P. R. Shaver (Ed.), *Handbook of attachment: Theory, research, and clinical applications* (pp. 469–496). New York, NY: Guilford Press.

This chapter reviews what is currently known about the relations between attachment and psychopathology in childhood, specifically, the more common externalizing and internalizing disorders of childhood.

Johnson, S. (Ed.). *Attachment processes in couple and family therapy*. New York, NY: Guilford Press.

The authors in this book use attachment theory as the basis for a clinical understanding of couples and family therapy. Insights are provided on the nature of interactions between adult partners and among parents and children, the role of attachment in distressed and satisfying relationships, and the ways attachment-oriented interventions can address individual problems, as well as marital conflict and difficult family transitions.

Kobak, R., & Duemmler, S. (1994). Attachment and conversation: Toward a discourse analysis of adolescent and adult security. *Advances in Personal Relationships, 5*, 121–149.

This article considers the pivotal developmental change of the acquisition of language and its implications for how attachment relationships are transformed into "goal-corrected partnerships."

Kobak, R., & Madsen, S. D. (2011). Attachment. In B. B. Brown & M. J. Prinstein (Eds.), *Encyclopedia of adolescence* (Vol. 2, pp. 18–24). Boston, MA: Academic Press.

Kobak and Madsen examine how to extend attachment theory and research to understand adolescents' relationships with parents and peers. The article reviews the following: formation and maintenance of attachment bonds; adolescence and transformations in attachment bonds with caregivers; the emergence of affectional bonds to close friends and sexual partners; organizing attachment bonds with parents and peers; attachment-related aspects of adolescent personality; behavioral systems in adolescence and risky behaviors, states of mind, and disrupted bonds; and psychopathology.

Slade, A., Grienenberger, J., Bernbach, E., Levy, D., & Locker, A. (2005). Maternal reflective functioning, attachment, and the transmission gap: A preliminary study. *Attachment & Human Development, 7*, 283–298.

The study reported here looked at the association between maternal reflective functioning (the ability of the mother to be aware of her child's mental states as well as her own) and attachment. Both adult attachment status and infant attachment status were found to be significantly correlated with parental reflective functioning. This suggests that parental reflective functioning may serve as a link between the attachment status of the mother and that of her infant and, perhaps, may be a better predictor of infant attachment than adult attachment classification itself.

Waters, S. F., Virmani, E. A., Thompson, R. A., Meyer, S., Raikes, H. A., & Jochem, R. J. (2010). Emotion regulation and attachment: Unpacking two constructs and their association. *Journal of Psychopathology and Behavioral Assessment, 32*, 37–47.

This study sought to better understand the link between attachment style and emotion regulation by inducing a feeling of mild frustration in the child and then interviewing the child and mother separately about the emotions evoked. Overall, mother–child concordance of emotional attribution was low, but secure attachment was associated with higher concordance. Implications regarding the influences of attachment on the ability to regulate emotion in childhood are discussed.

Emotion

Angus, L. E., & Greenberg, L. S. (2011). *Working with narrative in emotion-focused therapy: Changing stories, healing lives*. Washington, DC: American Psychological Association.

The authors examine the role of narratives—or personal stories—in both impacting and being impacted by a person's emotional experience, and what this means for the treatment of mental illness. They also consider how these stories change over the course of therapy and how changing the ways a patient interprets the world can ultimately contribute to the healing process. The book concludes with case examples that consider how narrative and emotional processes affect individuals' experiences with depression and trauma.

Carryer, J. R., & Greenberg, L. S. (2010). Optimal levels of emotional arousal in experiential therapy of depression. *Journal of Consulting and Clinical Psychology, 78*, 190–199.

This study found that moderate amounts of heightened emotional arousal improve predictions of therapeutic outcome.

Greenberg, L. S. (2002). Integrating an emotion-focused approach to treatment into psychotherapy integration. *Journal of Psychotherapy Integration, 12*, 154–189.

This article discusses the three major principles of emotional change (emotional awareness, regulation, and transformation).

Greenberg, L. S., & Pascual-Leone, A. (2006). Emotion in psychotherapy: A practice-friendly research review. *Journal of Clinical Psychology, 62*, 611–630.

This article reviews four distinct types of emotion processes that have been found to be useful in therapy and their practical implications for psychotherapy.

Greenberg, L. S., & J. C. Watson. (2005). *Emotion-focused therapy for depression*. Washington, DC: American Psychological Association.

This book outlines how to make distinctions between different types of emotional experience and expression that require different types of in-session intervention when working with emotions in depression.

Parenting

Gottman, J. M, Katz, L. F., & Hooven, C. (1996). Parental meta-emotion philosophy and the emotional life of families: Theoretical models and preliminary data. *Journal of Family Psychology, 10*, 243–268.

This article introduces and researches the concepts of parental meta-emotion and meta-emotion philosophy. In a 3-year longitudinal study of children and their parents, the researchers developed a theoretical model and path-analytic models linking parental meta-emotion philosophy to parenting, to child regulatory physiology, to emotion regulation abilities in the child, and to child outcomes in middle childhood.

Katz, L., & Hunter, E. (2007). Maternal meta-emotion philosophy and adolescent depressive symptomatology. *Social Development, 16*, 2, 343–360.

The study reported here examined the relationship between parental beliefs about their own emotions and adolescent depressive symptoms. A mother's acceptance of her own emotions was inversely related to adolescent depressive symptoms and externalizing behaviors and positively correlated with self-esteem. The implications of these findings in terms of creating parental intervention programs aimed at reducing adolescent depression are discussed.

Sharp, C., & Fonagy, P. (2008). The parent's capacity to treat the child as a psychological agent: Constructs, measures and implications for developmental psychopathology. *Social Development, 17*, 737–754.

The authors present an overview of past attempts to operationalize parental ability to treat the child as a psychological agent. They tie together a wide array of diverse theoretical constructs and consider the implications these theories have in terms of child development.

Tokic, A., & Pecnik, N. (2010). Parental behaviors related to adolescents' self-disclosure: Adolescents' views. *Journal of Social and Personal Relationships, 28*, 201–222.

Tokic and Pecnik describe a study that explored adolescent perceptions of their parents' behaviors that inhibited or facilitated adolescents' self-disclosures to them.

Enactment

Allen-Eckert, H., Fong, E., Nichols, M. P., Watson, N., & Liddle, H. A. (2001). Development of the Family Therapy Enactment Scale. *Family Process, 40*, 469–478.

This report describes the development of a new scale designed to establish how therapists intervene and clients respond during effective enactments in family therapy sessions. The Family Therapy Enactment Rating Scale (FTERS) was developed by clinically trained investigators who observed 27 videotaped family therapy sessions and listed therapist interventions and client responses during four phases of enactments: pre-enactment preparation, initiation, facilitation, and closing commentary. Findings on the FTERS were used to offer tentative guidelines for effective initiation and facilitation of enactments in family therapy sessions.

Nichols, M. P., & Fellenberg, S. (2000). The effective use of enactments in family therapy: Discovery-oriented process study. *Journal of Marital and Family Therapy, 26*, 143–152.

This study investigated the elements of enactments-in-session to observe and modify family interactions in structural family therapy. Judges were able to reliably describe therapist interventions that led to successful enactments, as well as what therapists did or failed to do that led to unproductive outcomes. The authors discuss the clinical implications of these findings.

FOR PARENTS

Parents can benefit from education about parenting adolescents, adolescent depression, and suicide. The following are helpful books we often recommend to parents.

Parenting and Emotions

Faber, A., & Mazlish, E. (2012). *How to talk so kids will listen and listen so kids will talk*. New York, NY: Simon & Schuster.

This self-help guide is for parents frustrated by ineffective communication with their children. This book provides real-life examples and expert techniques aimed at producing smoother, more effective communication between parent and child.

Ginott, H. G. (1967). *Between parent and teenager*. New York, NY: Macmillan.

A classic work that examines parent–adolescent misunderstandings, as well as ways to address breakdowns in communication.

Gottman, J. M., & DeClaire, J. (1997). *The heart of parenting: How to raise an emotionally intelligent child*. New York, NY: Simon & Schuster.

This is a guide to raising a child who is well-equipped to attend to and regulate his or her emotions. It includes advice for parents whose children may be facing difficult emotional experiences. Case studies and examples are intertwined with parenting advice across different parenting scenarios to illustrate the authors' points.

Teen Suicide, Directed at Parents

Garfinkel, L. F., & Slaby, A. E. (1996). *No one saw my pain: Why teens kill themselves*. New York, NY: Norton.

Drawing on actual accounts of completed teen suicides, this book explores similarities across each of these secondhand narratives in an attempt to shed light on a tragic subject. The authors share the lessons they have learned from these tragedies and formulate advice for the next generation of struggling teens.

Williams, K. (1995). *A parent's guide for suicidal and depressed teens. A first person account of what she learned when her own child became suicidal*. Minnesota, MN: Hazelden Foundation.

This book explores the antedating components of adolescent depression and suicidal thinking, as well as ways for parents to help a child who may be struggling with these same thoughts and feelings. As a parent whose own daughter dealt with the same issues, Williams wrote through the lens of her own experiences, exploring the challenges she faced as a mother trying to help both herself and her daughter along this difficult journey.

About Teen Depression, Directed at Parents

The first book includes a chapter on suicide and focuses more on therapies than the second book; the second reports more extensively on biology, medications, and so on, for depression.

Aarseth, E. J. (2002). *Adolescent depression: A guide for parents*. Baltimore, MD: The Johns Hopkins University Press.

Conceptualizing depression as a serious illness, Aarseth details the symptoms of depression, its associations with other psychiatric disorders, and how treatments can effectively combat this debilitating disorder. The goal is for parents to help their adolescents get help now so that they can ultimately lead normally, healthy, symptom-free lives.

Bakalar, N. (2001). *Understanding teenage depression: Diagnosis and management*. New York, NY: Holt.

Bakalar provides a psychiatrist's account of how depression in adolescents is assessed and effectively treated. This work combines scientific evidence with firsthand accounts of depressed and suicidal adolescents to guide parents whose children are facing similar struggles.

REFERENCES

Abela, J. R. Z., Hankin, B. L., Haigh, E. A. P., Adams, P., Vinokuroff, T., & Trayhern, L. (2005). Interpersonal vulnerability to depression in high-risk children: The role of insecure attachment and reassurance seeking. *Journal of Clinical Child and Adolescent Psychology, 34,* 182–192. doi:10.1207/s15374424jccp3401_17

Ainsworth, M. S. (1989). Attachments beyond infancy. *American Psychologist, 44,* 709–716. doi:10.1037/0003-066X.44.4.709

Allen, J. G., & Fonagy, P. (Eds.). (2006). *Handbook of mentalization-based treatment.* Chichester, England: Wiley. doi:10.1002/9780470712986

Allen, J. P., & Land, D. (1999). Attachment in adolescence. In J. Cassidy & P. R. Shaver (Eds.), *Handbook of attachment: Theory, research, and clinical applications* (pp. 319–335). New York, NY: Guilford Press.

Allen, J. P., Marsh, P., McFarland, C., McElhaney, K. B., Land, D. J., Jodl, K. M., & Peck, S. (2002). Attachment and autonomy as predictors of the development of social skills and delinquency during midadolescence. *Journal of Consulting and Clinical Psychology, 70,* 56–66. doi:10.1037/0022-006X.70.1.56

Allen, J. P., McElhaney, K. B., Land, D. J., Kuperminc, G. P., Moore, C. W., O'Beirne-Kelly, H., & Kilmer, S. L. (2003). A secure base in adolescence: Markers of attachment security in the mother–adolescent relationship. *Child Development, 74,* 292–307. doi:10.1111/1467-8624.t01-1-00536

Allen, J. P., Moore, C., Kuperminc, G., & Bell, K. (1998). Attachment and adolescent psychosocial functioning. *Child Development, 69,* 1406–1419. doi:10.2307/1132274

Anderson, H. (1997). *Conversation, language, and possibilities: A postmodern approach to therapy.* New York, NY: Basic Books.

Angus, L., Levitt, H., &,Hardtke, K. (1999). The narrative processes coding system: Research applications and implications for psychotherapy practice. *Journal of Clinical Psychology, 55,* 1255–1270. doi:10.1002/(SICI)1097-4679(199910)55:10<1255::AID-JCLP7>3.0.CO;2-F

Arnett, J. J. (2000). Emerging adulthood: A theory of development from late teens through the twenties. *American Psychologist, 55,* 469–480. doi:10.1037/0003-066X.55.5.469

Asarnow, J. R., Emslie, G., Clarke, G., Wagner, K. D., Spirito, A., Vitiello, B., . . . Brent, D. (2009). Treatment of selective serotonin reuptake inhibitor–resistant depression in adolescents: Predictors and moderators of treatment response. *Journal of the American Academy of Child & Adolescent Psychiatry, 48,* 330–339.

Asarnow, J. R., Tompson, M., Hamilton, E. B., & Goldstein, M. J. (1994). Family expressed emotion, childhood-onset depression, and childhood-onset schizophrenia spectrum disorders: Is expressed emotion a nonspecific correlate of child psychopathology or a specific risk factor for depression? *Journal of Abnormal Child Psychology, 22,* 129–146. doi:10.1007/BF02167896

Barbe, R. P., Bridge, J. A., Birmaher, B., Kolko, D. J., & Brent, D. A. (2004). Lifetime history of sexual abuse, clinical presentation, and outcome in a clinical trial for adolescent depression. *The Journal of Clinical Psychiatry, 65*, 77–83. doi:10.4088/JCP.v65n0113

Barber, B. K. (Ed.). (2002). *Intrusive parenting: How psychological control affects children and adolescents*. Washington, DC: American Psychological Association. doi:10.1037/10422-000

Barkley, R. A. (1997). *Defiant children: A clinician's manual for assessment and parent training*. New York, NY: Guilford Press.

Bateson, G. (1972). *Steps to an ecology of mind: Collected essays in anthropology, psychiatry, evolution, and epistemology*. Lanham, MD: Aronson.

Baumrind, D. (1989). *Rearing competent children*. San Francisco, CA: Jossey-Bass.

Beardslee, W. R. (2003). *When a parent is depressed: How to protect your children from the effects of depression in the family*. New York, NY: Little, Brown.

Beck, A. T. (1967). *Depression: Clinical, experimental, and theoretical aspects*. New York, NY: Hoeber.

Becker, D. (2005). *The myth of empowerment: Women and the therapeutic culture in America*. New York, NY: New York University Press.

Belsky, J. (1984). The determinants of parenting: A process model. *Child Development, 5*, 83–96. doi:10.2307/1129836

Belsky, J., & Pluess, M. (2009). Beyond diathesis stress: Differential susceptibility to environmental influences. *Psychological Bulletin, 135*, 885–908. doi:10.1037/a0017376

Berger, P., & Luckmann, T. (1966). *The social construction of reality: A treatise in the sociology of knowledge* (1st ed.). Garden City, NJ: Anchor Books.

Bertalanffy, L. V. (2003). *General system theory*. New York, NY: Braziller.

Bhandari, K. P., & Barnett, D. (2007). Restrictive parenting buffers Head Start students from stress. *Infants & Young Children, 20*, 55–63. doi:10.1097/00001163-200701000-00006

Birmaher, B., Brent, D., AACAP Work Group on Quality Issues, Bernet, W., Bukstein, O., Walter, H., . . . Medicus, J. (2007). Practice parameter for the assessment and treatment of children and adolescents with depressive disorders. *Journal of the American Academy of Child & Adolescent Psychiatry, 46*, 1503–1526. doi:10.1097/chi.0b013e318145ae1c

Bordin, E. S. (1979). The generalizability of the psychoanalytic concept of the working alliance. *Psychotherapy: Theory, Research, and Practice, 16*, 252–260. doi:10.1037/h0085885

Bosmans, G., Braet, C., & Van Vlierberghe, L. (2010). Attachment and symptoms of psychopathology: Early maladaptive schemas as a cognitive link? *Clinical Psychology & Psychotherapy, 17*, 374–385. doi:10.1002/cpp.667

Böszörményi-Nagy, I., & Spark, G. M. (1973). *Invisible loyalties: Reciprocity in intergenerational family therapy*. Hagerstown, MD: Routledge.

Bowlby, J. (1969). *Attachment and loss: Vol. 1. Attachment.* New York, NY: Basic Books.

Bowlby, J. (1988). *A secure base: Parent–child attachment and healthy human development.* New York, NY: Basic Books.

Brendler, J., Silver, M., Haber, M., & Sargent, J. (1991). *Madness, chaos, and violence: Therapy with families at the brink.* New York, NY: Basic Books.

Brenning, K. M., Soenens, B., Braet, C., & Bosmans, G. (2012). Attachment and depressive symptoms in middle childhood and early adolescence: Testing the validity of the emotion regulation model of attachment. *Personal Relationships, 19,* 445–464.

Brent, D., Emslie, G., Clarke, G., Wagner, K. D., & Asarnow, J. R. (2008). Switching to another SSRI or to venlafaxine with or without cognitive behavioral therapy for adolescents with SSRI-resistant depression: The TORDIA randomized controlled trial. *JAMA, 299,* 901–913. doi:10.1001/jama.299.8.901

Brent, D. A. (2006). Glad for what TADS adds, but many TADS grads still sad. *Journal of the American Academy of Child & Adolescent Psychiatry, 45,* 1461–1464. doi:10.1097/01.chi.0000237708.28013.2a

Bridge, J. A., Iyengar, S., Salary, C. B., Barbe, R., Birmaher, B., Pincus, H. A., . . . Brent, D. A. (2007). Clinical response and risk for reported suicidal ideation and suicide attempts in pediatric antidepressant treatment: A meta-analysis of randomized controlled trials. *JAMA, 297,* 1683–1696. doi:10.1001/jama.297.15.1683

Bronfenbrenner, U. (1979). Contexts of child rearing: Problems and prospects. *American Psychologist, 34,* 844. doi:10.1037/0003-066X.34.10.844

Buber, M. (1937). *I and thou.* (R. G. Smith, Trans.). Edinburgh, Scotland: Clark.

Bugental, J. F. (1992). *The art of the psychotherapist.* New York, NY: Norton.

Butler, M. H., & Gardner, B. C. (2003). Adapting enactments to couple reactivity: Five developmental stages. *Journal of Marital and Family Therapy, 29,* 311–327. doi:10.1111/j.1752-0606.2003.tb01209.x

Byng-Hall, J. (1995). Creating a secure family base: Some implications of attachment theory for family therapy. *Family Process, 34,* 45–58. doi:10.1111/j.1545-5300.1995.00045.x

Byng-Hall, J. (1998). *Rewriting family scripts: Improvisation and systems change.* New York, NY: Guilford Press.

Cheung, A. H., Zuckerbrot, R. A., Jensen, P. S., Ghalib, K., Laraque, D., Stein, R. E. K. & The GLAD–PC Steering Group. (2007). Guidelines for adolescent depression in primary care (GLAD–PC): II. Treatment and ongoing management. *Pediatrics, 120,* 1313–1326. doi:10.1542/peds.2006-1395

Cicchetti, D., & Lynch, M. (1993). Toward an ecological/transactional model of community violence and child maltreatment: Consequences for children's development. *Psychiatry: Interpersonal and Biological Processes, 56,* 96–118.

Cicchetti, D., & Toth, S. L. (1998). The development of depression in children and adolescents. *American Psychologist, 53*, 221–241. doi:10.1037/0003-066X.53.2.221

Cicchetti, D., Toth, S. L., & Lynch, M. (1995). Bowlby's dream comes full circle: The application of attachment theory to risk and psychopathology. *Advances in Clinical Child Psychology, 17*, 1–75. doi:10.1007/978-1-4757-9044-3_1

Cole, D. A., Martin, J. M., & Powers, B. (1997). A competency-based model of child depression: A longitudinal study of peer, parent, teacher, and self-evaluations. *Journal of Child Psychology and Psychiatry and Allied Disciplines, 38*, 505–514. doi:10.1111/j.1469-7610.1997.tb01537.x

Coulehan, R., Friedlander, M. L., & Heatherington, L. (1998). Transforming narratives: A change event in constructivist family therapy. *Family Process, 37*, 17–33. doi:10.1111/j.1545-5300.1998.00017.x

Creed, T. A., Reisweber, J., & Beck, A. T. (2011). *Cognitive therapy for adolescents in school settings*. New York, NY: Guilford Press.

Csikszentmihalyi, M. (1997). *Creativity: Flow and the psychology of discovery and invention*. New York, NY: HarperCollins.

Cummings, E. M., & Davies, P. T. (2010). *Marital conflict and children: An emotional security perspective*. New York, NY: Guilford Press.

Curry, J., Rohde, P., Simons, A., Silva, S., Vitiello, B., Kratochvil, C., . . . March, J. (2006). Predictors and moderators of acute outcome in the Treatment for Adolescents With Depression Study (TADS). *Journal of the American Academy of Child & Adolescent Psychiatry, 45*, 1427–1439. doi:10.1097/01.chi.0000240838.78984.e2

Dallos, R. (2006). *Attachment narrative therapy: Integrating systemic, narrative, and attachment therapies*. New York, NY: Open University Press.

David-Ferdon, C., & Kaslow, N. J. (2008). Evidence-based psychosocial treatments for child and adolescent depression. *Journal of Clinical Child and Adolescent Psychology, 37*, 62–104. doi:10.1080/15374410701817865

Diamond, G., & Liddle, H. A. (1996). Resolving a therapeutic impasse between parents and adolescents in multidimensional family therapy. *Journal of Consulting and Clinical Psychology, 64*, 481–488. doi:10.1037/0022-006X.64.3.481

Diamond, G. M., Diamond, G. S., Levy, S., Closs, C., Ladipo, T., & Siqueland, L. (2012). Attachment-based family therapy for suicidal lesbian, gay, and bisexual adolescents: A treatment development study and open trial with preliminary findings. *Psychotherapy: Theory, Research, and Practice, 49*, 62–71. doi:10.1037/a0026247

Diamond, G. M., Liddle, H. A., Hogue, A., & Dakof, G. A. (1999). Alliance-building interventions with adolescents in family therapy: A process study. *Psychotherapy: Theory, Research, and Practice, 36*, 355–368. doi:10.1037/h0087729

Diamond, G. S., Creed, T., Gillham, J., Gallop, R., & Hamilton, J. L. (2012). Sexual trauma history does not moderate treatment outcome in attachment-based family therapy (ABFT) for adolescents with suicide ideation. *Journal of Family Psychology*, *26*, 595–605. doi:10.1037/a0028414

Diamond, G. S., & Diamond, G. M. (2002). Studying a matrix of change mechanisms: An agenda for family-based process research. In H. A. Liddle, D. A. Santisteban, R. F. Levant, and J. H. Bray (Eds.), *Family psychology: Science-based interventions* (pp. 41–66). Washington, DC: American Psychological Association.

Diamond, G. S., Levy, S., & Creed, T. (2013). *Attachment-based family therapy as hospital care after a suicide attempt*. Manuscript in preparation.

Diamond, G. S., & Liddle, H. A. (1999). Transforming negative parent–adolescent interactions: From impasse to dialogue. *Family Process*, *38*, 5–26. doi:10.1111/j.1545-5300.1999.00005.x

Diamond, G. S., Reis, B. F., Diamond, G. M., Siqueland, L., & Isaacs, L. (2002). Attachment-based family therapy for depressed adolescents: A treatment development study. *Journal of the American Academy of Child & Adolescent Psychiatry*, *41*, 1190–1196. doi:10.1097/00004583-200210000-00008

Diamond, G. S., Siqueland, L., & Diamond, G. M. (2003). Attachment-based family therapy: Programmatic treatment development. *Clinical Child and Family Psychology Review*, 6, 107–127. doi:10.1023/A:1023782510786

Diamond, G. S., & Stern, R. (2003). Attachment-based family therapy for depressed adolescents: Repairing attachment ruptures. In S. Johnson & V. E. Whiffen (Eds.), *Attachment process in couple and family therapy* (pp. 191–212). New York, NY: Guilford Press.

Diamond, G. S., Wintersteen, M.B., Brown, G.K., Diamond, G.M., Gallop, R., Shelef, K., & Levy, S. (2010). Attachment-based family therapy for adolescents with suicidal ideation: A randomized controlled trial. *Journal of the American Academy of Child & Adolescent Psychiatry*, 49, 122–131.

Eisenberg, N., Spinrad, T. L., Eggum, N. D., Silva, K. M., & Reiser, M. (2010). Relations among maternal socialization, effortful control, and maladjustment in early childhood. *Development and Psychopathology*, *22*, 507–525. doi:2110/10.1017/S0954579410000246

Erikson, E. H. (1950). *Childhood and society*. New York, NY: Norton.

Essau, C. A. (2009). *Treatments for adolescent depression*. New York, NY: Oxford University Press.

Foa, E. B., Hembree, E. A., & Rothbaum, B. O. (2007). *Prolonged exposure therapy for PTSD: Emotional processing of traumatic experiences therapist guide*. New York, NY: Oxford University Press.

Foa, E. B., Huppert, J. D., & Cahill, S. P. (2006). Emotional processing theory: An update. In B. O. Rothbaum (Ed.), *The nature and treatment of pathological anxiety* (pp. 3–24). New York, NY: Guilford Press.

Fonagy, P., Gyorgy, G., Jurist, E., & Target, M. (2005). *Affect regulation, mentalization, and the development of self*. New York, NY: Other Press.

Forehand, R., & Long, N. (1996). *Parenting the strong-willed child: The clinically proven five-week program for parents of two- to six-year-olds*. Chicago, IL: Contemporary Books.

Fosha, D. (2000). *The transforming power of affect: A model for accelerated change*. New York, NY: Basic Books.

Fraley, R. C. (2002). Attachment stability from infancy to adulthood: Meta-analysis and dynamic modeling of developmental mechanisms. *Personality and Social Psychology Review, 6*, 123–151. doi:10.1207/S15327957PSPR0602_03

Framo, J. L. (1976). Family of origin as a therapeutic resource for adults in marital and family therapy: You can and should go home again. *Family Process, 15*, 193–210.

Friedlander, M. L., Escudero, V., Heatherington, L., & Diamond, G. M. (2011). Alliance in couple and family therapy. *Psychotherapy Relationships That Work, 2*, 92–109.

Friedlander, M. L., Heatherington, L., Johnson, B., & Skowron, E. A. (1994). Sustaining engagement: A change event in family therapy. *Journal of Counseling Psychology, 41*, 438. doi:10.1037/0022-0167.41.4.438

Garber, J., Ciesla, J. A., McCauley, E., Diamond, G., & Schloredt, K. A. (2011). Remission of depression in parents: Links to healthy functioning in their children. *Child Development, 82*, 226–243. doi:10.1111/j.1467-8624.2010.01552.x

Garner, P. W., & Spears, F. M. (2000). Emotion regulation in low-income preschoolers. *Social Development, 9*, 246–264. doi:10.1111/1467-9507.00122

Gergen, K. (1991). *The saturated self*. New York, NY: Basic Books.

Ginott, H. G. (2009). *Between parent and child: The bestselling classic that revolutionized parent–child communication*. New York, NY: Crown Archetype.

Gomez, J., Miranda, R., & Polanco, L. (2011). Acculturative stress, perceived discrimination and vulnerability to suicide attempts among emerging adults. *Journal of Youth and Adolescence, 40*, 1465–1476. doi:10.1007/s10964-011-9688-9

Goodman, S. H., & Gotlib, I. H. (1999). Risk for psychopathology in the children of depressed mothers: A developmental model for understanding mechanisms of transmission. *Psychological Review, 106*, 458–490. doi:10.1037/0033-295X.106.3.458

Goodyer, I., Dubicka, B., Wilkinson, P., Kelvin, R., Roberts, C., Byford, S., . . . Harrington, R. (2007). Selective serotonin reuptake inhibitors (SSRIs) and routine specialist care with and without cognitive behaviour therapy in adolescents with major depression: Randomised controlled trial. *British Medical Journal, 335*, 142–146. doi:10.1136/bmj.39224.494340.55

Gotlib, I. H., & Hammen, C. L. (1992). *Psychological aspects of depression: Toward a cognitive–interpersonal integration*. Oxford, England: Wiley.

Gotlib, I. H., & Hammen, C. L. (2009). *Handbook of depression* (2nd ed.). New York, NY: Guilford Press.

Gottman, J. (2011). *Raising an emotionally intelligent child*. New York, NY: Simon & Schuster.

Gottman, J. M., Katz, L. F., & Hooven, C. (1996). Parental meta-emotion philosophy and the emotional life of families: Theoretical models and preliminary data. *Journal of Family Psychology, 10,* 243–268. doi:10.1037/0893-3200.10.3.243

Greenberg, L., & Watson, J. (1998). Experiential therapy of depression: Differential effects of client-centered relationship conditions and process experiential interventions. *Psychotherapy Research, 8,* 210–224.

Greenberg, L. S. (2002). *Emotion-focused therapy: Coaching clients to work through their feelings.* Washington, DC: American Psychological Association. doi:10.1037/10447-000

Greenberg, L. S. (2011). *Emotion-focused therapy.* Baltimore, MD: United Book Press.

Greenberg, L. S., Auszra, L., & Herrmann, I. R. (2007). The relationship among emotional productivity, emotional arousal, and outcome in experiential therapy of depression. *Psychotherapy Research, 17,* 482–493. doi:10.1080/10503300600977800

Greenberg, L. S., & Johnson, S. M. (1988). *Emotionally focused therapy for couples.* New York, NY: Guilford Press.

Greenberg, L. S., & Paivio, S. C. (2003). *Working with emotions in psychotherapy.* New York, NY: Guilford Press.

Greenberg, L. S., & Safran, J. D. (1987). *Emotion in psychotherapy: Affect, cognition, and the process of change.* New York, NY: Guilford Press.

Greenberg, L. S., & Watson, J. C. (2005). *Emotion-focused therapy for depression.* Washington, DC: American Psychological Association.

Grice, H. P. (1975). Logic and conversation. In P. Cole & J. L. Morgan, *Syntax and semantics: Vol. 3. Speech acts* (pp. 41–58). New York, NY: Academic Press.

Groh, A. M., Roisman, G. I., Van IJzendoorn, M. H., Bakermans-Kranenburg, M. J., & Fearon, R. (2012). The significance of insecure and disorganized attachment for children's internalizing symptoms: A meta-analytic study. *Child Development, 83,* 591–610. doi:10.1111/j.1467-8624.2011.01711.x

Grych, J. H., & Fincham, F. D. (1990). Marital conflict and children's adjustment: A cognitive–contextual framework. *Psychological Bulletin, 108,* 267. doi:10.1037/0033-2909.108.2.267

Haley, J. (1987). *Problem-solving therapy.* San Francisco, CA: Jossey-Bass.

Hall, G. S. (1904). *Adolescence: Its psychology and its relations to physiology, anthropology, sociology, sex, crime, religion, and education.* New York, NY: Appleton. doi:10.1037/10616-000

Hammen, C. (2009). Adolescent depression: Stressful interpersonal contexts and risk for recurrence. *Current Directions in Psychological Science, 18,* 200–204. doi:10.1111/j.1467-8721.2009.01636.x

Hesse, E. (1999). The adult attachment interview: historical and current perspectives. In J. Cassidy & P. Shaver (Eds.), *Handbook of attachment* (pp. 395–433). New York, NY: Guilford Press.

Hollon, S. D., Garber, J., & Shelton, R. C. (2005). Treatment of depression in adolescents with cognitive behavior therapy and medications: A commentary on the TADS project. *Cognitive and Behavioral Practice, 12*, 149–155. doi:10.1016/S1077-7229(05)80019-7

Holmes, J. (2001). *The search for the secure base: Attachment theory and psychotherapy*. London, England: Brunner-Routledge.

Holmes, J. (2010). *Exploring in security: Towards an attachment-informed psychoanalytic psychotherapy*. New York, NY: Routledge.

Hooley, J. M., Orley, J., & Teasdale, J. D. (1986). Levels of expressed emotion and relapse in depressed patients. *The British Journal of Psychiatry, 148*, 642–647. doi:10.1192/bjp.148.6.642

Horvath, A. O. (2006). The alliance in context: Accomplishments, challenges, and future directions. *Psychotherapy: Theory, Research, and Practice, 43*, 258–263. doi:10.1037/0033-3204.43.3.258

Hughes, C. W., Emslie, G. J., Crismon, M. L., Posner, K., Birmaher, B., Ryan, N., . . . Trivedi, M. H. (2007). Texas children's medication algorithm project: Update from Texas consensus conference panel on medication treatment of childhood major depressive disorder. *Journal of the American Academy of Child & Adolescent Psychiatry, 46*, 667–686. doi:10.1097/chi.0b013e31804a859b

Hughes, D. A. (2007). Attachment-focused family therapy. New York, NY: Norton.

Israel, P. & Diamond, G. S. (2012). Feasibility of attachment based family therapy for depressed clinic-referred Norwegian Adolescents. *Clinical Child Psychology and Psychiatry*. Advance online publication. Retrieved from http://ccp.sagepub.com/content/early/2012/08/27/1359104512455811.abstract

Izard, C. E. (2011). Forms and functions of emotions: Matters of emotion–cognition interactions. *Emotion Review, 3*, 371–378. doi:10.1177/1754073911410737

Izard, C. E., Woodburn, E. M., Finlon, K. J., Krauthamer-Ewing, E., Grossman, S. R., & Seidenfeld, A. (2011). Emotion knowledge, emotion utilization, and emotion regulation. *Emotion Review, 3*, 44–52. doi:10.1177/1754073910380972

Jensen, P. S. (2006). After TADS, can we measure up, catch up, and ante up? *Journal of the American Academy of Child & Adolescent Psychiatry, 45*, 1456–1460. doi:10.1097/01.chi.0000237712.81378.9d

Johnson, S. M. (2004). *The practice of emotionally focused marital therapy: Creating connection* (2nd ed.). New York, NY: Brunner/Routledge.

Joiner, T. E., Jr., & Coyne, J. C. (Eds.). (1999). *The interactional nature of depression: Advances in interpersonal approaches*. Washington, DC: American Psychological Association.

Julian, T. W., McHenry, P. C., & McKelvey, M. W. (1994). Cultural variations in parenting, perceptions of Caucasian, African American, Hispanic, and Asian American parents. *Family Relations, 43*, 30–37. doi:10.2307/585139

Kazdin, A. E. (2000). *Parent management training: Treatment for oppositional, aggressive, and antisocial behavior in children and adolescents*. New York, NY: Oxford University Press.

Keels, M. (2009). Ethnic group differences in early Head Start parents' parenting beliefs and practices and links to children's early cognitive development. *Early Childhood Research Quarterly, 24,* 381–397. doi:10.1016/j.ecresq.2009.08.002

Kelley, M. L., Power, T. G., & Wimbush, D. D. (1992). Determinants of disciplinary practices in low-income Black mothers. *Child Development, 63,* 573–582. doi:10.2307/1131347

Kendall, P. C. (Ed.). (2011). *Child and adolescent therapy: Cognitive–behavioral procedures.* New York, NY: Guilford Press.

Kennard, B., Silva, S., Vitiello, B., Curry, J., Kratochvil, C., Simons, A., . . . March, J. (2006). Remission and residual symptoms after short-term treatment in the Treatment of Adolescents with Depression Study (TADS). *Journal of the American Academy of Child & Adolescent Psychiatry, 45,* 1404–1411. doi:10.1097/01.chi.0000242228.75516.21

Kobak, R., Cassidy, J., Lyons-Ruth, K., & Ziv, Y. (2006). Attachment, stress, and psychopathology: A developmental pathways model. In D. Cicchetti, & D. J. Cohen (Eds.), *Developmental psychopathology: Vol. 1. Theory and method* (2nd ed., pp. 333–369). Hoboken, NJ: Wiley.

Kobak, R., & Duemmler, S. (1994). Attachment and conversation: Toward a discourse analysis of adolescent and adult security. In K. Bartholomew & D. Perlman (Eds.), *Attachment processes in adulthood* (pp. 121–149). London, England: Kingsley.

Kobak, R., & Esposito, A. (2004). Levels of processing in parent–child relationships: Implications for clinical assessment and treatment. *Attachment issues in psychopathology and intervention,* 139–166.

Kobak, R., Grassetti, S., Close, H. & Krauthamer Ewing, E. S. (2013). *Attachment-based treatments for adolescents: Toward a theory of change.* Manuscript submitted for publication.

Kobak, R., Rosenthal, N, & Serwik, A. (2005). The attachment hierarchy in middle childhood. In In K. A. Kerns & R. A. Richardson (Eds.), *Attachment in middle childhood* (pp. 71–88). Mahwah, NJ: Erlbaum.

Kobak, R. R., Cole, H. E., Ferenz-Gillies, R., Fleming, W. S., & Gamble, W. (1993). Attachment and emotion regulation during mother–teen problem solving: A control theory analysis. *Child Development, 64,* 231–245. doi:10.2307/1131448

Kobak, R. R., Sudler, N., & Gamble, W. (1991). Attachment and depressive symptoms during adolescence: A developmental pathways analysis. *Development and Psychopathology, 3,* 461–474. doi:10.1017/S095457940000763X

Laing, R. D. (1998). *Self and others: Selected works of R. D. Laing* (Vol. 2). New York, NY: Routledge.

Lewinsohn, P. M., Clarke, G. N., Hops, H., & Andrews, J. (1990). Cognitive–behavioral treatment for depressed adolescents. *Behavior Therapy, 21,* 385–401. doi:10.1016/S0005-7894(05)80353-3

Lewinsohn, P. M., Clarke, G. N., Rohde, P., Hops, H., & Seeley, J. R. (1996). A course in coping: A cognitive–behavioral approach to the treatment of adolescent depression. In E. D. Hibbs & P. S. Jensen (Eds.), *Psychosocial treatment of child and adolescent disorders: Empirically based approaches* (pp. 109–135). Washington, DC: American Psychological Association. doi:10.1037/10196-005

Liddle, H. A. (1987). Family psychology: Tasks of an emerging (and emerging) discipline. *Journal of Family Psychology, 1*, 149–167. doi:10.1037/h0084976

Liddle, H. A. (1994). The anatomy of emotions in family therapy with adolescents. *Journal of Adolescent Research, 9*, 120–157. doi:10.1177/074355489491009

Liddle, H. A. (1995). Conceptual and clinical dimensions of a multidimensional, multisystems engagement strategy in family-based adolescent treatment. *Psychotherapy: Theory, Research, and Practice, 32*, 39–58. doi:10.1037/0033-3204.32.1.39

Liddle, H. A. (1999). Theory development in a family-based treatment for adolescent drug abuse. *Journal of Clinical Child Psychology, 28*, 521–532. doi:10.1207/S15374424JCCP2804_12

Liddle, H. A. (2002). *Multidimensional family therapy (MDFT) for adolescent cannabis users* (DHHS Publication No. SMA 02-3660). Rockville, MD: Center for Substance Abuse Treatment, Substance Abuse and Mental Health Services Administration.

Liddle, H. A. (2010). Multidimensional family therapy: A science-based treatment system. *Australian and New Zealand Journal of Family Therapy, 31*, 133–148.

Liddle, H. A., Bray, J. H., Levant, R. F., & Santisteban, D. A. (2002). Family psychology intervention science: An emerging area of science and practice. In H. Liddle, D. Santisteban, R. F. Levant, & J. H. Bray (Eds.), *Family psychology: Science-based interventions* (pp. 3–15). Washington, DC: American Psychological Association. doi:10.1037/10438-000

Liddle, H. A., Dakof, G. A., Parker, K., Diamond, G. S., Barrett, K., & Tejeda, M. (2001). Multidimensional family therapy for adolescent drug abuse: Results of a randomized clinical trial. *The American Journal of Drug and Alcohol Abuse, 27*, 651–688. doi:10.1081/ADA-100107661

Liddle, H. A., & Diamond, G. (1991). Adolescent substance abusers in family therapy: The critical initial phase of treatment. *Family Dynamics of Addiction Quarterly, 1*, 55–68.

Luborsky, L. (1984). *Principles of psychoanalytic psychotherapy: A manual for supportive-expressive treatment*. New York, NY: Basic Books.

Maccoby, E. E. (1992). The role of parents in the socialization of children: An historical overview. *Developmental Psychology, 28*, 1006. doi:10.1037/0012-1649.28.6.1006

Mackey, S. K. (2003). *Adolescence and attachment: From theory to treatment implications* (pp. 79–113). New York, NY: Brunner-Routledge.

Main, M. (1995). *Recent studies in attachment: Overview, with selected implications for clinical work* (pp. 407–474). Hillsdale, NJ: Analytic Press.

Main, M., & Goldwyn, R. (1998). *Adult Attachment scoring and classification system* Unpublished manuscript, University of California, Berkeley.

Martinez, R. O., & Dukes, R. L. (1997). The effects of ethnic identity, ethnicity, and gender on adolescent well-being. *Journal of Youth and Adolescence, 26*, 503–516. doi:10.1023/A:1024525821078

Maturana, H., & Varela, F. (1984). *The tree of knowledge: Biological roots of human understanding*. London, England: Shambhala.

McCullough, M. E., Pargament, K. I., & Thoresen, C. E. (2000). *Forgiveness, theory, research, and practice*. New York, NY: Guilford Press.

McLoyd, V. C., Aikens, N., & Burton, L. (2006). Childhood poverty, policy, and practice. In W. Damon, R. Lerner, A. Renninger, & I. Sigel (Eds.), *Handbook of child psychology: Vol. 4. Child psychology in practice* (6th ed., pp. 700–775). New York, NY: Wiley.

Micucci, J. A. (1998). *The adolescent in family therapy: Breaking the cycle of conflict and control*. New York, NY: Guilford Press.

Mikulincer, M., & Florian, V. (2004). Attachment style and affect regulation: Implications for coping with stress and mental health. *Applied social psychology*, 28–49.

Minuchin, S. (1974). *Families and family therapy*. Cambridge, MA: Harvard University Press.

Minuchin, S. (1980). *Taming monsters* [videotape]. Philadelphia, PA: Philadelphia Child Guidance Clinic.

Minuchin, S. (1998). Where is the family in narrative therapy? *Journal of Marital and Family Therapy, 24*, 397–403. doi:10.1111/j.1752-0606.1998.tb01094.x

Minuchin, S., & Fishman, H. C. (1981). *Techniques of family therapy*. Cambridge, MA: Harvard University Press.

Minuchin, S., & Fishman, H. C. (2009). *Family therapy techniques*. Cambridge, MA: Harvard University Press.

Minuchin, S., Nichols, M., & Lee, Y. (2007). *Assessing families and couples: From symptoms to systems*. Boston, MA: Allyn & Bacon.

Moed, H. (2002). *Building alliances with parents of depressed adolescents in family therapy: A task analysis* (Master's thesis). Ben-Gurion University of the Negev, Beer-Sheva, Israel.

Moran, G., & Diamond, G. (2008). Generating nonnegative attitudes among parents of depressed adolescents: The power of empathy, concern, and positive regard. *Psychotherapy Research, 18*, 97–107. doi:10.1080/10503300701408325

Moran, G., Diamond, G. M., & Diamond, G. S. (2005). The relational reframe and parents' problem constructions in attachment-based family therapy. *Psychotherapy Research, 15*, 226–235. doi:10.1080/10503300512331387780

Moretti, M. M., Holland, R., Moore, K., & McKay, S. (2004). An attachment-based parenting program for caregivers of severely conduct disordered adolescents: Preliminary findings. *Journal of Child and Youth Care Work, 19*, 170–179.

Moretti, M. M., & Obsuth, I. (2009). Effectiveness of an attachment-focused manualized intervention for parents of teens at risk for aggressive behavior:

The connect program. *Journal of Adolescence, 32,* 1347–1357. doi:10.1016/j.adolescence.2009.07.013

Mufson, L., Dorta, K. P., Moreau, D., & Weissman, M. M. (2004). *Interpersonal psychotherapy for depressed adolescents* (2nd ed.). New York, NY: Guilford Press.

Mufson, L., Gallagher, T., Dorta, K. P., & Young, J. F. (2004). A group adaptation of interpersonal psychotherapy for depressed adolescents. *American Journal of Psychotherapy, 58,* 220–237.

Mufson, L., Weissman, M. M., Moreau, D., & Garfinkel, R. (1999). Efficacy of interpersonal psychotherapy for depressed adolescents. *Archives of General Psychiatry, 56,* 573–579. doi:10.1001/archpsyc.56.6.573

Neborsky, R. J. (2003). A clinical model for the comprehensive treatment of trauma using an affect experiencing–attachment theory approach. *Healing trauma: Attachment, mind, body, and brain,* 282–321.

Nichols, M. P., & Schwartz, R. C. (1984). *Family therapy.* Allyn and Bacon.

Palmer, S., & Woolfe, R. (Eds.). (2003). *Integrative and eclectic counseling and psychotherapy.* London, England: Sage.

Patterson, G. R. (1975). *Families: Applications of social learning to family life.* Champaign, IL: Research Press.

Patterson, G. R., DeBaryshe, B. D., & Ramsey, E. (1989). A developmental perspective on antisocial behavior. *American Psychologist, 44,* 329–335. doi:10.1037/0003-066X.44.2.329

Paul, G. L. (1967). Strategy of outcome research in psychotherapy. *Journal of Consulting Psychology, 31,* 109–118. doi:10.1037/h0024436

Perls, F., Hefferline, G., & Goodman, P. (1951). *Gestalt therapy.* New York, NY: Delta Books.

Pinsof, W. M., & Hambright, A. B. (2002). Toward prevention and clinical relevance: A preventive intervention model for family therapy research and practice. In H. A. Liddle, D. A., Sanisteban, R. F. Levant, & J. H. Bray (Eds.), *Family psychology: Science-based interventions* (pp. 177–195). Washington, DC: American Psychological Association.

Pinsof, W. M., & Lebow, J. (2005). A scientific paradigm for family psychology. In W. M. Pinsof & J. L. Lebow (Eds.), *Family psychology: The art of the science* (pp. 3–19). New York, NY: Oxford University Press.

Polanco-Roman, L., & Miranda, R. (2013). Culturally related stress, hopelessness, and vulnerability to depressive symptoms and suicidal ideation in emerging adulthood. *Behavior Therapy, 44,* 75–87. doi:10.1016/j.beth.2012.07.002

Promising Practices Network. (2011). *Attachment-based family therapy.* Retrieved from http://www.promisingpractices.net

Rachman, S. J. (1990). *Fear and courage* (2nd ed.). New York, NY: Holt.

Radke-Yarrow, M., Nottelmann, E., Belmont, B., & Welsh, J. D. (1993). Affective interactions of depressed and nondepressed mothers and their children. *Journal of Abnormal Child Psychology, 21,* 683–695. doi:10.1007/BF00916450

Restifo, K. & Bogels, S. (2009). Family processes in the development of youth depression: Translating the evidence to treatment. *Clinical Psychology Review, 29*, 294–316. doi:2110/10/1016/j.cpr.2009.02.005

Rice, L. N., & Greenberg, L. S. (1984). *Patterns of change: Intensive analysis of psychotherapy process*. New York, NY: Guilford Press.

Robin, A. L., & Foster, S. L. (2002). *Negotiating parent–adolescent conflict: A behavioral–family systems approach*. New York, NY: Guilford Press.

Roisman, G. L., Padrón, E., Sroufe, L. A., & Egeland, B. (2002). Earned–secure attachment status in retrospect and prospect. *Child Development, 73*, 1204–1219. doi:10.1111/1467-8624.00467

Rosselló, J., & Bernal, G. (1999). The efficacy of cognitive–behavioral and interpersonal treatments for depression in Puerto Rican adolescents. *Journal of Consulting and Clinical Psychology, 67*, 734–745. doi:10.1037/0022-006X.67.5.734

Schore, A. N. (2001). Effects of a secure attachment relationship on right brain development, affect regulation, and infant mental health. *Infant Mental Health Journal, 22*(1–2), 7–66. doi:10.1002/1097-0355(200101/04)22:1<7::AID-IMHJ2>3.0.CO;2-N

Sheeber, L., Hops, H., & Davis, B. (2001). Family processes in adolescent depression. *Clinical Child and Family Psychology Review, 4*, 19–35. doi:10.1023/A:1009524626436

Sheeber, L., & Sorensen, E. (1998). Family relationships of depressed adolescents: A multimethod assessment. *Journal of Clinical Child Psychology, 27*, 268–277. doi:10.1207/s15374424jccp2703_4

Sheeber, L. B., Davis, B., Leve, C., Hops, H., & Tildesley, E. (2007). Adolescents' relationships with their mothers and fathers: Associations with depressive disorder and subdiagnostic symptomatology. *Journal of Abnormal Psychology, 116*, 144. doi:10.1037/0021-843X.116.1.144

Shelef, K., Diamond, G. M., Diamond, G. S., & Liddle, H. A. (2005). Adolescent and parent alliance and treatment outcome in multidimensional family therapy. *Journal of Consulting and Clinical Psychology, 73*, 689–698. doi:10.1037/0022-006X.73.4.689

Shpigel, M. S., Diamond, G. M., & Diamond, G. S. (2012). Changes in parenting behaviors, attachment, depressive symptoms, and suicidal ideation in attachment-based family therapy for depressive and suicidal adolescents. *Journal of Marital and Family Therapy, 38*, 271–283. doi:10.1111/j.1752-0606.2012.00295.x

Siegel, D. J. (2012). *The developing mind: How relationships and the brain interact to shape who we are* (2nd ed.). New York, NY: Guilford Press.

Smith, C. L. (2010). Multiple determinants of parenting: Predicting individual differences in maternal parenting behavior with toddlers. *Parenting: Science and Practice, 10*, 1–17. doi:10.1080/15295190903014588

Steinberg, L. (1990). Autonomy, conflict, and harmony in the family relationships. In S. S. Feldman & G. R. Elliot (Eds.), *At the threshold: The developing adolescent* (pp. 255–276). Cambridge, MA: Harvard University Press.

Stern, D. (1985). *The interpersonal world of the infant*. New York, NY: Basic Books.

Thompson, K. L., & Gullone, E. (2008). Prosocial and antisocial behaviors in adolescents: An investigation into associations with attachment and empathy. *Anthrozoös, 21*, 123–137. doi:10.2752/175303708X305774

Thompson, R. A. (2008). Early attachment and later development: Familiar questions, new answers. In J. Cassidy & P. Shaver (Eds.), *Handbook of attachment* (2nd ed., pp. 348–365). New York, NY: Guilford Press.

Treatment for Adolescents With Depression Study (TADS) Team. (2004). Fluoxetine, cognitive–behavioral therapy, and their combination for adolescents with depression: Treatment for Adolescents With Depression Study (TADS) randomized controlled trial. *JAMA, 292*, 807–820.

Van IJzendoorn, M. (1995). Adult attachment representations, parental responsiveness, and infant attachment: A meta-analysis on the predictive validity of the Adult Attachment Interview. *Psychological Bulletin, 117*, 387. doi:10.1037/0033-2909.117.3.387

Van IJzendoorn, M. H., Bakermans-Kranenburg, M. J., & Sagi-Schwartz, A. B. R. A. H. A. M. (2006). Attachment across diverse sociocultural contexts: the limits of universality. *Parenting beliefs, behaviors, and parent–child relations: A cross-cultural perspective*, 107–142.

Van IJzendoorn, M. H., & Sagi, A. (1999). Cross-cultural patterns of attachment. In J. Cassidy & Shaver, P. R. (Eds.), *Handbook of attachment, theory, research, and clinical applications* (pp. 713–734). New York, NY: Guilford Press.

Vitiello, B. (2009). Treatment of adolescent depression: What we have come to know. *Depression and Anxiety, 26*, 393–395. doi:10.1002/da.20572

Wallin, D. J. (2007). *Attachment in psychotherapy*. New York, NY: Guilford Press.

Walsh, F. (2006). *Strengthening family resilience* (2nd ed.). New York, NY: Guilford Press.

Waters, H. S., & Waters, E. (2006). The attachment working models concept: Among other things, we build script-like representations of secure base experiences. *Attachment & Human Development, 8*, 185–197. doi:10.1080/14616730600856016

Waters, S. F., Virmani, E. A., Thompson, R. A., Meyer, S., Raikes, H. A., & Jochem, R. (2010). Emotion regulation and attachment: Unpacking two constructs and their association. *Journal of Psychopathology and Behavioral Assessment, 32*, 37–47. doi:10.1007/s10862-009-9163-z

Weersing, V. R., Rozenman, M., & González, A. (2009). Core components of therapy in youth: Do we know what to disseminate? *Behavior Modification, 33*, 24–47. doi:10.1177/0145445508322629

Weissman, M. M., Markowitz, J. C., & Klerman, G. L. (2000). *Comprehensive guide to interpersonal psychotherapy*. New York, NY: Basic Books.

Weisz, J. R., McCarty, C. A., & Valeri, S. M. (2006). Effects of psychotherapy for depression in children and adolescents: A meta-analysis. *Psychological Bulletin, 132*, 132–149. doi:10.1037/0033-2909.132.1.132

Wells, K. C., & Albano, A. M. (2005). Parent involvement in CBT treatment of adolescent depression: Experiences in the Treatment for Adolescents With Depression Study (TADS). *Cognitive and Behavioral Practice, 12*, 209–220. doi:10.1016/S1077-7229(05)80026-4

White, M., & Epston, D. (1990). *Narrative means to therapeutic ends*. New York, NY: Norton.

Wiener, N. (1973). *Cybernetics or control and communication in the animal and the machine*. (2nd ed.). Boston, MA: Massachusetts Institute of Technology.

Winnicott, D. W. (1953). Transitional objects and transitional phenomena—A study of the first not-me possession. *The International Journal of Psychoanalysis, 34*, 89–97.

Wolpe, J. (1973). *The practice of behavior therapy*. New York, NY: Pergamon.

Yap, M. B. H., Allen, N. B., & Sheeber, L. (2007). Using an emotion regulation framework to understand the role of temperament and family processes in risk for adolescent depressive disorders. *Clinical Child and Family Psychology Review, 10*, 180–196. doi:10.1007/s10567-006-0014-0

Young, J. E., Klosko, J. S., & Weishaar, M. E. (2003). *Schema therapy: A practitioner's guide*. New York, NY: Guilford Press.

Zanetti, C. A., Powell, B., Cooper, G., & Hoffman, K. (2011). *The circle of security intervention: Using the therapeutic relationship to ameliorate attachment security in disorganized dyads* (pp. 318–342). New York, NY: Guilford Press.

INDEX

ABOUT THE AUTHORS

Guy S. Diamond, PhD, is an associate professor of psychology in the Department of Psychiatry at the University of Pennsylvania School of Medicine, and the director of the Center for Family Intervention Science at The Children's Hospital of Philadelphia. In 2014, he will move the Center for Family Intervention Science to Drexel University's College of Nursing and Health Professions. At Drexel, he will also become the director of the Couples and Family Therapy Doctoral Program and establish the Attachment-Based Family Therapy Training Program (ABFT; see http://www.ABFTtraining.com and https://www.facebook.com/Attachment.Based.Family.Therapy for more information).

Gary M. Diamond, PhD, is a clinical psychologist and associate professor in the Department of Psychology at Ben-Gurion University of the Negev in Beer Sheva, Israel. His research focuses on the processes and outcomes of family-based treatments. He is particularly interested in the therapeutic alliance, emotional processing, and the development and testing of family therapy for lesbian/gay/bisexual individuals and their parents.

Suzanne A. Levy, PhD, is a licensed clinical psychologist and director of the ABFT Training Program at Drexel University's College of Nursing and Health Professions. Prior to this she was the training director and a clinical child psychologist at the Center for Family Intervention Science at The Children's Hospital of Philadelphia. She conducts ABFT training workshops and supervision for therapists involved in the center's clinical trials, as well as therapists both nationally and internationally. She has presented regionally, nationally, and internationally on ABFT, emotion coaching, child and adolescent therapies, adolescent depression, adolescent development, and adolescent substance use.